Lecture Notes
in Business Information Processing 39

Series Editors

Wil van der Aalst
Eindhoven Technical University, The Netherlands
John Mylopoulos
University of Trento, Italy
Norman M. Sadeh
Carnegie Mellon University, Pittsburgh, PA, USA
Michael J. Shaw
University of Illinois, Urbana-Champaign, IL, USA
Clemens Szyperski
Microsoft Research, Redmond, WA, USA

D1570578

Anne Persson   Janis Stirna (Eds.)

The Practice of Enterprise Modeling

Second IFIP WG 8.1 Working Conference, PoEM 2009
Stockholm, Sweden, November 18-19, 2009
Proceedings

 Springer

Volume Editors

Anne Persson
University of Skövde
School of Humanities and Informatics
P.O. Box 408, 54128 Skövde, Sweden
E-mail: anne.persson@his.se

Janis Stirna
Royal Institute of Technology and Stockholm University
Department of Computer and Systems Sciences
FORUM 100, 16440 Kista, Sweden
E-mail: js@dsv.su.se

Library of Congress Control Number: 2009938211

ACM Computing Classification (1998): J.1, H.4, I.6

ISSN   1865-1348
ISBN-10   3-642-05351-3 Springer Berlin Heidelberg New York
ISBN-13   978-3-642-05351-1 Springer Berlin Heidelberg New York

springer.com

© IFIP International Federation for Information Processing, Hofstrasse 3, A-2361 Laxenburg, Austria 2009
Printed in Germany

Typesetting: Camera-ready by author, data conversion by Scientific Publishing Services, Chennai, India
Printed on acid-free paper   SPIN: 12786671   06/3180   5 4 3 2 1 0

Preface

Enterprise modeling (EM) has gained substantial popularity both in the academic community and among practitioners. A variety of EM methods, approaches, and tools are being developed and offered on the market. In practice they are used for various purposes such as business strategy development, process restructuring, as well as business and IT architecture alignment and governance.

PoEM 2009 – the second IFIP WG 8.1 Working Conference on The Practice of Enterprise Modeling took place in November in Stockholm, Sweden. The conference series is a dedicated forum where the use of EM in practice is addressed by bringing together researchers, users, and practitioners in order to develop a better understanding of the practice of EM, to contribute to improved EM practice as well as to share knowledge and experiences.

PoEM 2009 attracted 41 submissions from many different parts of the world, out of which the Program Committee selected 17 high-quality papers. Among the authors of these papers we find both researchers and practitioners. The resulting program reflects the fact that the topic of EM encompasses human, organizational issues, as well as more technical aspects related to the development of information systems. The program was organized in six thematic sessions:

- Experiences in EM
- The process of modeling
- EM in information systems development
- Model quality and reuse
- EM for Services modeling
- New ventures in EM

The program also featured two keynotes by experienced EM practitioners. Håvard D. Jørgensen's talk focused on practical experiences collected from a number of applications of EM, while Christer Nellborn discussed how EM can become an institutionalized tool in business development. Following the positive experiences from the 2008 edition of the conference, the program also included a joint working session where researchers and practitioners had the opportunity to discuss emerging issues in the field of EM practice.

We devote a special thanks to the members of the international Program Committee for promoting the conference and for providing excellent reviews of the submitted papers. Their dedicated work was vital for putting together a high-quality working conference. We also thank the external reviewers. Special thanks go to Stockholm University, University of Skövde, Jönköping University, and the Royal Institute of Technology in Stockholm for supporting the organization of the conference.

The PoEM 2009 organizers would also like to thank the conference sponsor – Fraunhofer Institute for Software and Systems Engineering (ISST), Germany.

September 2009   Anne Persson
Janis Stirna

PoEM 2009 Conference Organization

General Chair

Paul Johannesson   Royal Institute of Technology, Sweden

Program Committee Co-chairs

Anne Persson   University of Skövde, Sweden
Janis Stirna   Royal Institute of Technology, Sweden

Organizing Chair

Jelena Zdravkovic   Stockholm University, Sweden

Organizing Committee

Natalja Nikitina
Khurram Shahzad
Iyad Zikra

Program Committee

Marko Bajec   University of Ljubljana, Slovenia
Rimantas Butleris   Kaunas University of Technology, Lithuania
Wolfgang Deiters   Fraunhofer ISST, Germany
Eric Dubois   CRP Henri Tudor, Luxembourg
Mathias Ekstedt   Royal Institute of Technology, Sweden
Gustaf Ericsson   Alfa Laval AB, Sweden
Xavier Franch   Universitat Politècnica de Catalunya, Spain
Jaap Gordijn   VU University Amsterdam, The Netherlands
Remigijus Gustas   Karlstad University, Sweden
Terry Halpin   LogicBlox, Australia
Lennart Holmberg   Sweden
Stijn Hoppenbrouwers Radboud University Nijmegen, The Netherlands
Jarl Höglund   Allmentor AB, Sweden
Pontus Johnsson   Royal Institute of Technology, Sweden
Håvard Jørgensen   Commitment AS, Norway
John Krogstie   Norwegian University of Science and Technology, Norway

Marc Lankhorst	Novay, The Netherlands
Michel Leonard	Université de Genève, Switzerland
Peri Loucopoulos	Loughborough University, UK
Graham McLeod	PROMIS Solutions AG, South Africa
Christer Nellborn	Nellborn Management Consulting AB, Sweden
Björn Nilsson	Anatés AB, Luxembourg
Andreas Opdahl	University of Bergen, Norway
Oscar Pastor	Valencia University of Technology, Spain
Naveen Prakash	GCET, India
Erik Proper	Radboud University Nijmegen, The Netherlands
Jolita Ralyte	Université de Genève, Switzerland
Colette Rolland	Université Paris 1 Panthéon Sorbonne, France
Michael Rosemann	Queensland University of Technology, Australia
Camille Salinesi	Université Paris 1 Panthéon Sorbonne, France
Kurt Sandkuhl	Jönköping Technical University, Sweden
Ulf Seigerroth	Jönköping International Business School, Sweden
Keng Siau	University of Nebraska-Lincoln, USA
Guttorm Sindre	Norwegian University of Science and Technology, Norway
Pnina Soffer	University of Haifa, Israel
Renate Strazdina	Ernst & Young SIA, Latvia
Olegas Vasilecas	Vilnius Gediminas Technical University, Lithuania
Eric Yu	University of Toronto, Canada

External Reviewers

Jesper Holgersson
David Höök
Robert Lagerström
Ulrik Franke
Khurram Shahzad
Eriks Sneiders
Jelena Zdravkovic

Table of Contents

Model Quality and Reuse

Enterprise Modeling for Service Modeling

New Ventures in Enterprise Modeling

To Make Modeling a Natural Tool in Business Development We Need to Stop Talking about Modeling

Christer Nellborn

Nellborn Management Consulting AB
Spiselvägen 14
141 59 Huddinge, Sweden
christer@nellborn.se
www.nellborn.se

Abstract. To make enterprise modeling a natural tool for business development we need to integrate with other disciplines such as sociology, psychology and economy. We also need to focus more on the business problems to solve and the benefits and effects the business gets from using the models and less on the models themselves.

Keywords: Business modeling, enterprise modeling.

1   Background

Business modeling is nothing new. It has been around for a very long time. Some of the earliest documented examples can be found in the drawings our cavemen ancestors made of animals being hunted. Dressed in modern terminology these cave drawings are business models showing how to optimize the utilization of available enterprise resources in a gathering process in order to maximize the achievement of important short- and long term business goals – i.e. kill the beast to get food to eat and material for making clothes to keep us warm at winter.

Since the early stages of the industrial era, a lot of research and development has been put into developing models and techniques for analyzing and handling the complexity when enterprises grow from small and local to large and international. These models come from a wide variety of disciplines such as economy, psychology and sociology.

In the last 30 or so years, automated information systems have emerged as a crucial tool for organizations to manage complexity. One of the key questions for information systems development is getting good, sound, complete requirements. This has been a challenge for many years and proven to be a very elusive problem. Many models, techniques, tools and approaches have been developed to handle the problem.

2   Business Development and Models

Business development can be seen as consisting of three areas:

1. The development of the relations and interactions between the organization and its surroundings, i.e. customers, suppliers, competitors, society in general

A. Persson and J. Stirna (Eds.): PoEM 2009, LNBIP 39, pp. 1–2, 2009.

2. The development of resources and how the organization utilize them to support the external interactions
3. The development of computerized business resources

A significant difference between the first two and the third area is the implementation of changes. For the first two, the implementation is mainly in the way people in the organization work, interact and behave, whereas the implementation in the third area is mainly in the functions of a computer system.

The purposes of models for the three areas are therefor slightly different. When implementing changes in a computer system you need models for designing the system, preferably with as much detail as possible to remove guesswork and to get precise requirements.

When implementing changes in the behavior of people you need models that support communication, learning and understanding. Models for this purpose need to focus more on context, reason and motivation and less on detailed design of the organization. People will work out the details for themselves in discussions, interactions and in their practical day-by-day work.

3 The Proof of the Pudding Is in the Eating

To succeed in making enterprise modeling a natural tool in business development, we need to do three things:

1. Stop talking about the models and the modeling as such. Focus on how the models can support the change process
2. Integrate more with the traditional disciplines for enterprise modeling (i.e. economy, sociology, psychology et.c.). Cooperate in the development of new enterprise models.
3. Make models easier to use in communication with people without technical background. If people don't understand the models they will not use them no matter how good they are.

Enterprise Modeling – What We Have Learned, and What We Have Not

Håvard D. Jørgensen

Commitment AS, PO Box 534
N-1327 Lysaker, Norway
`havard.jorgensen@commitment.no`

Abstract. Over the last 25 years, enterprise modeling has evolved from a loose collection of business oriented modeling practices to comprehensive frameworks for enterprise architectures. What was initially a combination of industrial and software engineering methodologies applied to enterprise design and development, is today dominated by the concerns of IT development, management and governance. This talk summarizes experiences from years of practice, research and development in the field, and points out directions for future development.

Keywords: Enterprise architecture, Model-driven applications, Active knowledge architecture.

1 Background

Like many in the field, my involvement with enterprise modeling started with business process analysis, in this case in the early 90s [4]. Development of flexible process execution systems soon lead to customizable, model-driven application portals in general [3]. Process modeling was extended to cover modeling of other enterprise aspects. The techniques found utilization in interoperability and integration, and model-driven composition of applications from underlying services [5]. After some years of Enterprise Architecture (EA) methodology and tool development, we turned our focus towards industrial product development and design [2], looking to learn more from the area that enterprise modeling came from in the first place [6].

2 Lessons Learned

Many of the lessons presented below are obvious to enterprise modeling practitioners. They are included here because outsiders coming into the field sometimes get them wrong. Other lessons may be more controversial, and they may not be applicable in every situation.

First, let us look at four related lessons that concern the scope of enterprise modeling and enterprise architecture:

1. Don't reduce enterprise architecture to IT architecture.
2. "What can we automate" is not always the right question.

A. Persson and J. Stirna (Eds.): PoEM 2009, LNBIP 39, pp. 3–7, 2009.
© IFIP International Federation for Information Processing 2009

3. Don't frame business problems as IT problems.
4. Discuss purpose, scope and level of ambition throughout the architecture's lifecycle.

Some companies that provide enterprise application integration (EAI) describe their IT level integration platforms as enterprise architectures, and the people who develop them as enterprise architects. There is a clear danger that EA will go the same way as "business process", and be hi-jacked from the business domain to the IT domain.

In the overall practice of enterprise modeling, these lessons should be highlighted:

5. Don't confuse analysis and design.
6. Keep models and languages as simple as possible.
7. Don't let the language be a straight-jacket.

Enterprise modeling is used for analyzing the current situation, and for designing future solutions to identified problems, as in to-be business processes and architectures [7]. Analysis should focus on identifying the most important elements, dependencies and aspects of a domain. Often however, people perform a lot of synthesis during analysis, constructing complex structures of the elements, such as business processes and organizational hierarchies. Too much structuration during analysis is dangerous because the model will contain a lot of noise, and it makes the approach more conservative.

This leads on to the 6th principle, simplicity. A common condition is *analysis paralysis*, where decision making is continuously postponed in order to create a better foundation and justification. Enterprise modeling research also tends to violate the simplicity requirement. Countless papers are produced with extensions of modeling languages in order to represent some additional aspect more precisely. Often the added value is small, as the most important concerns could already be represented in existing languages. The cost in terms of increased complexity, on the other hand, is large. Validation that takes this issue into account is rare.

During modeling we have experienced a few common challenges:

8. Beware of hierarchies, they are often local to a viewpoint and not shared by everyone.
9. Beware of matrices and streamlined frameworks, often you need to break the system.
10. Beware of leaving important things out at the boundaries.
11. Don't confuse views with the underlying architecture elements.

Multiple, aspect oriented classification of model elements is important in order to allow overlapping hierarchies and multiple views for different stakeholders' perspectives.

With respect to the enterprise model content, we often found that

12. Product models are more important and fundamental than process models.
13. Processes are better understood by focusing on the decisions to make, the issues to solve, and the results to produce, than on the administrative ordering of steps.
14. Multi-dimensional analysis, combining e.g. processes with the data it manipulates and the organizational roles responsible, is superior to single-dimensional data modeling and business process modeling.

15. During decomposition, don't expect to "go all the way down" using a single modeling language. Another language is likely to be a better match for detailed models than the one used for high-level overviews.
16. Aspects that can be separated on one level of detail may be inherently woven together on another level. Products, processes and organization models do for instance become thoroughly intertwined in work execution.
17. Relationships are the most important kind of element in most models.

For managing dependencies, relationships should be modeled at the right level of detail. If every element is related to every other element, you're at a too high level of abstraction. If there is a clear one-to-one correspondence between two sets of elements, you have probably included too much detail.

In modeling tool development, and in selecting the right modeling tools for your needs, it is important to

18. Decide whether you need a multi-purpose modeling platform, or a modeling application specialized for one usage area.

Tool vendors struggle to find their place in the large number of applications domains for business oriented modeling. Establishing a general purpose architecture that can support the analyses needed by a wide range of stakeholders, requires a flexible and extensible modeling platform.

Finally, here is some advice for how an architect should behave:

19. Be open, humble, and willing to expose your mistakes.
20. Take charge, set directions.
21. Don't listen to management.
22. An architecture that is not actively used will die. Motivating stakeholders to participate, is an ongoing challenge.

Some architects treat the architecture as their own property, and see organizational stakeholders primarily as sources of information. Other inexperienced architects see themselves too much as enablers, and become followers of the whims of strong forces in the organization. Managers are of course important stakeholders, and generally also important sources of information for an architecture. We should however be cautious, as relying to one-sided on management perspectives can make it difficult to capture the concerns of the core, value-adding work performance. A typical result is business process models that include several activities for administration, planning, monitoring, reporting, reviewing, quality control, setting up, and closing etc., but very few details about how the actual work is to be performed. Management views should be complemented by operational views.

3 Future Directions

In the short term, the future development of enterprise modeling practice is likely to remain dominated by enterprise architectures for IT management. In this area, standardization of modeling languages is beginning, e.g. BPMN, and it will probably be a major trend in the next five years. Compared to e.g. UML, enterprise modeling deals with a much larger scope of content, and aims to support a much larger set of practices.

Standardization will be more difficult in this domain. Whether any single dominant vendor will emerge with a strong enough position to establish a de facto industry standard, is difficult to tell. If we end up relying on a poorly suited metamodeling framework from another domain, such as UML/MOF, the complexity of even a limited general purpose enterprise modeling language may prevent its use in practice [5].

Over the past decade, more and more EA frameworks have been proposed, often targeting different industries and application areas. Most proposals position themselves with reference to general purpose frameworks such as Zachman and TOGAF, but further alignment is hampered by the great complexity. A simplified TOGAF core should probably be established as a first step towards a consolidated, extensible standard EA framework, capable of supporting domain specific extensions. The core framework should include the definition of standard modeling concepts, but it is difficult to predict whether the framework or the language standard will arrive first.

Industrial design and development is in need of a language for capturing and sharing knowledge throughout the entire product lifecycle. While interoperability is becoming a reality between the tools used in the later stages of product development, conceptual and functional systems design is still not integrated. In these early stages, documents, rather than structured data/models, are still dominating. To develop enterprise modeling languages for conceptual and functional design is thus a major challenge for future research.

Finally, we see *enterprise model driven applications* as a promising approach to construct more customizable, agile, modular and service-oriented IT solutions. Pilot solutions applying what we call "active knowledge architectures" (AKA) show that applications can indeed be put together from simple building blocks, using high level enterprise models. AKA execution environments combine

- Model-driven data definition and management,
- Model-driven process, task, and rule execution,
- Model-driven views and user interfaces,
- Model-driven role-based filtering and access control.

From this perspective, standard enterprise modeling languages should be aligned with industry standards for data exchange. More information about our ideas for future modeling approaches and model-driven applications is found in the *Active Knowledge Modeling* blog [1].

Acknowledgements

This presentation draws on the experience of several colleagues and collaborators, in particular Frank Lillehagen, who founded Metis in 1986 and has been developing enterprise modeling ever since.

References

1. Active Knowledge Modeling blog, http://activeknowledgemodeling.com
2. Johnsen, S., et al.: Model-based Adaptive Product and Process Engineering. In: Rabe (ed.) Ambient Intelligence Technologies for the Product Lifecycle (2007)

3. Jørgensen, H.D., Krogstie, J., Ohren, O.P., Johnsen, S.G.: Interactive Models for Tailorable and Evolving Information Systems. Journal of Applied Systems Studies 6(1) (2005)
4. Jørgensen, H.D.: Interactive Process Models. PhD thesis, Norwegian University of Science and Technology, Trondheim, Norway (2004),
   http://ntnu.diva-portal.org/smash/record.jsf?pid=diva2:125137
5. Jørgensen, H.D., Karlsen, D., Lillehagen, F.: Collaborative Modeling and Metamodeling with the Enterprise Knowledge Architecture. An International Journal on Enterprise Modeling and Information Systems Architectures 1(1) (2005)
6. Lillehagen, F., Krogstie, J.: Active Knowledge Modeling for Enterprises. Springer, Heidelberg (2008)
7. Stirna, J., Persson, A., Sandkuhl, K.: Participative Enterprise Modeling: Experiences and Recommendations. In: Krogstie, J., Opdahl, A.L., Sindre, G. (eds.) CAiSE 2007 and WES 2007. LNCS, vol. 4495, pp. 546–560. Springer, Heidelberg (2007)

Information Demand Context Modelling for Improved Information Flow: Experiences and Practices

Magnus Lundqvist[1], Eva Holmquist[2], Kurt Sandkuhl[1],
Ulf Seigerroth[1], and Jan Strandesjö[3]

[1] School of Engineering at Jönköping University,
P.O. Box 1026, 55111 Jönköping, Sweden
{Magnus.Lundqvist,Kurt.Sandkuhl}@jth.hj.se
Ulf.Seigerroth@ihh.hj.se
[2] SYSteam Management AB, Box 439, 561 25 Huskvarna, Sweden
Eva.Holmquist@systeam.se
[3] Proton Finishing, Box 1002, 331 29 Värnamo, Sweden
Jan.Strandesjo@proton.se

Abstract. The paper addresses the field of modelling information demand context, which can be considered as an application of enterprise modelling techniques with focus on capturing information demands. Based on industrial cases from automotive industries, experiences and practices of information demand modelling are presented and investigated. This includes the specific perspective taken in the method for information demand analysis, common challenges experienced in demand modelling, the validity of practices from participative enterprise modelling for context modelling and practices of context modelling.

Keywords: Enterprise Modelling, Information Demand, Information Logistics, Context Modelling, Information Demand Context.

1 Introduction

Since more than 20 years, one of the traditional application purposes of enterprise modelling has been to understand the current situation in an enterprise under consideration, in order to be able to propose improvements [1]. Various approaches and methods dedicated for this purpose were developed in areas such as business process reengineering [2], process improvement [3], process innovation or organisational renewal [4]. This significant body of knowledge is the basis for the work presented in this paper.

Another field of relevance is the area of information logistics [5]. Information logistics addresses the challenge of improving information flow in organisations. Recent studies showed that information overload is increasingly perceived as a problem even on an enterprise level [6] calling for innovative approaches to overcome this challenge.

In order to improve information flow in organisations, the development of context models has been found useful [7]. Context models – to be more precise information demand context models – can be considered as application of enterprise modelling

A. Persson and J. Stirna (Eds.): PoEM 2009, LNBIP 39, pp. 8–22, 2009.

techniques for capturing selected parts of an enterprise using a representation and modelling method tailored for the purpose of capturing information demand.

This paper summarise the background, presents an industrial case for information demand modelling and includes examples of the use of information demand contexts based on that case. Finally it discusses practices and experiences from context modelling in comparison to enterprise modelling practices.

2   The Constituent of Information Demand

Information demand as a concept is based upon empirical work performed by the Centre for Evolving IT in Networked Organisations during the period 2005-2007. The results from this work resulted in a number of verified conjectures regarding the nature of information demand as well as a deeper understanding of how information is used with regards to work-related tasks [8]. These results have been used as the foundation on which the method discussed in Section 4. has been developed. The definition of information demand used throughout the paper is:

Information demand is the constantly changing need for relevant, current, accurate, reliable, and integrated information to support (business) activities, when ever and where ever it is needed.

While this definition gives an initial conceptual view on information demand it is not sufficient as a basis for method development. Consequently, additional analysis and conceptualisation was performed to identify different dimensions of information demand. It was concluded [8] that contextual aspects such as role, tasks and resources define information demand while it is affected by situational and individual aspect such as competence, time, location and social networks etc. Since the contextual aspects are considered most important [7], focus in this paper will be on parts in the developed method that are relevant for modelling information demand contexts.

Information demand as it is defined and referred to here, has a strong relation to the context in which such a demand exists. In order to know something about information demand, something need to be known about the organisational role having the demand and for what task the information is demanded as well as the setting in which such tasks are performed. Thus, the concept of information demand context has been defined both conceptually and as the core of the method with respect to modelling, evaluating and analysing of information demand. The definition of information demand context that has been used during the method development is the following:

An Information Demand Context is the formalised representation of information about the setting in which information demands exist and comprises the organisational role of the party having the demand, work tasks related, and any resources and informal information exchange channels available, to that role.

This definition and the empirical data that supports it, conclude that information demand not only is connected to a role, and therefore also always is considered to be role-based, but also to additional enterprise related aspects as illustrated in Figure 1. below. The informal aspects of information demand mentioned in the definition above can, although not covered in this paper, also be a part of the context by considering social networks as resources.

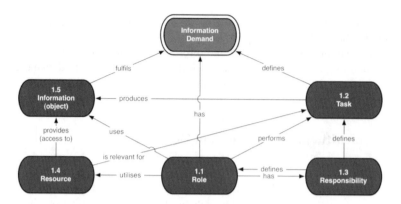

Fig. 1. Context-related concepts with respect to information demand

This view on information demand context allows traditional enterprise modelling techniques to be used, with a somewhat different focus, in order to reach an initial understanding of role-based information demand. In Section 4. a number of practical experiences from an industrial case and the implication it has for the development of a method component for analysing information demand will be described in more detail.

3 Industrial Application Cases

Within InfoFLOW, modelling of information demand context was performed in a number of industrial cases in order to collect experiences from various situations and domains in order to iteratively develop and improve the modelling approach. This paper will briefly discuss just one industrial case in order to expose typical modelling purpose, the process of modelling, the organisation frame, and results.

The industrial case defining the context for work presented in this paper is taken from manufacturing industries and focuses on engineering change management within one of the industrial partners. Proton Finishing (henceforth Proton) is a sub-supplier to different first-tier suppliers in automotive and telecommunication industries and performs various surface treatment services of metal components. Surface treatment in this context includes different technical or decorative coatings to achieve certain functionality or appearance.

In the Proton case four major activities were conducted in accordance with the list below. These activities have had a framing focus of dealing with change management in the finishing production process where Proton is a subcontractor to an OEM in the automotive industry. The challenge for Proton is to handle the continuously incoming changed specifications for the products that they are producing for the OEM. The major activities in this project was therefore:

1. General modelling of how Proton was handling change management in the production processes. The major result from this activity was descriptions of Proton's processes and a number of described change areas.
2. Validation of process descriptions, prioritisation of change areas, and planning of how to proceed.

3. Detailed process modelling and refinement of improvement areas at Proton.
4. Information demand analysis of a specific part of Proton's sales process (from quotation to production planning).

In this paper focus is on the fourth session in the list above since it has served as the major basis for development of a method component for information demand context modelling and analysis. While there usually are a number of scoping activities preceding the context modelling, such activities were not needed here as the scope was defined in activity 1, 2, and 3 in the list above. The fourth session, the actual modelling, was divided into two main activities, 1) interviews, and 2) an information demand modelling seminar. During these two activities the following persons were involved, two researcher from Jönköping University, one consultant from SYSteam and four persons from Proton (head of quality, sales representative, technical support/technical in-house sales, and production planner).

The interviews were performed in a semi-structured manner during two hours where one researcher was guiding the interview and the other researcher together with the consultant took notes. The interview was also recorded as basis for later analysis and further development of the information demand analysis method. The main purpose with the interviews was to set the stage and decide the focus for the next activity; a seminar under which an initial version of the information demand analysis method (a method hypothesis) was tested.

After the interviews and a short planning meeting the information demand modelling seminar was performed. During this modelling seminar one researcher acted as modelling facilitator to move the modelling activities forward. The major purpose of the modelling seminar was to describe the information demand for different roles based on their assignments in the sales process. The modelling seminar was performed in a participative way where the representatives from Proton were actively involved in the modelling. The modelling was performed on plastic sheets with sticky notes and whiteboard markers. The remaining researcher and the consultant participated during the modelling seminar by observing, documenting and asking questions regarding clarification of aspects of the domain that was in focus. The result from the modelling seminar was the empirical foundation to a method component for information demand context modelling, specifying a number of procedures, a notation and a number of concepts on which to focus. The result from the seminar has also been used by the head of quality at Proton to elucidate and share knowledge amongst the employees about certain dimensions in the change management process. The models have served as an instrument to develop shared knowledge amongst roles at Proton about different aspects of the practice in terms of information demand and information flow.

4 Practices of Information Demand Modelling

In this section information demand and information context modelling as concepts are discussed in the light of the implications from the industrial case covered in Section 3. with respect to common problems and methodological support.

4.1 Common Problems Related to Information Demand

Most organisations have problems related to information demand in some way or another and many of them are also quite common independently of organisation or domain. However, the effects of most of these problems can also be reduced relatively simply by visualising the information demand of the organisation. In this section some of those problems will be describe and exemplified, partly based on experiences from the industrial case covered in Section 3. but also grounded in SYSteam's many years of system analysis experience within industrial contexts. Similar problems are known from the area of data quality.

4.1.1 Superfluous Information

A very common problem in the industry is the constant stream of information being supplied to roles despite there being no need for it. Often the reason behind this is that the information once was needed, but the information demand changed over time. This results in unnecessary work having to be performed, work that in the current market no longer can be afforded.

One example of this is the administrator which every month spends a couple of days computing statistics for the sales department. These statistics were used to plan the sales department work for the next month, but nowadays reports from an ERP-system are used instead. The administrator is however not aware that the information is no longer needed.

Another example is the construction department, which produces a lot of drawings and specifications to be used by the production department. They are not certain that all these documents are needed anymore, but they do not dare stop producing them if someone actually does need them.

4.1.2 Gap in the Information Flow

Another very common problem is that there often is a gap in the information flow. The information is supplied, but the roles needing the information are not receiving it. One reason can be that the roles supplying the information are not aware of all roles that need the produced information and therefore do not distribute it accordingly. Another reason can be that the roles in demand of the information do not know where the information is available or how it is distributed. A third reason is that the information is supplied through a gateway role, i.e. the only purpose for this role to get the information is to supply it to any role needing it. A final reason might be lack in technical support; information is simply not stored in a system or location that supports the proper distribution of it.

One example of this is customer relationship related information. The production department has all information regarding any problems the customers have had with the delivery of their products, but this information does not reach the sales department sometimes resulting in awkward situations with customers and possible loss of sales as a consequence.

Another example is the specification of the raw material in an ERP-system needed by the purchase department and the production planners. The relevant information is gathered by the warehouse personnel upon arrival and then handed to the machine operators to input it into the ERP-system. As the operators have no need for this information on their own, this task is always down prioritized and consequently raw material is always specified too late.

4.1.3 Information Gathered at the Wrong Time

It is also very common that information is gathered at the wrong time. The reason for this often is that roles, which easily can gather information at the correct time, are not aware that they should.

One example of this is customer invoice information. It is practical to, when the sale is made, gather the information about where to send the invoice. Most sales department however, does not do this because they are not thinking about invoicing as one of their activities and are therefore not aware of what information is needed. This results in the roles performing the invoicing trying to find this information when the invoice should be sent. At that time it is much harder to get the information.

4.1.4 Outdated and/or Incorrect Information

Another common problem is the use of outdated and/or incorrect information. This is often due to that individuals do not use the correct source of information. They can be asking another person who they think has the most recent information or information stored elsewhere.

One very common example of this is the use of outdated contract templates. The correct templates are often stored on the intranet but people tend to use the latest contract they wrote as a template resulting in faulty contracts.

4.2 Information Demand Modelling

Based on the industrial case and the typical problems described above, various approaches to modelling information demand have been used. The result is a suggestion on a highly flexible component-based method defining a framework for analysing information demand guided by a set of important principles through the application of a number of method components and a unified representation. In this paper focus is on the method component for modelling and analysing information demand contexts, as this is the core of the method.

From a principle point-of-view, modelling information demand relies heavily on stakeholder participations. While it certainly would be possible to base the analysis on existing enterprise descriptions this would not ensure the strong connection to roles required. Therefore it is considered of crucial importance that the modelling is performed in cooperation with the actual individuals having the roles to be modelled. Furthermore, as supported by the underlying, and empirically supported, theory, information demand is always role-based. Consequently, the investigative focus of information demand modelling should not be process-based since this would take focus from many of the relevant aspects of information demand.

4.2.1 A Method for Information Demand Modelling and Analysis

Identifying, modelling and analysing information demand is, based on the empirical background, considered as a prerequisite to building various technical solutions for providing demand-driven information supply. As mentioned in Section 2. understanding information demand requires understanding of information demand contexts in addition to a number of aspects. In Figure 2. below an overview of a framework for achieving such understanding is presented. Since context is considered central to information demand analysis, methodological support for modelling such contexts is at the core of the framework. However, in order to be able to perform any meaningful context modelling a clear scope is needed. Consequently, the process starts with scoping activities. Also, depending on the requirements and needs relevant for the specific case additional aspects of information demand might be analysed and modelled.

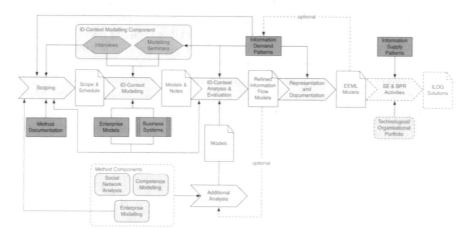

Fig. 2. An overview of the process of analysing information demand

In order for any context modelling and analysis to be possible a clear scope is considered as a prerequisite. Scoping is the process of defining the area of analysis and is done with the purpose of selecting the part of an organisation to analyze with respect to information demand as well as identifying the individuals that will be providing the necessary information during the continued analysis activities. Scoping also serves the purpose of facilitating the understanding and identification of the analysed party's perceived problems motivating them to engage in information demand analysis. Furthermore, it also facilitate the identification of intensions, goals and expectation such parties might have with doing so.

Supporting the method user in the various scoping activities there are a number of different tools, techniques and information. Using traditional enterprise techniques as process modelling, goal modelling and concept graphs can facilitate a shared understanding between all involved parties and thereby ensuring minimising of time and effort needed for continued activities. As the scoping was an integrated part of the case described in Section 3. and aspects of information demand modelling such as competence modelling, documentation and representation etc. are outside the scope of this paper, the rest of this section will focus mainly on the context modelling and analysis parts of the method in relation to the industrial case.

Information Demand Context Modelling
Due to the nature of information demand the next step of the process after scoping, is to identify and capture contexts. Doing so rely heavily on participative activities such

as joint modelling seminaries where the informants themselves construct models and the method user facilitates the process by supporting and helping the informants. As illustrated in Figure 1. the conceptual focus is rather small during this phase of the process and furthermore, the focus is solely on information demand within the defined scope. No regards are given to the sequence of activities and resource availability etc. The key to context modelling is instead to identify the interrelationship between roles, tasks, resources and information.

The format and appearance of the actual models produced during these seminars is not important as long as the models capture the information relevant for the continued process. Rather, the choice of techniques used has to be dependent on the situation and the requirements following from it. However, Figure 3. below introduce a notation that can be used for this purpose by giving an example taken from the academic world (the reason behind using this example rather than the models resulting from the industrial case is due to confidentiality regarding Proton Finishing's business processes).

Information Demand Context Analysis and Evaluation
Once the necessary knowledge about information demand contexts within the scope is gained it can be used for a number of different purposes. From Figure 3. a number of constructs relating to problems identified in Section 4.1. can be identified. The notation allows for representing superfluous information (relating to 4.1.1.) as exemplified by the information object *"Registration Status"* supplied to the role *Examiner*. The same is true for gaps between information demand and information actually supplied (relating to 4.1.2.) exemplified by amongst others *"Course Evaluation"* in Figure 3. Furthermore, the problems relating to dated information (4.1.4), can be partially dealt with by applying temporal conditions to information demand as is done with the task *"Sign up for Exam"* for the role *"Course Participant"*. Such temporal attributes can also be connected directly to information objects and not only to the tasks motivating the demand for information as in this example.

Visualising information demand and flow in this manner also helps with reducing the effects of problems relating to information gathered at the wrong time (4.1.3.) as the visualisation in itself facilitates the understanding of the information demand in a wider organisational perspective. There is also an inherent value in grouping information by role independently of processes as this gives an overview of each roles general situation with respect to information flow.

During this phase of the process it also suitable to evaluate the results with respect to motivation and purposes expressed during the scoping activities. Focusing on information demand contexts only provide an initial view of information demand without any consideration given to such aspects as individual competence, organisational expectations and requirements in terms of goals, processes etc. Depending on the intentions behind performing the analysis further activities might be required. The method provides a number of method components supporting such activities. Since the main focus of the method presented here is on information demand it utilises existing procedures and notations for such additional aspects rather than defining new ones. Consequently, if the method user wishes to investigate such additional aspects of information demand, he or she can do this by using subsets of the following methods, notations and languages:

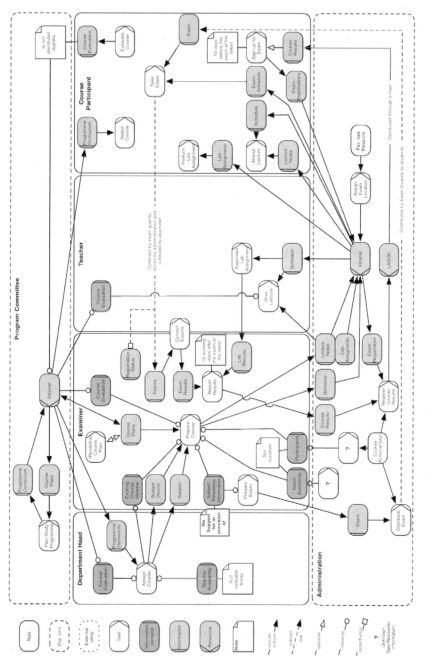

Fig. 3. A notation for modelling information demand contexts

- **Enterprise Knowledge Development (EKD)** – a method for generating knowledge about organisational functioning and reasons for change by analysing traditional enterprise aspects in a participative manner with support of a number of description techniques and guidelines.
- **I-star (i*)** – a method for modelling social networks in terms of the concepts typically found within the area of enterprise modelling.
- **Unified Enterprise Competence Modelling Language (UECML)** – an extension to the Unified Enterprise Modelling Language focusing on modelling competence with respect to mainly roles and activities.

Whilst no further details on utilising these methods, notations and languages are given in this paper the results from doing so always have to be evaluated with respect to the contexts identified during the previous phase. The reasoning behind this is simply that the method presented here is not a method for analysing traditional enterprise aspects. Its only goal is to identify and understand the information demand within an organisation. Everything that is done as part of the analysis efforts should therefore also be focused on the role-based nature of information demand. Doing so requires one to relate any knowledge gained to the information demand contexts. That is to say, such additional aspects are only relevant in the sense that they influence the initial view on information demand generated by the context modelling and analysis. Examples of this might be individual competence that differentiates between the information needed by two separate individuals having the same role and performing the same tasks within an organisation. Consequently, this phase of the process has to be iterated over for every additional analysis activity that is performed to ensure that the strong connection to the contexts is kept.

5 Reflections and Discussion

5.1 Methods Supporting Action

There are several things that influence, guide and inspire us, when performing qualified investigations, modelling and analysis. The sources of guidance and influence can be more or less explicit. They can be of a tacit nature in terms of different experiences that we have and that we are recalling in the actual work situation. They can also be explicitly formulated in different method descriptions that we follow. Somewhere between experiences and methods we also have theories that directs us without giving such explicit prescriptive directives as methods. In addition to this we can also use computerised tools in which the method has been implemented. The use of methods, theories and tools can therefore be regarded as action knowledge that we can agree with and seek support from during information demand analysis, i.e. methods, theories, and tools are examples of supporting instruments that we can use when we are performing information demand analysis. This conceptualisation of support for actions is also described in Figure 4.

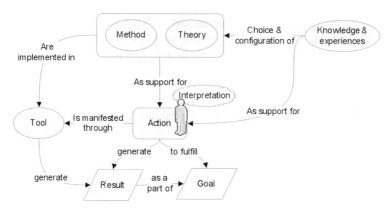

Fig. 4. Support for information demand analysis

The main reason for this elaboration on different types of support for actions is to structure, formalise and clarify different types of support that are used during information demand analysis. In this paper we have put a method as support for information demand analysis in focus and therefore we also need to present a conceptualisation that describes method as a phenomenon.

A method is prescriptive in character since it gives us guidance on what to do in different situations in order to reach certain goals. During modelling there is usually a need to document different aspects and many methods therefore include roles for representation, which often is called modelling techniques or notations. Such methods also provide procedural guidelines, which many times are tightly coupled to notation. The procedure involves some meta-concepts as process, activity, information, and object, which are parts of the prescribed procedure. They are also parts of the semantics of the notation. The concepts are the cement and the overlapping parts between procedure and notation. Methods can thus be crystallised into:

Perform action A, in order to reach goal G
It has now been stated that procedure, notation and concepts, amongst other things, constitute methods. When there is a close link between procedure, notation, and concepts, it is referred to as a method component [9]. The concept of method component is similar to the concept Method Chunk [10] and [11] and the notion of method fragment [12]. A method is often a compound of several method components to what many times is called a methodology [13]. These different method components together form a structure called a framework, which includes the phase structure of the method.

All methods build on some implicit (tacit) or explicit perspective. Such a perspective includes values, principles and categories (with definitions), which are more fully expressed in the method and its method components. The perspective is the conceptual and value basis of the method and its rationality.

An additional aspect of methods is labelled co-operation principle; i.e. how different persons interact and co-operate when performing method guided work. Co-operation principles have to do with roles and division of work in the process. This aspect is labelled collection principles and it is conceptually important to distinguish between a procedure ("what question to ask"), a co-operation principle ("whom is asking the question") and a collection principle ("how is the answer collected"). A method component (with procedures) can be used within several different co-operation and collection principles, as e.g. seminars, brainstorm sessions, interviews and questionnaires. The central parts of this method theory are illustrated in Figure 5. below [14] [15] [9]. This notion of methods is the conceptual base that we have used for structuring the method for information demand analysis.

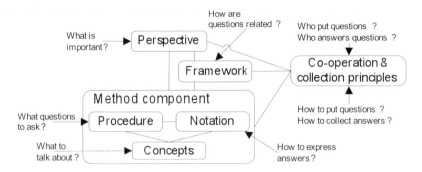

Fig. 5. The notion of method

5.2   Validity of Practices from EM

Context modelling in the industrial cases presented in Section 3. was conducted in a participative manner, as the researchers involved had experience in this way of work-ing, considered it as best practice for the problem at hand and it created a shared un-derstanding of the current situation [16]. Information demand context modelling is similar to enterprise modelling, but still a different approach due to the different per-spective taken. Thus, it should be examined whether proven experiences and recom-mendations for participative modelling can be transferred to context modelling. This section will present the lessons learned in this area by discussing how and to what extent the recommendations for participative modelling proposed by Stirna et al [17] were used in the context modelling cases.

Table 1. shows the recommendations published in Stirna et al [17] and compares them to the experiences from the context modelling cases. The recommendations were divided into five groups, which are reflected in the table. When describing the experiences, we will use

- "confirmed", if the practice was applied in the cases and usefulness for context modelling was confirmed,
- "not applied", if the practice was not applied, i.e. no statement can be made regarding validity for context modelling
- "not confirmed", if the number of cases was too small in order to confirm the validity. However, this does not necessarily mean that the practice is not valid.
- "modified", if the practice was enhanced or changed.

Table 1. Comparison of recommendations and experiences

Recommendation from Stirna et al (2007)	Experiences from Context Modelling
1. Assess the organisational context	
understanding the organisation's *power and decision-making structure is essential*	Confirmed, but in only one of the cases, since the other three cases were part of the already established InfoFLOW project.
Organisational culture has significant impact	Not confirmed. The culture in the cases was quite similar, i.e. there was an insufficient basis to confirm the practice
Interviews with stakeholders before starting the project may reveal hidden agendas	Confirmed. Not all participants were interviewed before the modelling sessions, but most of them, which proved to be a good preparation
2. Assess the problem at hand	
Interview key decision maker or conduct participative EM sessions for understanding the actual problem	Confirmed. Both ways were used (interviews and sessions)
Understand the complexity of the project (fairly simple, complex or wicked	Not confirmed. Too few cases were considered; none of them can be categorised as wicked problem.
3. Assign roles in the modelling process	
Modelling facilitator	Confirmed. This role is considered as essential.
Tool operator	Modified: the tool was used after the session. The tool operator was rather an assisting facilitator.
Modelling participant / domain expert	Confirmed.
4. Acquire resources for the project in general and for preparation efforts in particular	Not applicable in 3 of the cases as they were part of the InfoFLOW project. Confirmed in one case.
5. Conduct modelling sessions	
clear objectives of practical value	Confirmed. The objectives were always related to information demand and information flow issues.
modelling notation that everyone understands	Confirmed. Notation was introduced very thoroughly.
Do not "train" the modelling participants in method knowledge	Confirmed. This would not contribute to context modelling.
Keep everyone involved and focused	Confirmed. This is essential for success of the sessions.
Do not accept unknown participants	Not applied, i.e. there were no "intruders" to be taken care of.
problem owner should not dominate the seminar	Not confirmed. There always were several problem owners, i.e. dominance of only a few participants was not an issue.
Establish a common vocabulary	Confirmed.
Develop models in parallel	Not applied. Models were developed after the sessions.

Table 1. (*Continued*)

	Make concrete decisions in the session	Confirmed regarding decisions about first changes in information flow and regarding next steps to take
	Model should deliver a solution	Not applied. Model aimed at creating a joint understanding.
	Make sure that everyone knows what will happen after the seminar	Confirmed.

The overall impression is – not surprisingly – that an overwhelming part of the recommendations for participative modelling were found useful and accurate for context modelling. However, the number of cases this result is based on was rather small. Furthermore, there is the danger of a certain bias regarding utility of the original recommendations, due to tight working relationships of the authors.

6 Summary and Future Work

The paper presented practices and experiences from information demand context modelling based on several industrial cases. The modelling approach used is a newly developed method for this purpose, which takes a role-centric view and focuses on capturing the role's tasks and responsibilities and the information required for these tasks and responsibilities. The method consists of several method components, which to a substantial part are grounded in enterprise modelling traditions.

Based on industrial cases from automotive industries, experiences and practices of information demand modelling are presented and investigated. This includes the specific perspective taken in the method for information demand analysis, common challenges experienced in demand modelling, the validity of practices from participative enterprise modelling for context modelling and practices of context modelling.

Acknowledgements

Some parts of the research presented were financed by the Swedish Knowledge Foundation (KK-Stiftelsen) through grant 2005/0252, project "Information Logistics for SME (InfoFLOW)".

References

1. Harmon, P.: The Scope and Evolution of Business Process Management. In: vom Brocke, J., Rosemann, M. (eds.) Handbook on Business Process Management. Springer, Heidelberg (2009)
2. Davenport, T.H.: Process Innovation. Reengineering Work Through Information Technology. Harvard Business School Press, Boston (1993)

3. Humphrey, W.S.: Software Process The improvement – A Personal View: How it Started and Where it is Going. Software Process The Improvement and Practice 12, 223–227 (2007)
4. Warner, B.W.: Organisational Development - A Process of Learning and Changing. Addison Wesley, Reading (1994)
5. Deiters, W., Löffeler, T., Pfenningschmidt, S.: The Information Logistical Approach Toward a User Demand-driven Information Supply. In: Spinellis, D. (ed.) Cross-Media Service Delivery, pp. 37–48. Kluwer Academic Publisher, Dordrecht (2003)
6. Öhgren, A., Sandkuhl, K.: Information Overload in Industrial Enterprises - Results of an Empirical Investigation. In: Proceedings ECIME 2008, London, UK (2008)
7. Lundqvist, M.: Context as a Key Concept in Information Demand Analysis. In: Proceedings of the Doctoral Consortium associated with the 5th Intl. and Interdisciplinary Conference on Modelling and Using Context (Context 2005), Paris, France, pp. 63–73 (2005)
8. Lundqvist, M.: Information Demand and Use: Improving Information Flow within Small-scale Business Contexts. Linköping studies in science and technology, Linköping University, Department of Computer and Information Science, Linköping, Sweden (2007)
9. Röstlinger, A., Goldkuhl, G.: På väg mot en komponentbaserad metodsyn (in Swedish). Presented at VITS Höstseminarium 1994, Linköping University, Linköping, Sweden (1994)
10. Ralyté, J., Backlund, P., Kühn, H., Jeusfeld, M.A.: Method Chunks for Interoperability. In: Embley, D.W., Olivé, A., Ram, S. (eds.) ER 2006. LNCS, vol. 4215, pp. 339–353. Springer, Heidelberg (2006)
11. Mirbel, I., Ralyté, J.: Situational method engineering: combining assembly-based and roadmap-driven approaches. Requirements Eng. 11, 58–78 (2006)
12. Brinkkemper, S.: Method engineering: engineering of information systems development methods and tools. Information and Software Technology 1995, 37 (1995)
13. Avison, D.E., Fitzgerald, G.: Information Systems Development: Methodologies, Techniques and Tools. McGraw Hill, Berkshire (1995)
14. Goldkuhl, G., Cronholm, S.: Customizable CASE environments: A Framework for Design and Evaluation. Accepted to COPE IT 1993/NordDATA, Copenhagen, June 14-16 (1993)
15. Goldkuhl, G., Lind, M., Seigerroth, U.: Method integration: the need for a learning perspective. IEE Proceedings, Software (special issue on Information System Methodologies) 145(4) (August 1998)
16. Lind, M., Seigerroth, U.: Team-based reconstruction for expanding organisational ability. Journal of the Operational Society 54, 119–129 (2003)
17. Stirna, J., Persson, A., Sandkuhl, K.: Participative enterprise modeling: Experiences and recommendations. In: Krogstie, J., Opdahl, A.L., Sindre, G. (eds.) CAiSE 2007 and WES 2007. LNCS, vol. 4495, pp. 546–560. Springer, Heidelberg (2007)

The Common Model of an Enterprise's Value Objects, Presented in Relevant Business Views

Jan Gustafsson[1] and Jarl Höglund[2]

[1] Ferrologic Enterprise Design AB, Stora Nygatan 14, 111 27 Stockholm, Sweden
jan.gustafsson@ferrologic.se
[2] ALLMENTOR AB, Storsvängen 66, 129 43 Hägersten, Sweden
jarl.hoglund@allmentor.se

Abstract. The purpose of the paper is to report on the experiences from four linked product structuring cases at large Swedish companies involving substantial concept modeling. Case by case will be described in brief, and we will discuss how the experiences from previous case add to the next. The main issues have been: one business view of the product dominates information access, the terminology and communication. We will discuss the value of having one common product model and unified terminology that is accepted in all processes adding value to the product. The modeling method will be discussed, including the way of working when many contributors must be on the arena. The paper analyzes the fact that what is supposed to be very company/product unique objects/relations, in fact often are generic. The most recent case introduces context as an object into an already complex product structure.

Keywords: Product, perspectives, participation, value objects, context, complete value chain, generics, complexity, resistance.

1 Introduction

The journey we have experienced started in a crucial phase at the to-be analysis of a product management process in a global telecom industrial environment. The purpose of the process is to control and maximize the product profitability over the complete life-cycle, considering three areas of responsibility– market needs, product characteristics and business control. That, in fact, implies interfaces to all other main processes and stakeholders in both the time-to-market flow and the time-to-customer flow, and their specific views on the product.

Our objective in the project was to find out if there were some commonalities in how the product was structured, and if people communicated using the same terminology regarding the product, and other product related terms, and to identify points of measurement. The initial as-is study gave us the immediate answer that this was not the case.

The main question was: What is the "product"? To some parts of the enterprise it is only what is sold and delivered. To other parts it is something else. Subsequently it is very important to regard the product as the value-carrying object throughout the

A. Persson and J. Stirna (Eds.): PoEM 2009, LNBIP 39, pp. 23–37, 2009.

enterprise. This means it includes the sold product, the parts it consists of, included functions, configured models, etc. Actually it includes all objects that time, money or effort is spent on, or that generates money, or the investment object. This also means that the "product" exists as a value-carrying object long before it is developed or produced, and in fact, as soon as someone spends working time thinking about it.

At this time we got an inquiry from the CFO: What does the company make money on? Which products are profitable? Suddenly we had a sponsor to at least start an analysis of how to structure the product to please all stakeholders.

The method for all coming cases, represented by this "meta case" is Conceptual Modeling, based on the Entity-Relation modeling principles [2].

We know that the method is a pre-requisite, but not the only key to success. The key is rather how we have applied the method to the identified situation, and the outcome [Astrakan reference here].

The first issue is to have a clear and common understanding about and difference between "concepts and terms" [3].

It is also important to realize and accept that everything may be looked at from different viewpoints, and may have different meaning to different viewers. All views are correct, and relevant, but to different viewers in different situations, or business functions. In this case it is important not to confuse the organizational division of the enterprise with the functional views. A functional view gathers all parts/roles that regard a common "thing" in the same way. The thing being the "product" as defined earlier, as a value-carrying object.

In order to visualize this and to make it pedagogical, we used the metaphor of a flower. The petals of the flower each represent a business functional view of a shared/common object in the centre of the flower, the seed-pod.

The business views most likely like to see the information sorted in some sort of structure of the product, and mostly in a hierarchical way, suitable for their view. The different views have a need for different sorting, and thereby different hierarchical structures. In order to produce theses different structures without storing information more than once, it is essential to build a logical model of information objects and business rules in the centre of the flower, the seed-pod. The logic of the central model may the present information in different hierarchical context, to different business views.

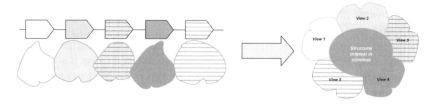

Fig. 1. Each process/business function, and their views on the product

When modeling the "product" of an enterprise it is essential to model on appropriate abstraction level. This means to focus on the concepts rather than the information. The concepts are the objects/information holders and the "thing" you want to know something about. The information is attributes of the concepts, initially utilized to identify the correct concepts and their inter-relational logic.

Another extremely important issue is to define the relevant projection of the effort. Projection is to set the scope for the model according to the mission of your business, the business idea.

An example of projection -- for a producer of speed boats the boats are their products, being the result of their efforts. So is the hull, the keel and the deck. Even if their products are "things", not all "things" are products to them. They use drills, grinders and lathes when producing their products, but these are not products to their business. They are means/tools.

To the company producing tools, they are products, of course. That is a different projection. The reason is to ensure that the content will be the "product" in the sense of value-carriers, not assets in general.

1.1 Work Procedure for the Effort

The analysis was performed in a number of workshops, starting with identifying the business views by the means of Stakeholders Diagram Analysis. This workshop was conducted together with representatives of the stakeholders, in order to cover the enterprise in a rational way.

After deciding the accepted business views (by management based on a recommendation from the participating stakeholders), the planning of one workshop per business view (petal of the flower) was initiated.

In each workshop, the participants were asked to focus on finding concepts/products that they use when communicating with other business views. In other words the participants were instructed to focus on finding the concepts/products that would be their "candidates" for the core model (the seed-pod of the flower). Objects and information that are proprietary to the view, is of less interest in order to define the common object model of product information.

After modeling all business views, a number (4-5) of candidates to become the common object model existed.

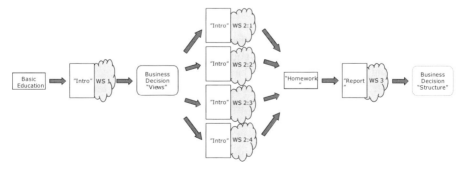

Fig. 2. Work procedure for the modeling effort

At this stage in the procedure, the facilitators (us) had some homework to do. All the different versions/candidates to become the core model had to be analyzed, both separately and together. All concepts/products that existed in more than one view, had to be represented in the final core model.

After concluding "our homework" it was presented to the final workshop with representatives from all business views for final "massaging", leading to the concluded core model that was accepted by a management decision.

1.2 Organization of the Paper

The remainder of the paper is organized as follows. In section 2 there is a presentation of the cases, the reason for conducting them and the remaining results. In section 3 we summarize the experiences from the cases and the advantages in conducting this work procedure. In section 4 we make some concluding remarks and discuss issues for future work.

2 The Cases

There is no single case. We are now sharing our experiences from four selected cases. It is the sum of experiences from four different assignments that is evolving this way of performing modeling. The motivations for the different cases are specific, not the same, yet leading to the same need for analysis, of the "product model logic".

The cases that we summarize in our meta-case are from three different branches of business:

- Case 1 - A large manufacturer within telecom
- Case 2 - A portal business start-up during the dot-com era
- Case 3 - A large manufacturer of vehicles (corporate core)
- Case 4 – A large manufacturer of vehicles (service market's view of corporate core)

They all aim to run a profitable business, offering something that attracts the chosen marketplace, while producing and delivering it with a fair margin.

2.1 Case 1 - Matching Revenue to Cost of the Products

The controller of one company stated a question to the managers of the different business units – "Last year we had a very good result within the company. Which products created that result?" The managers had to assemble the information, and get back to the controller, but their reply was "We don't know. We have no idea!" The controller replied "Lucky for you that we had a good result!"

At this time we belonged to a team responsible to map and establish the product management process at the company, and the controller asked us for help – "I need a way to be able to match cost, and investments to the revenue of a product!" Since we regarded this as a core issue within product management, we responded that we would gladly take on this assignment.

At this time the revenue of each "order" was registered under one of hundred "product codes". There was also one product code named "other", where about 80% of all orders were booked! The controller asked if we could help him to reduce the number of "product codes", to less than ten, just to make it manageable. We responded with a desire to map the product, as a value-object through-out the entire business, from each applicable business perspective. This implied making a conceptual core model of "product".

The controller gave us "carte blanche" as long as we reduced the number of "product codes" within three months.

We realized that the enterprise had a premium product data management system support for the existing product structures. However, the structures represented the development view of the products. This was perfect for designers, but less suitable for sales and production staff. We defined the need for the business to look at the "product" from different view-points, depending on the business view.

The modeling job was performed according to the work procedure described earlier, with the metaphor of the flower with business views sharing a common product core model.

In a first workshop, where a variety of business functions, derived from the main process map, were represented we analyzed that five different perspectives of the product, would cover the desired control. The views were: Product Management, Marketing & Sales, Supply, Development and Operation & Maintenance.

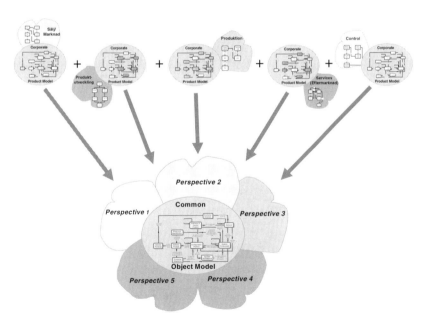

Fig. 3. The flower as a metaphor, and the work procedure for developing the common object model

We had realized that the different views had to see different, or the same, information of the products, but placed in different contexts. We also realized that we had to
find some common "core logic" that kept the information and products in some sort
of order, so information could be generated into structures suitable for the different
business views need of product information.

This was actually the first time we utilized the metaphor with the flower to the full
extent.

In order to find the logic of the common object model that would fulfill the needs
of each business view, we decided to model with the representatives from each view
separately. The reason for that was to prevent arguments between people representing
different views to arise at this early stage, and the problems to facilitate the number of
representatives needed in only one big workshop.

The instruction to the workshops in each view, was to ask them: regarding which
product objects are you sharing information with other business views?

Our finding was also that people in the business are quite used to model their
business, but mostly in terms of processes and activities. The change in focus was to
concentrate on the prerequisites for a specific task, as input, and the result, as an
output, finding and modeling the product, as the "back-bone" value carrier in the
business flow.

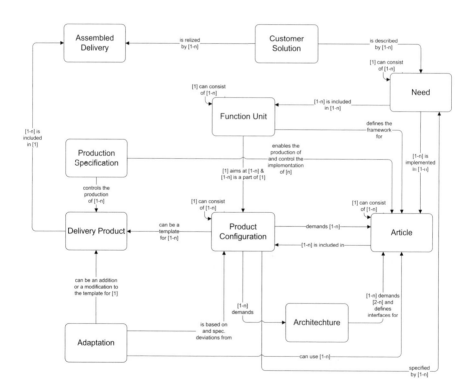

Fig. 4. The common object model of the product

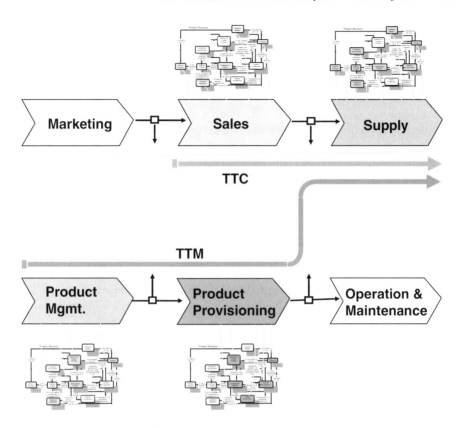

Fig. 5. The different petals of the flower metaphor, laid out in the product flow at the company

After having results from each and every business view, in this case five, we would stack them on top of each other, and "x-ray" the stack, in order to find commonalities, and differences. Everything that existed in two or more business views was selected as a candidate to be a core object. In this normalization effort, performed in a workshop with a few representatives from each previous view workshops, we created the logical pattern with all core objects (shared by at least two business views).

2.2   Case 2 - A Portal Business Start-Up during the Dot-Com Era

A start-up company had found a niche on the internet market, where a portal could be positioned in order to orchestrate a bonus redemption program for a number of under-laying e-business retail portals (e-biz partners).

Our assignment was to "categorize the product" to enable, the business idea. We realized that the way to go was to analyze and model the product in a corporate core model in order to present it in several appropriate views. The problem however was that categorization is much like sorting something into different boxes -- fine for one situation at one particular moment in time. But different viewers may want to see the things sorted in different ways for different situations. And the things may only be placed in one box at a time…

The business idea was to identify a certain product that was sold to a customer on internet, by one or possibly several members. Except for the needed possibility to identify a particular sold item regardless of retailer within the "portal". Additionally the idea was to analyze the customer's combination of purchased items (customer's shopping cart) and recommend what to buy next. In this "portal sphere" there would also be providers of content (advertisers, editors, etc.) as well as providers of the bonus rewards. A part of the financing of the business would also be based on advertising. The company for this "top portal endeavor" was based on venture capital and two persons to administer the portal (run the business).

We started by analyzing the vision, mission, goals and strategy defined for the business. We also identified the "e-biz partners" being the e-business portals to be connected to the bonus/redemption program. In parallel with our investigation to "categorize the product", another part of the project had already started to build the "redemption engine", the solution that would keep track of all products, customers, retailers, purchase transactions, bonus accounts as well as realized and pending redemptions.

Again we utilized the work procedure that we presented in the introduction - identifying business views, modeling workshops per business view, conducting normalization homework, and finalizing the core model.

The views were defined as Business Control, Member Services, Individual visitor and/or member, E-biz Partner, Space Customer, Advertisers, Media Brokers and Provider of Content, Public Services and Rewards.

In this case we experienced something new – since this was a start-up, the business staff to involve in the modeling workshops did not exist. The modeling per view had to be simulated as homework. We had to interview the two founders in order to understand their intension with the business, and thereby simulate the business-to-be, in workshops "at home". We also interviewed companies (e-biz partners) from each view about the forthcoming business set-up. The core model was created from all the business views and their need to control and benefit from the business.

The basis of the idea to map, log and analyze the demographic patterns of purchases, as well as common product portfolio among a number of retailers, was found to be very hard, if not impossible, due to the fact that products did not have unique identifiers. For example, a specific sports shoe from one retailer was called "gymnastics shoe" from another, and "tennis shoe" from a third. The only product that was possible to handle, within the specified portfolio, was books based on the ISBN global numbering standard.

It also became quite obvious that this would not become a "pianola" for the two founders. The interaction to administer this logical core was to become enormous.

The effort to run this portal enterprise was very demanding. The founders realized this, after being presented to the facts and the whole business idea was changed. Instead of actually running this "portal sphere" for bonuses and redemption, they would capitalize on the developed solution by making a product of that and selling it to other companies to run a redemption scheme.

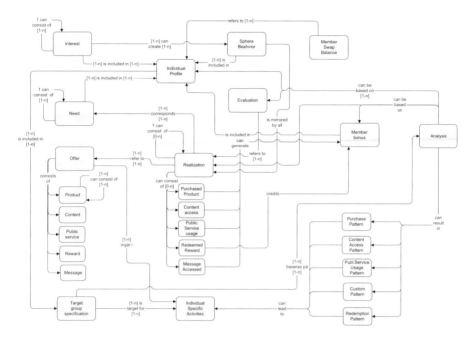

Fig. 6. The common object model of the product for the portal enterprise

2.3 Case 3 - A Large Manufacturer of Vehicles (Common Object Model)

Case 3 took place at an industrial company that is well known to the market, as being very efficient in utilizing few parts combined in many configured products.

The reason to re-investigate how this is handled is due to the fact that the principles for re-use and modularity have been practiced within the company since the 1950s, but applied to mechanical products. Mechanics can be perceived as easy to understand due to the visibility. During the last few decades there has been an increasing involvement of electronics, and recently also computers and software. The existence of these things is not as obvious, due to the lack of physical presence. Additionally the new technology brought in new terminology, such as, for instance, "system".

A system was now considered to be a logical context, which utilized components to fulfill a desired function/service for electronics and software.

It is worth pointing out that a vehicle has had a lot of "systems" historically, but they are mechanical such as exhaust, steering, brake, propulsion, etc.

The new technologies, like electronics and SW, have brought in a capability to meet new needs and fulfill new functions in a completely new way of realizing it. That has led to an exponential increase in number of functions on a vehicle, and thereby the complexity is increasing continuously.

The company has early on, at least earlier than others, realized the need to have different structures for different business views. The fact to let the two perspectives for development and production interact, has placed the company far ahead of their competitors.

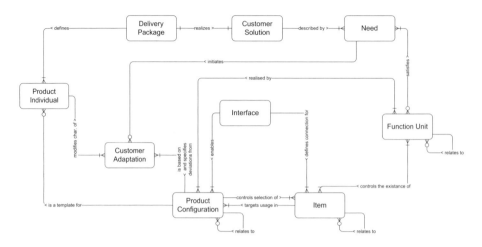

Fig. 7. The central common object model of the product

The stakeholders diagram was defined to the following views, or perspectives as this company decided to call them: Sales & Marketing, Production, and Service Market, Research & Development, and Control. We also decided to call the evolving common object model the "Corporate Product Model".

The greatest interest and largest need to achieve a better support to the business was from Service Market. So we decided to start with that business view. The workshops would be run in the backward order of the product life-cycle: Service Market, Production, Sales & Marketing and Research & Development. The last perspective Control was handled through project interwork between the development and marketing functions. The common object logic induced by "control" was however captured.

During the project we observed the low level of tool support that was addressed to Service Market and to Sales/Marketing. The production organization is used to handle total mass-customization and have accepted that all vehicles are unique and different. No commonality, no models and no patterns are of interest. Models are however essential for any sales effort since the buyers would identify models based on utilization. Within Service Market it is also of interest to see/utilize models or similar abstractions of commonality, in order to prepare service workshops with repair manuals for typical product configurations (models).

When assembling the common object model we found "clusters of information" without any obvious concept/object to hold it. We also found same or similar "clusters" in many /all business views. Obviously we had discovered a well known, but undefined object that was extremely central to the business. The object was the Product Configuration which is central object to all perspectives. It has six relations to other objects in the common object model, as well as it has it's own multiple structures.

This led us to the fact that when the final presentation of the result was made to the main stakeholders, as well as most of the involved persons from all workshops, everyone involved said: "That's our model!". None of the workshops had seen the final model, but they could all relate to the final result to come.

A notable difference between the common object model in Case 1 and Case 3 is that the relations "can consist of" has been replaced by "relates to" for the configuration. This means that the structural need differ between the business views, and one single structure in the common object model, would be wrong. (See Case 4).

2.4 Case 4 – A Large Manufacturer of Vehicles (Service Market View of Corporate Common Object Model)

After the effort to map and create the business logic on corporate level, supporting all business perspectives, there was a direct interest from some views to proceed with the next level of business analysis.

The service market was in a troublesome situation, due to the fact that they are not only working with the latest products and their information, but are also forced to handle information for the product during 5-10 years to come.

Within the Service Market perspective an assignment was defined, in order to analyze the as-is and the to-be situation for Service Market specifically.

The staff within service market has to define and maintain information for products and parts that exist on the market. One of the objects identified during the modeling of the common object model (Case 3) is the Product Configuration. That is one of the few objects that is regarded/seen from all views. It was concluded earlier that the relations of that object differed between the views, and even how the recursive relations would be applied. A very interesting finding in this perspective is that product configurations have to be presented having a hierarchical structure that is unique to Service Market, and has to have a different structures presented to other perspectives.

The solution was when we realized that Product Configurations had a structure based on "Components" playing a role in a specific "Context". This means that the context does not "own" the component, as it would in a traditional hierarchy, but instead is "utilizing" it.

One component may subsequently play a role in several contexts. It also became very obvious that the component is not equal to a physical item. The component is the logical "space" or "position" defined by the context. The item can play the role as a component in a context.

Another notable finding is that there are two different break-down structures important to Service Market: logical and physical. Physical is important to find the need

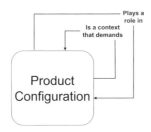

Fig. 8. The recursive Product Configuration

for specific spare parts, and logical is crucial for analyzing faults and errors in the functionality of the final product.

This also calls for the need to keep information on abstract object level (product without instances) in an applied logical structure. Information that would need this level is for instance "system". A system is a logical context, which may be applied physically different, on different instances of a product, thus having the exact same function and characteristics regardless of implementation.

The culture of this company is to re-use few parts in different contexts, creating modularity. Therefore no hierarchical structures may be stored for re-use, thus needed to be utilized with different sorting, depending of purpose.

In the view for service market a component is to be regarded as a role in a logical context. A part/item may take that role, or several roles in different contexts.

On the contrary, within production a "component" may be a role in a "physical" context, being parts at the assembly line.

3   Experiences

Our experiences from the four product structuring cases have been as a relay race, each case has added value to the next etc. The predominant experience is probably the break-through in Case #4 where the principle of roles in contexts was introduced.

3.1 Deliverables Case #1

The prime assignment was to architect the future product management process, and an additional request from the CFO was to find a way to reduce the number of product codes (class of goods).The result ended up in a reduction of the number of product codes from more than 100 to less than 10. Revenue could now be tied to chosen level in the structure of business control products (see fig 4), enabling monitoring of product profitability. Furthermore the establishment of product configuration as a key central object paved the way for a potential efficiency increase in all processes from sales to delivery in the range of 50%.

3.2 Deliverable Case #2

The assignment was to set a model to qualify and further specify a completely new business model on the dot.com arena. The result ended up in a new strategy. Instead of actually running the portal sphere for bonuses and redemption, the strategy became to capitalize on the developed solution, by making it a product and sell it to other companies to run redemption schemes.

3.3 Deliverable Case #3

The assignment was to map all key stakeholders view of the product, in addition to enabling phase-out of the current IT platform for product data management.

The resulting core product model, explicitly illustrated the importance of controlling complex product configurations in order to reuse information regarding the configuration of the delivered product, not only in development and production, but also in sales and the long lasting and profitable service market. This created a new basis for enhancement of efficiency in terms of lead time and quality, as well as basis for IT requirements on future product data support. The service market representatives in the assignment realized there potential value and initiated the next case.

3.4 Deliverable Case #4

The assignment was to utilize the common object model developed in case #3, in order to find and detail the product structure tailored to service market's needs. Configuration objects to "hang" information on, was needed in order to keep structure information to supply spare parts, create and maintain repair instructions, and functional instructions for service workshops.

The key result was to allow unique structures to exist for the use of service market, respecting similarities between delivered products (models), even-though all delivered product unique by the means of mass-customization in production. The structures in the service market view are not a base to store information, but to generate and present from the common object model.

4   Conclusions and Future Work

It has been a very awarding journey to go through all these four cases, in different business environments, which has created an enormous increase in insight, while we have been having a real good time!

The metaphor of the flower is a prerequisite for success. The same object may be seen from different view-points, both demanding attribute filtering, as well as seeing an object in relation to different surroundings (other objects), depending on the purpose of that view-point.

Essential to all the efforts of conceptual modeling is to be really precise in delimiting the scope of the domain to model.

A key insight from Case #1 was to find the configuration product being a value carrier in the whole enterprise. That was the last object to appear in the model, thus being the most central, with the most number of relations to other object, as well as being regarded from all business views. The object appeared by the gathering, or a cluster, of information with no object to "hang it" on. Key insights from Case #2 – the common object model was proved to be useful even in a non industrial environment. It is more generic than we initially realized. If the "product" was regarded, not only as a physical thing, but as anything in an enterprise being the result of effort and carrying value, it really became an eye-opener to us all.

Key insights from Case #3 – this time we were addressing an enterprise that already has done this effort, leading to combination of two business views. The challenge was now to first address an addition/shift in technology. All structural work previously performed, was related to mechanical products. Now the business is adding electronics and software which was less tangible.

Adding two more business views also proved the fact that the imbedded structure in our previous core model no longer could remain hierarchical. "Consists of" was replaced by "relates to". The reason for that is that "structure" was handled as a synonym to hierarchical. The structures had to be different in the different business views. Therefore the information origin in the common object model had to be non-hierarchical and the stricter had to be generated on demand.

Key insights from Case #4 – the imperative finding in this effort was that there may be needs to have multiple break-down structures of the same product configuration, depending of utilization. Role and "Context" becomes obviously crucial in order to create the necessary logic in the common object model. There must be both a logical and physical breakdown of the delivered product in order to navigate and coordinate the information.

The following insights come from all cases:

– The applied approach, e.g. to be very focused on the WHAT-perspective and its structures, after the analysis of WHY and HOW, have been part of the success in all cases [1].
– The access to a sponsor, with driving spirit in the management team is a prerequisite in order to get competent people to the analyses and to reach out with the result and obtain the expected effect. In one case we did not have a supporting sponsor, and that made it much harder to proceed as planned. This is in line with the recommendation in [4] of acquiring the management support which helps securing authority and resources for the modeling project.
– The chosen order in running workshops by view was according to reversed product lifecycle, i.e. services first and end with product development. The project should begin with one workshop per chosen view. In this way the stakeholders become confident with their "structures" before we start to find the common object model content. By doing so we got less irrelevant and time consuming discussions.
– The missing object, which "always" appears in the centre of the structure model, came in place as we have a way to identify it. By testing alternatives, and listen to the spoken language we are able to find it. To ask the question "why" and "to be used as", usually gives the answer. Experienced facilitators are needed.
– The importance of communication, both during the analysis in order to obtain quality and participation, as well as when reporting the outcome, e.g. never presenting the whole structure at once, making an animated presentation so the complexity can be digested in logical portions, etc.
– The common object model must not inherit any hierarchical structures of any kind, since they lock the information in a specific context. The model shall instead contain the "atomic" information and necessary logic represented by business rules, to enable generation of information in hierarchical to the proper business perspectives.

We think there are interesting areas for further research, such as:

– We realize again and again that "unique" structures and processes/value chains in fact are generic. To what extent can we know/assume what´s unique or generic?
– How to calculate/illustrate/argue the potential business value in having the common structure of products/services/offerings?

References

[1] Astrakan Method, http://www.astrakan.se
[2] Chen, P.P.S.: The Entity Relationship Model – Towards an Unified View of Data. ACM Transactions of Database Systems 1(1) (1976)
[3] Ogdens Triangle, http://www.ogden.com
[4] Stirna, J., Persson, A., Sandkuhl, K.: Participative Enterprise Modeling: Experiences and Recommendations. In: Krogstie, J., Opdahl, A.L., Sindre, G. (eds.) CAiSE 2007 and WES 2007. LNCS, vol. 4495, pp. 546–560. Springer, Heidelberg (2007)

On the Use of *i** for Architecting Hybrid Systems: A Method and an Evaluation Report[*]

Juan Pablo Carvallo[1] and Xavier Franch[2]

[1] Universidad Del Pacifico
Carlos Arizaga Toral S/N y Luis Moscoso, Cuenca, Ecuador
jpcarvallo@upacifico.edu.ec
[2] Universitat Politècnica de Catalunya (UPC)
c/Jordi Girona, 1-3, E-08034 Barcelona, Spain
franch@lsi.upc.edu

Abstract. The architectural definition of hybrid software systems is a challenging problem that demands to reconcile stakeholders' strategic needs and components marketplace, whilst defining an appropriate set of services. We have defined a method called DHARMA based on the *i** framework. The goal of this paper is to present an experience report about the use of *i** in large-scale projects. We provide two different viewpoints: the viewpoint of the stakeholder and the viewpoint of the modeller. Apart from general lessons learned, we also provide some insights about the use of *i** in the specific context of architecting hybrid systems using DHARMA.

Keywords: hybrid systems, goal-oriented models, *i**, software architecture.

1 Introduction

Most of current software systems are built as the integration of software components of different nature and origins in which sometimes is referred to as *Hybrid Architecture Systems* [1]. The software components used in these systems include software packages developed by third parties, commonly known as Off-The-Shelf (OTS) components [2] (e.g., commercial OTS components or COTS; free components open source or FOSS [4]; and web services [5]), and also bespoke software and legacy systems.

In this development context, systems are built in an opportunistic manner [6], considering at the same time the environment and the strategy of the organization, the components available in the marketplace (e.g., OTS marketplace, FOSS community), their capacity for being integrated into a single system and interoperate in a transparent manner, and the resources required by their adoption and integration.

The specification of requirements, the selection of the required components, and their adaptation and integration into a single architecture, are some of the problems that have been extensively studied and documented in the literature [7, 8]. However, there are some other problems that remain as challenges and demand more study from

---

[*] This work has been partially supported by the Spanish project TIN2007-64753.

A. Persson and J. Stirna (Eds.): PoEM 2009, LNBIP 39, pp. 38–53, 2009.

the scientific community. Among them, we mention: the identification of the strategic needs for which the system is required; the identification of the specific services (bound to these needs) that the system shall offer; and the grouping of the services into atomic domains, which structure the generic architecture of the system and describe the minimum functionality that must be covered for each of the components that will be part of the system.

This paper proposes the DHARMA method to identify the architecture of a component-based system. The generic components that form this architecture may be later substituted in an opportunistic manner (in the sense of [6]) by components of different nature and origins forming a hybrid system. Specifically, DHARMA is based on the use of the *i** framework [9], exploiting its ability to represent actors, dependencies and intentions. And in fact this use yields to the main goal of the paper, namely to provide an empirical assessment on the use of the *i** framework in large-scale projects, both from the point of view of stakeholders and modellers.

The rest of the paper is organized as follows. Section 2 briefly describes the two case studies that have provided most of the feedback for this evaluation report. Section 3 provides a summary of the DHARMA method. Sections 4 and 5 give the details about the use of *i** in the experiences described in Section 2. Finally, Section 6 presents conclusions and future work.

2   The Experience

The work described in this paper in based on two projects developed in Ecuador: the renovation of the IS inside the company ETAPATELECOM, and the elaboration of an IT strategic plan for the Cuenca Airport. We briefly describe both projects in this section.

2.1 The ETAPATELECOM Case

ETAPATELECOM is a new entrant telecom company, based in Cuenca, Ecuador. Established in 2002, it currently provides nationwide internet access, data carrying and public and residential fixed telephone services.

To fulfil its deployment strategy, ETAPATELECOM had to face the selection and adoption of several technologies, including several COTS components required by the information system that supports its operation. During this process, the company has used quality models [10] under different forms, and modelling techniques based on *i** to support several activities linked with the adoption and development of information technologies, with more than satisfactory results. Finally, both techniques (quality models and the *i** framework) were combined by means of the COSTUME method aimed at construction quality models for composite systems [11].

2.2 The Cuenca Airport Case

Due to the decentralization process conducted in Ecuador in the last few years, the administration of Cuenca's airport was handed from the national Civil Aviation Direction (DAC) to its local municipality. Although the airport was at that moment the

3rd largest in the country, it was severally underused, managing only few domestic flights during the day. The new administration decided to change this situation and developed a strategic plan, designed to increase the airport usage with additional national and international frequencies, as well as other services including the implementation of cargo transportation fleet, a convention center and shopping facilities.

An important part of the strategic plan was oriented to the implementation of the IT services required to support its operation. The $i*$ framework was used to define basic hardware (network and domotic services required) and the software system architecture. Once the architecture was outlined, several projects were defined to support is implementation. Projects were categorized regarding the hardware-software and generic-strategic dimensions, and prioritized base on the current criticality and time available before they become essential e.g., in relation to the approximate dates in which new services were to be implemented according to the strategic plan.

The defined projects were part of the IT strategic plan which also included the Function and Organization Manual (MOF, acronym for the Spanish term) and the outline of the process manual to be used by the IT staff in software and hardware acquisition, software development and systems operation.

3   The DHARMA Method

The DHARMA method (Discovering Hybrid ARchitectures by Modelling Actors) aims at the definition of software architectures using the $i*$ framework. It has been defined as a result of the experiences reported in Section 2. The process resulting from the method is initiated by modelling the organizational context and ends with the identification of the generic architecture of the software system. By "generic architecture" we mean the identification of the actors that form part of the system, the services that must be covered by each of them and the relationships among them.

The concept of actor is therefore central to the DHARMA method and this is reason that makes the $i*$ framework highly convenient. System actors represent atomic domains for which OTS components may be identified. By "atomic domain" we mean a group of functions or services that bring some value to the user, such that not other proper subset of this group represents a different significant domain.

The objective of the DHARMA method is not the identification of the final architecture of the system, in which every actor represents a subsystem that may be directly mapped into an individual OTS component (although this may be a particular case). Instead, other cases are possible: an OTS component may cover the services of more than one actor; the services of an actor may be covered by more than one OTS component that altogether provide the required functionality; an actor may be covered by several OTS components that overlap for dependability purposes; or some services of an actor may not be covered by existing OTS components, requiring some bespoke development.

The method has been structured into four basic activities that may iterate or intertwine as needed (see Fig. 1):

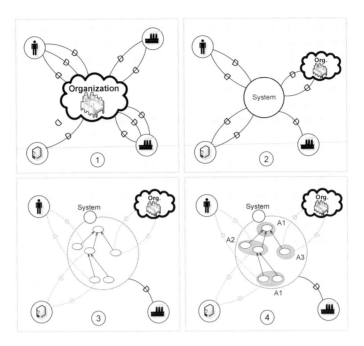

Fig. 1. Activities of the DHARMA method

- **Activity 1:** *Modelling the organizational context.* The organization and its business model are analysed in detail, in order to identify the role that it plays inside its environment. This analysis surfaces the different types of actors that exist in its contexts, and the strategic needs among them and the organization. The *i** SD diagrams are used to elicit and represent the actors and relationships.

- **Activity 2:** *Modelling the environment of the system.* In this activity, a new system is inserted into the organization and the impact that this system has over the context is analysed. The system may be a typical information system, or it may be a hybrid system including hardware components, maybe with some embedded software. The strategic dependencies identified in the former activity are analysed with the aim of determining which of them may be directly satisfied by the system, and which others are needed by the system providing its operational level. As a result, the dependencies are redirected inside the *i** SD diagram, and also new dependencies arise. The model includes also the organization itself as an actor in the system environment, in which its needs are modelled as strategic dependencies over the system.

- **Activity 3:** *Decomposition of system goals.* In this activity, the system is analysed and decomposed into a hierarchy of goals that are needed to satisfy the strategic dependencies stated by the environment actors. The goals represent the services that the system must provide, to interact with the actors in the environment. An SR diagram for the system is built, using decompositions means-end of type goal-goal (representing then a decomposition of objectives into subobjectives).

- **Activity 4:** *Identification of the system actors.* The goals included in the SR model are analysed and systematically grouped into subactors that represent atomic domains. The objectives are grouped into services, according to an analysis of the strategic dependencies with the environment and an exploration of the existing OTS marketplace. The relationships between the different actors that form the basic structure of the system are described according to the direction of the means-end links that exist among the objectives included inside them.

4   The *i** Framework from the Stakeholder Point of View

In this section we outline the issues that we found when using *i** models in conjunction with the system stakeholders.

4.1   Initial Modeling

The DHARMA method requires at its first step the construction of an SD diagram modeling the organization environment. Instead of the classical elicitation approach in which the RE expert elicits requirements from stakeholders and represents them using *i**, we opted for a different approach: stakeholders received some training in *i** and were committed to develop their own partial vision of the organization in a SD model.

A first consideration was needed: were the stakeholders going to learn the whole *i** language? Some authors have reported about the difficulty of using the full expressive power of *i** with stakeholders that are not skilled in advanced requirements engineer techniques [12, 13]. After a careful consideration and some feedback, we took several decisions that are reported below and described in the metamodel of Fig. 2, which shows some simplifications with respect to the one defined by Ayala et al. [14]:

- Actors. We treat all actors in a generic manner, without distinguishing roles, positions and agents. The barrier between these concepts is sometime fuzzy, especially when considering the combination of these types and links like is-a, and may provoke some confusion to the *i** novice. Instead, we considered useful to distinguish among four types of actors: human, software, hardware and organizations. Although we didn't bring the distinction into the model itself graphically, we kept traceability of the type through comments.
- Actor links. We kept the two types of main actor links, i.e. is-a and is-part-of. Especially the is-a specialization link became very useful when declaring hierarchies of human roles represented by actors of human type. Note that the actors' type may be used here for correctness conditions, e.g. the specialization of a human actor must also be human.
- Dependencies. contrary to what was expected beforehand, stakeholders very intuitively grasped the difference between goal and soft goal. The concept of subjectiveness was crucial to understanding this difference. Therefore, we kept both types of dependencies. Also resource dependencies had a very clear meaning, namely informational need. On the contrary, task dependencies were considered too much low level, stakeholders found easier to focus on the level of goals (what the task is going to provide) than

on the task itself. We avoid this fourth type of dependency (that may appear later when the expert takes the lead).

–   Intentional elements. The most significant difference between the standard *i**
    and the way we used it was the type of intentional elements inside actors'
    boundaries. We just supported goals and then, as intentional elements' links,
    goal decomposition. This decision reduced complexity a lot (sometimes the
    distinction among goal, task and resource depends on the point of view or the
    emphasis) and aligned with most stakeholders' way of thinking, where goals
    play a central role.

The three tasks that were undertaken during the first activity of DHARMA were then:

–   Initial training of stakeholders. Initial Stakeholders' training was conducted
    more in a workshop-brainstorm formatted session than in formal teacher-
    students session. After a quick explanation of the basic *i** concepts, con-
    ducted by the moderator (a expert in *i**), the concepts were used to create the
    initial models of the organizational environment. With the guidance of the
    moderator a first set of environmental actors was brainstormed and then
    some basic dependencies were proposed and analyzed by participants. The
    session was about three hours long, and included stakeholders of several ar-
    eas of the organizations (e.g., financial, administrative, legal, and tech-nical).
    Blackboards and projectors were used as tools to support the process.

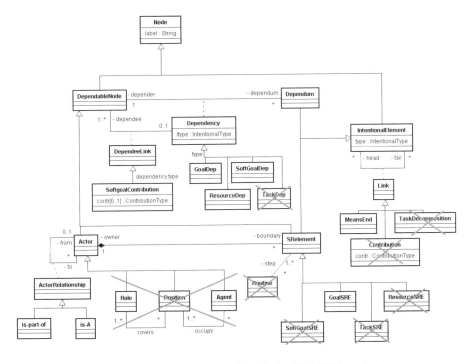

Fig. 2. The *i** metamodel as defined in the DHARMA method

- Individual models built by stakeholders. With the first models constructed, stakeholders were given a week to carefully study them and to propose changes or new versions of the models. Once the resulting models were handled, they were reviewed by an expert in $i*$ which helped stakeholders to validate the correct usage of the different types of dependencies. It was interesting to find that some of the reviewed models included dependencies among environmental actors and third party actors, even if they didn't have a direct relation with the organization. In some cases they were seen by stakeholders as relevant to complement their understanding of the environment (e.g. the dependency among telephony service regulators and radio and TV services regulators, which were perceived as potential environmental actors, in the case of future joint ventures with that kind of service providers). This confirmed us that even if they were not technical staff, they got a good understanding of the basic $i*$ modeling skills.
- Consolidation of the different models into one. Once the individual models were validated, the team of $i*$ experts created a consolidated version including all the identified actors and the proposed dependencies. Redundancies were eliminated and similarities were marked in order to validate if different stakeholders were referring to the same concepts. After the consolidated models were completed, final workshops ware conducted in order for stakeholders to validate the resulting models and to align their views on the problem. At this point it was obvious that stakeholders were already very familiar with more abstract concepts such as soft-goals. This made easy the communication among technical and non technical staff and helped to conduct the workshops in a very proactive way.

Another point worth to mention is tool support. There are several $i*$ modelling tools available in the community (see [15] for a survey) and even recently an XML model interchange format named iStarML [16] based on the $i*$ metamodel proposed in [14] has been defined and is being adopted by several tools. But of course, using these tools implies learning a new technology. And it must be remarked that the use of $i*$ in these projects was limited to modeling, no further treatments were required. As a consequence, the functionalities needed from these tools were quite limited. To sum up, we decided to use a generic drawing tool like MS Visio instead of using a new technology. This decision reduced the stakeholders' learning curve and allowed to take use of some facilities of MS Visio that became useful:

- The use of connection links to easily and permanently link actors and intentional elements.
- The use of the grouping by layers to control the visibility of the model. We assigned each stakeholder partial model to one layer, therefore during the analysis if a part of the model (developed by a stakeholder) was not relevant, it was easily hidden. Of course this was possible because of the particular characteristics of our SD models, which are radial (dependencies always stem/go from/to the system to/from a context actor).

- We took the chance to change the graphical representation of dependencies from the standard definition (use of oriented "D") by a standard directed arrow (this change is also recommended by [17] in a recent work).
- Some diagrammatic advices were issued. For instance, use of straight lines instead of curved lines for representing dependencies, making easier manual reallocation and the preliminary drawing of quadrants, as a mean to delimit the areas of the diagram to be filled by each actor and their particular dependencies, proved useful to support this activity.

4.2 The Model as a Communication Mean

In projects involving people with different background and skills, it is quite normal to find that many of them have their own view of the problem and goals on the project. *i** has proven to be a good way to align the different views and make people work together towards the achievement of the project, with the same concepts in mind.

During the workshops, the organization and its goals were discussed among participants. The produced environmental draft models were used as framework to drive the discussion. In the process several mismatches were identified; among them we can mention the following cases (illustrated with some examples from the ETAPA-TELECOM case):

- Addition of actors: Some actors were not originally included in the model, but after some discussion they became obviously required. This was the case of the *Prepaid Services Vendor* actor, proposed by the commercial staff. It was required by the organization to satisfy the goal *Prepaid Services Sold*, whilst it required from the organization the *Services Activation Cards* as a resource and the *Prepaid Services Consumption Controlled* as a goal.
- Elimination of actors: Some of the participants proposed the incorporation of new actors at some stage of the process, but after a more detailed review it became clear that they were not relevant. This is the case of the *Technology Provider* actor; it was originally introduced because of the concern of the financial staff, in relation to the criticality of the provision of several components required by the organization to construct its operations platform. After some discussion it was removed because it was perceived as an incidental actor, for which no permanent dependencies existed.
- Refinement of dependencies: During the workshops, it was quite normal to identify new dependencies or to remove some of them in order to refine the model. In addition, some dependencies were redefined as other kinds of dependencies, e.g. the *Provide Quality of Service* soft-goal originally proposed by the technical staff was later changed to a goal; in order to maintain the operation license it is required as a non negotiable goal by the *Regulation Authority* actor.

5 The *i** Framework from the Modeler Point of View

In this section we report our experience as requirements engineering experts about the use of *i** in industrial projects.

5.1 Drawing of the Diagram

Although it may seem strange that we start this section by the issue of drawing, in fact *i** is a visual notation that heavily relies on the graphical representation of its models. As explained in the former section, stakeholders build their partial vision of the system using MS Visio and producing an *i** SD model. These models have to be merged into one after some consolidation conducted by the requirements engineer expert. As a result, we get a big single *i** model. This model is:

– Difficult to build. The different partial SD models have to be integrated into one. This integration must be done by hand (copy&paste plus manual reallocation of elements). Diagrammatic tools in the *i** community do not support this functionality neither. Therefore, this task becomes cumbersome.
– Difficult to modify. After the SD model is consolidated, it is modified in the next steps. These modifications are addition and removal of actors and intentional elements, and reallocation of links. Also these tasks are cumbersome.

We may say that there is a lot of work to do with *i** diagrammatic tools until they can be considered satisfactory for large-scale projects. As an alternative, we have started to represent *i** SD models as tables with the same rows and columns, and cells represent links between them. This representation solves the problems above, although the model is more difficult to be comprehended as a whole. Probably, a model-view-controller architecture supporting these two views altogether (and even some other, like the directory-like structure promoted by the J-PR*i*M tool [18]), and the addition of features like the layered control mentioned in Section 4, are the key to overcome the inherent difficulty of representing *i** models.

5.2 Reusability

We may consider three types of reusability:

– **Intra-process reusability.** SD Environmental Models describe the dependencies among the organization (or the system) and the actors on their environment. Thus, when describing the dependencies with respect to a particular environmental actor, we are implicitly describing the dependencies in the environment of the given actor with respect to the organization (or the system). This intra-process reusability became evident from the beginning when performing our first industrial experiences (prior to the ones described in Section 2). Whilst studying the *e-Mail Systems* domain, *Mail Clients* where included as actors in their environment (see Fig. 3, Top, for an excerpt of the e-Mail Systems environmental mode). When studding the *Mail Clients* domain in a latter process, the *e-Mail Systems* actor was included as environmental actor together with all the dependencies already identified.

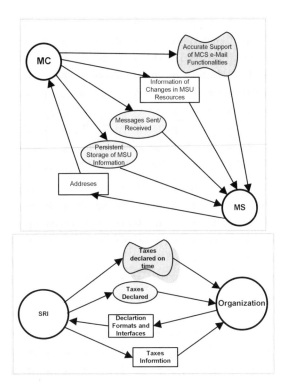

Fig. 3. Top: Excerpt of the Mail Client (MC) and Mail Server (MS) SD model; Bottom: Excerpt of environmental model showing the dependencies among the Ecuadorian Tax Agency and the Organization (ETAPATELECOM / Cuenca's Airport)

– **Inter-process reusability.** Different organizations may share sets of elements in their environment. This is a well-known fact not only for organizations sharing the same vertical segment, but also for those in different market segments. Thus, regarding this issue two kinds of reusability exist:

  • Vertical reusability. When performing different DHARMA processes in organizations sharing the same vertical market segment. In these cases, most of the elements in the environmental model of one organization (or system) can be reused in the environmental models of others, e.g., telecommunications companies sharing the same regulators, users, interconnection providers, dealers, etc.

  • Horizontal reusability: When performing different DHARMA processes in organizations with different vertical market segments. In these cases some commonalities can be found and model elements reused. For instance, both ETAPATELECOM and the Cuenca Airport shall periodically report about their income and expenses to the Ecuadorian Taxes Agency (SRI). Thus, the area of the model describing this environmental actor that was first constructed for the ETAPATELECOM case (see Fig. 3, Bottom), was latter reused in the airport experience.

In general, inter-process reusability increases as the explored domains are more simi-lar. Regarding this issue, four levels of abstraction regarding simil-arity of their busi-ness strategy (e.g., service-oriented CRM, manufacture-oriented ERP, logistics- and transportation-oriented SCM, etc.) can be established. From the most similar to the most dissimilar: organizations in the same vertical market sharing the same business strategy; organizations in the same vertical market with different business strategies; organizations in different vertical markets but sharing business strategies; organiza-tions in different vertical markets with different business strategies.

- **Knowledge reusability.** As stated in the previous paragraphs, organizations share commonalities at different levels. Therefore it is not an unusual fact to find parts of models that can be reused as detailed patterns in other experi-ences. For instance, let's consider again the e-Mail Systems case, which used the activities of the COSTUME method [11] to identify the system architec-ture and to build the artifacts required for the selection of its components. Some of the actors (with their respective SR models as goal-subgoals de-compositions) identified in this case were reused both in the ETAPATELE-COM and the Cuenca's airport cases, namely the ones corres-ponding to the Mail Servers and Directory Servers system actors (see Fig. 4).

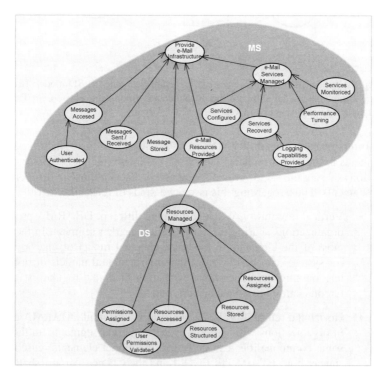

Fig. 4. Mail Server (MS) and Directory Services (DS) system actors with their SR decomposition

5.3 DHARMA-Related Lessons Learned

There are some additional lessons that emerged from the application of DHARMA:

– **Environmental models refinement.** Although the refinement of dependencies in environmental models was mainly driven by stakeholders' participation and understanding on the problem, there are some tips that help the modeler:

- Base the identification of environmental actors on several sources of information: use case diagrams; goal-oriented modeling techniques; identification of organizational roles supported by: the review of ontologies (e.g. OpenCyc), standards of professional bodies (e.g. SWEBOK), or organizational theory literature [19]; or the adoption of social patterns [20].
- To define environmental dependencies: first, identify which goals of the environmental actors depend on the organization (or the system) and vice versa, and represent them by goal dependencies. To simplify the process, omit the dependencies that do not involve the organization (or the system) as an actor. Environmental models shall be kept as simple as possible focusing only on the services required from the organization (or the system).
- Next, identify the resources needed to satisfy these goal dependencies and model them with resource dependencies. Note that resources may be physical or informational.
- Finally, analyze each goal dependency over the organization (or the system) with respect to catalogues of non-functional requirements e.g. the ISO/IEC 9126-1 standard, and include in the model a soft-goal for every subcharacteristic considered crucial to satisfy this goal.
- Tend to avoid task dependencies in the model, since they are rather prescriptive. A task dependency represents one particular way of attaining a goal; it can be considered as a detailed description of how to accomplish a goal.

– **System models refinement.** We found the following guidelines useful to conduct this activity:

- To construct the SR model of the system, first identify the main goal of the system and draw it as the root goal of the diagram.
- Reduce this goal into sub-goals by means of goal-goal links, representing the main identifiable functional areas that the system is expected to provide and link external dependencies to them whenever appropriated. This first decomposition is achieved by exploring the dependencies that environmental actors have on the system.
- Repeat the previous process for each of the sub-goals identified until the obtained sub-goals represent services atomic enough, such that it does not makes sense to further reduce them. A rule of the thumb to validate the decomposition is that all of the leaf goals of the hierarchy must be linked to at least one environmental dependency. If one leaf goal is not linked to any external dependency it can be removed, unless it is considered critical for the fulfillment of its predecessor.
- The process is complete when all the environmental dependencies have been considered and linked to the appropriated sub-goals required for their

fulfillment, in case of incoming dependencies, or to the ones which depend on them, in the case of outgoing dependencies.

– **System actors' identification.** We identify two kinds of system actors that can be present in system models:

• *Core system actors.* This kind of actors provides the core functionality of the system. Because of this, in many cases the system as a whole adopts their name. Most of the committed and critical dependencies of environmental actors are usually linked to them. Some examples of core system actors are the Mail Server in e-Mail Systems, the telecom billing system and the ERP system in the ETAPATELECOM case, or the airplane guidance and monitoring system in the Cuenca's airport case.

• *Supporting system actors.* Supporting actors do not provide the core functionality of the system. Instead they offer services required by the core actors in order to fulfill some of their external dependencies with environmental actors (e.g., the telecom billing services system relies on the platform mediation interfaces for services to be automatically activated / deactivated). All supporting actors have dependency links with core actors, but not necessarily among them. They may also have dependency links with environmental actors, but usually not in relation to the core functionality of the system.

• Systems may include more than one core actor. Regarding supporting system actors, they are not mandatory and some systems may not include them (although this is not the usual case). With these considerations in mind, in the extreme case, a system will include one core system actor and at least one additional actor.

• The identification of system actors is guided by the goals identified in the SR model of the system. These goals reveal services that are expected to be covered by system actors. Their assignment to system actors can be supported by reviewing several sources of information, such as online COTS components markets or COTS components taxonomies. Experience, Internet browsing and Google search for key words included in the defined goals, proved to be the most effective ways to conduct this activity.

– **Components interoperability.** Decisions on system architecture rely in several aspects but mainly in the ability of components to interoperate and work together as whole system. To support the decision making process, we found very useful to create an enriched SD model of the system after system actors were identified. To obtain the model we follow the process below:

• The set of goals and sub-goals assigned to a system actor (see Fig. 5, a) have to be abstracted to a circle representing the actor (see Fig. 5, b).

• The circles representing the actors inherit all the environmental dependencies assigned to the goals that define their services (see Fig. 5, b).

• The end links among the actors are replaced by goal dependency links. In these links the actor of the end goal is the depender, the actor of the means goal the dependee and the goal the dependum (see Fig. 5, c).

• Internal goal dependencies among system actors can be refined with a process similar to the one proposed for environmental process refinement, for obtaining a detailed interoperability model (see Fig. 5, d).

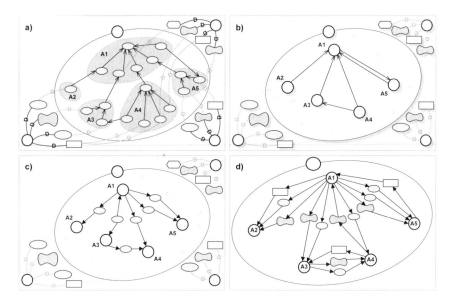

Fig. 5. Process to obtain an interoperability model

6   Conclusions and Future Work

In this paper we have presented an experience report about the use of *i** in the particular case of architecting hybrid systems using the DHARMA method. In a few words, the framework has demonstrated to be useful both for stakeholders and modellers provided that some simplifications of the model are done, remarkably the conversion of the rich SR models into goal-subgoal decomposition graphs.

We summarise in a sentence our view of each of the issues evaluated in [12]:

– **Refinement.** (1) SD: the three modeling steps, i.e. first joint workshop, then each stakeholder, last the modeler, seem to support stepwise refinement of the SD model; (2) SR: much easier than usual since decomposition is just goal-goal.
– **Modularity.** Somehow supported by the use of the MS Visio layer concept.
– **Repeatability**. Considering the sense given by [12], the use of a reduced *i** framework makes easier to use the framework in a uniform way.
– **Complexity management.** Again the use of a reduced framework supports this.
– **Expressiveness.** On the contrary, our proposal clearly damages the high expressiveness of *i**, although throughout the paper it has been argued that the concepts kept are the fundamental ones for stakeholders.
– **Traceability.** Not explicitly supported, although it has been said that comments are used to trace which stakeholder provided which part of the model.
– **Reusability.** Both intra- and inter-process reuse are supported.
– **Scalability.** The use of a reduced set of concepts and some diagrammatic conventions make the *i** models a bit more scalable than usual (trade-off with expressiveness). But it is not clear yet how much significant are the differences.
– **Domain Applicability.** It applies well to the hybrid systems architecting domain.

As future work, we are planning to extend a preliminary work in relation to hybrid systems evolution. In this work the modules of several legacy systems have been modeled as system actors and the dependencies among them have been stated, to make explicit the interoperability among them. In a second stage of the process, an ordering sequence has been established in relation to the priority in which some of the modules need to evolve to new versions. In this way the impact of the replacement of the modules in relation to other system components is made evident using a visual notation; as a consequence system evolution can be planned with more evidence of the effort required.

References

[1] Proceedings of the 7th International Intl. Conference on Composition-Based Software Systems (ICCBSS). IEEE, Los Alamitos (2008)
[2] Li, J., et al.: A State-of-the-Practice Survey of Risk Management in Development with Off-the-Shelf Software Components. IEEE TSE 34(2) (2008)
[3] Mohamed, A., Ruhe, G., Eberlein, A.: COTS Selection: Past, Present, and Future. In: CBSE 2007 (2007)
[4] Feller, J., Fitzgerald, B.: Understanding Open Source Software Development. Addison-Wesley, Reading (2002)
[5] Papazoglou, M.P.: Web Services: Principles and Technology. Prentice-Hall, Englewood Cliffs (2008)
[6] Kotonya, G., Lock, S., Mariani, J.: Opportunistic Reuse: Lessons from Scrapheap Software Development. In: Chaudron, M.R.V., Szyperski, C., Reussner, R. (eds.) CBSE 2008. LNCS, vol. 5282, pp. 302–309. Springer, Heidelberg (2008)
[7] Alves, C., Alencar, F.M.R., Castro, J.: Requirements Engineering for COTS Selection. In: WER 2000 (2000)
[8] Burgués, X., Estay, C., Franch, X., Pastor, J.A., Quer, C.: Combined Selection of COTS Components. In: Dean, J., Gravel, A. (eds.) ICCBSS 2002. LNCS, vol. 2255, p. 54. Springer, Heidelberg (2002)
[9] Yu, E.: Modelling Strategic Relationships for Process Reengineering. PhD Dissertation, University of Toronto (1995)
[10] Franch, X., Carvallo, J.P.: Using Quality Models in Software Package Selection. IEEE Software 20(1) (2003)
[11] Carvallo, J.P., et al.: COSTUME: A Method for Building Quality Models for Composite COTS-Based Software Systems. In: QSIC 2004. IEEE, Los Alamitos (2004)
[12] Estrada, H., Rebollar, A.M., Pastor, Ó., Mylopoulos, J.: An Empirical Evaluation of the i* Framework in a Model-Based Software Generation Environment. In: Dubois, E., Pohl, K. (eds.) CAiSE 2006. LNCS, vol. 4001, pp. 513–527. Springer, Heidelberg (2006)
[13] Annosi, M.C., et al.: Analyzing Knowledge Transfer in Software Maintenance Organizations using an Agent- and Goal-oriented Analysis Technique – an Experience Report. In: iStar 2008, CEUR Workshop Proceedings (2008)
[14] Ayala, C., et al.: A Comparative Analysis of i*-based Agent-Oriented Modeling Languages. In: SEKE 2005 (2005)
[15] http://istar.rwth-aachen.de/tiki-index.php?page_ref_id=21
[16] Cares, C., et al.: iStarML: an XML-based Model Interchange Format for i*". In: iStar 2008, CEUR Workshop Proceedings (2008)

[17] Moody, D.L., Heymans, P., Matulevicius, R.: Improving the Effectiveness of Visual Representations in Requirements Engineering: An Evaluation of i* Visual Syntax. In: RE 2009. IEEE, Los Alamitos (2009)

[18] Grau, G., Franch, X., Ávila, S.: J-PRiM: A Java Tool for a Process Reengineering i* Methodology. In: RE 2006. IEEE, Los Alamitos (2006)

[19] Daft, R.L.: Organization Theory and Design. Thomson (1992)

[20] Fuxman, A., et al.: Information Systems as Social Structures. In: FOIS 2001 (2001)

Interactions, Goals and Rules in a Collaborative Modelling Session

Denis Ssebuggwawo[1], Stijn Hoppenbrouwers[1],
and Erik Proper[1,2]

[1] Institute of Computing and Information Sciences, Radboud University Nijmegen
Heyendaalseweg 135, 6525 AJ Nijmegen, The Netherlands, EU
D.Ssebuggwawo@science.ru.nl, stijnh@cs.ru.nl
[2] Capgemini Nederland B.V.,
Papendorpseweg 100, 3528 BJ Utrecht, The Netherlands, EU
e.proper@acm.org

Abstract. Collaborative modeling can enhance productivity and quality of modeling in system development and enterprise engineering projects by helping to construct agreement and a sense of model ownership among stakeholders/modelers. Most of these stakeholders have relatively low expertise in formal modeling; advanced modeler-oriented support for collaborative modeling is a possible remedy. As a basis for further development of such support (methods, tools), we have carried out a detailed exploratory study of the interaction between modelers, involving diverse aspects of modeling: goal setting, modeling language concepts, planning, etc. Central in our approach is the study of how collaborative modelers negotiate, set, use, and deal with the various rules/goals governing interactive modeling sessions. We describe the conceptual framework and approach used for our analysis, and present findings from a case study which focused on the first phases of a session concerning basic Business Process Modeling. We also compare our findings to some existing work, to demonstrate the relevance of our approach.

Keywords: Collaborative Modeling, Business Process Modeling, Quality of Modeling, Modeling as a Game.

1 Introduction

System development, and conceptual modeling in particular (including, under our broad definition, information modeling, process/workflow modeling, and even business rule modeling), is a process in which communication plays a vital role [1]. In system development (including enterprise engineering) a number of stakeholders are usually brought aboard the system development ship with varying skills, expertise, and knowledge. This results in a heterogeneous group of stakeholders including, for example, project managers, (prospective) users who may act as domain experts, system architects, analysts, programmers, etc. In such environments, participants engage in various types of conversation during

A. Persson and J. Stirna (Eds.): PoEM 2009, LNBIP 39, pp. 54–68, 2009.

the creation of a *agreed models*. Such conversations involve *negotiation*, which results in *accepts, rejects, modifications*, etc., (see, for example, [2,3]).

Much has been written about (conceptual) modeling, mainly in the area of information systems. Some have developed frameworks to attain the desired qualities of the developed models [4,5]; others developed guidelines for modeling, see for example, [6]. Alternatively, we have worked toward understanding of the detailed process (act) of modeling; see for example [7]. During the collaborative process of system development, stakeholders *"move through a process in which they combine their expertise, insights and their resources to bring them to bear for the task at hand"* [8]. The importance of involving different hierarchical level representatives in a (re-)engineering process is recognized in [9]. However, the emphasis in the bulk of the literature is on tools and techniques used by the stakeholders in order to achieve the desired model quality (*completeness* and *correctness*). It is our contention, however, that when we are concerned with the quality of the final model, we also need to analyze the process that generates it. How a process is executed is a major influence (negatively or positively) on the quality of the model.

If the complex and dynamic collaborative interactions involved are not properly organized and supported, the benefits that potentially accrue from them may not be realized. This could, for example, be due to the limitations of the human mind, collaborative capacity, or of resources needed. To overcome some of these limitations, a number of approaches have been suggested, e.g. using *professional facilitators* in Group Support Systems (*GSS*) and Group Decision Support Systems (*GDSS*) [10], *group model building* in Systems Dynamics (*SD*) [11], etc.

The work of Peter Rittgen [3] is closely related to our own, based on similar principles, and therefore particularly relevant to this paper. His *Collaborative Modeling Architecture*(COMA) tool [12] reflects a similar approach to collaborative system analysis and design. However, while he focuses on negotiation of models as such (which is indeed the core activity), he largely ignores other aspects (like language setting, planning, sub-model definition, etc.), or sets default choices for them. While we consider his approach a good start, we believe more differentiated and in-depth analysis of real modeling processes will contribute to a broader and deeper understanding of *what concerns modelers when they do their thing*, leading to refinement and improvement of the collaborative modeling methods and tools.

The purpose of this paper is to propose, and report on results of, an approach for analyzing the process (act) of modeling by analyzing the *communication* between the modelers in a facilitator-free environment. Our in-depth analysis aims to reveal conventions/rules for interaction and collaboration in modeling. Knowledge of such patterns contributes to our understanding of the process of modeling *as it really occurs in operational modeling*. Consequently, we hope to advance our capability to design effective, more *"modeler*-oriented" support tools for collaborative modeling processes. Such tools should actively support the ways of thinking and interacting that lead to fulfillment of clear modeling goals [13]. This goes beyond the capabilities of the highly technical "*model-oriented*" editors that are currently the best we can offer modelers. In order to operationalize our approach, we hypothesize that the interactions that take place in collaborative modeling sessions can be looked at as *games* with *players* who may either explicitly or implicitly *determine and play by rules of a modeling game*. Taking this metaphorical gaming perspective helps us to home in on the rules and goals driving the modeling process, some of which may later feed *requirements* for support tools.

In the remainder of this paper, we explain our operational conceptual framework and methodological approach concerning the approach sketched above. We illustrate the framework and approach at the hand of data and results from a case collaborative modeling session. The main results are interaction and rule categories found (reflecting various concerns of modelers), and various relevant observations. We will also compare our findings with some existing work, mostly to demonstrate the relevance of our approach.

2   Analytical Setup

In this section we give a brief overview of the questions we try to answer (in view of our case study) in this paper. We then present an operational methodology designed to help us find answers to the questions raised. As discussed, we take the view that (conceptual) modeling in system and enterprise engineering can be regarded as a communicative process in which the modelers participate. We therefore mainly look at (categories in) *interactions* between modelers. This in turn helps us examine the *rules and goals* under which the development takes place. Crucially, the setting of rules and goals may itself be subject to interaction. Consequently, the rules can be changed and extended during the game, as part of the game.

2.1   Research Questions

We raise the following questions which motivate our way of thinking in this paper:

- What are modelers concerned with during the case modeling session?
- What are the main categories of the rules governing a (process) modeling session?
- How do rule categories found in the case study relate to the categories as proposed and used in previous relevant frameworks for analysis? (see Sect. 3 and Sect. 4.5 for details)
- What further observations can we make concerning rules, rule setting, and interaction?

2.2   General Set-Up of the Study

We created a fairly elaborate context and asked three subjects to create a process model together.

Assignment. Prior to the session, we provided the modelers with an elaborate written domain context (and enough time to read and digest it), even though we expected them not to get very far in producing an actual model (given the limited time available). The assignment we gave them was to start process modeling and see how far they could get, with the added requirement that they should *agree* on the outcome. We very deliberately did not dictate the use of a modeling language, but since the modelers had some experience in the use of UML Activity diagrams, we expected they would use this language (which indeed they did). Part of our interest is in how modelers deal with (agreeing about) modeling concepts to use. The business process scenario given to the modelers was based on a real life case, and concerned the development of a Hazardous Material Management System by the Materials Management Department of a city council through its Management Information Systems Department.

Researchers. The modeling session was organized and passively attended by two researchers. They took care of briefing and debriefing, observing and note-taking. One helped clarify a few concepts in the scenario description when this became necessary (i.e. he briefly acted as an informant, supplementing the written scenario provided before the session). Importantly, the researchers did not act as facilitators: the entire modeling session as such was intentionally left in the hands of the modelers.

Modelers. Three modelers participated in the actual session. They all had some experience in process modeling in a system development context, but were not expert modelers.

Recording the basic data. The session (which took 18 minutes) was video recorded with good sound quality. The modelers were also given a digital writing pad, which was recorded alongside the video. This provided us with a full, synchronized recording of all raw data we could wish for. See Fig. 1 for a snapshot of the recording.

Transcription. A complete transcription was made of the recording, including a detailed description of the drawings on the pad (which we consider a form of utterance, on par with verbal utterances). Table 1 shows a sample of the transcript. The three modelers are called M, D and R.

Data structuring and coding. To effectively study the conversation patterns in the modeling session, we identified atomic interactions (i.e., disentangled them if they were wrapped up in complex sentences) and annotated and categorized them. Table 2 shows an example of annotated and categorized data for the raw conversational data from Table 1. As usual in qualitative research with an explorative flavor, finding an optimal coding system is part of the effort. Hence, the coding system presented was in fact refined in the course of the analysis.

For the basics of our approach, we drew mainly on *Language-Action Perspective* (LAP) theory and *Discourse Analysis*, see for example [14]. The basic annotation structure will be discussed in the next section.

Table 1. Sample transcript of conversations from the video recording

Time	Actor	Speech Act
00:34	M	OK, we have to model...Process...Where shall we start?
00:41	D	Which language?
00:44	M	Hah. May be we just first...something on the fly, some arrows and some blocks, and then work it out later?
00:52	D	Then we have to draw it twice, but...(laughs)
00:55	M	So, What is the main process?
00:59	D	Those are here (laughs, points to the document), so may be swim lane diagrams
01:08	R	Yes, could be.
01:10	M	So as first ordering we see things ordering, dispensing and disposing
01:15	D	Yes, so 5 swim lane diagrams
01:17	M	So is it necessary for each process? Draw all five?
01:21	D	I guess so. Maybe you get short diagrams, but.....
01:25	M	Or we can make five first, so one for ordering, one for receiving, one for storing....
01:30	D	Yes?
01:32	R	That's what he meant I think.

Table 2. Sample coding and categorization of transcribed data

Time	Topic	Topic#	Categorization	Response to
0:34	Set Creation Goal	1	**Proposition**-[We must make a process model]	
	Set Planning	2	**Question**-[Where shall we start?]	
0:41	Set Grammar Goal	3	**Question**-[Which language?]	
0:44	Set Grammar Goal	4	**Proposition/Answer**-[Blocks and arrows]	3
	Set Planning	5	**Proposition/Answer** [First do something on the fly, then work It out later]	2
0:52	Set Planning	6	**Argument-against** [But then we have to draw it twice]	5
0:55	Set Content	7	**Question** -[What is the process?]	
0:59	Set Grammar Goal	8	**Proposition**-Counter [Let's use swim lanes]	5
1:08	Set Grammar Goals	9	**Agreement**-[Yes]	8
1:10	Set Content	10a	**Proposition** [We have Processes, Ordering, Dispensing and Disposing]	
1:15	Set Content	10b	**Agreement**-[Yes]	10a
	Set Creation Goal	10c	**Proposition**-[Let's create 5 swim lane diagrams]	
1:17	Set Creation Goal	11	**Question**-Doubt [Draw 5 swim lane diagrams for each of the 5 processes?]	10a
1:21	Set Creation Goal	12	**Answer**-[Yes]	11
	Set Creation Goal	13	**Argument for** [May be you get short diagrams but still this is the way to go]	10c
1:25	Set Creation Goal	14	**Proposition, Agreement** [Let's create 5 swim lane diagrams]	10a
1:30	Set Creation Goal	15	**Argument-Proposition** [Yes, Isn't that what I just proposed?]	14
1:32	Set creation Goal	16	**Agreement, Question** [Would 14 be OK?]	14

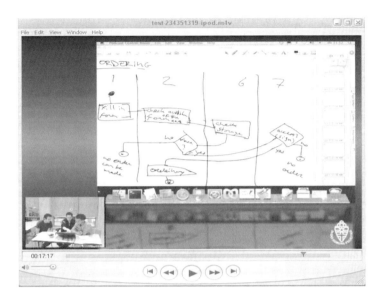

Fig. 1. Snap-shot of the recording

3   Framework and Concepts

In this section, we explain and demonstrate our analytical framework and approach at the hand of some selected fragments of the case; presenting the complete case analysis would take too much space. Our conceptual framework for analysis is based on previous theoretical work on the act of modeling, but pushes for operationalization of the theory in the form of qualitative analysis of (transcripts of) actual modeling sessions. It is rooted in discourse analysis, but extends into the definition and deployment of rules representing conventions and agreements concerning models and modeling processes.

In a collaborative modeling session modelers come together to perform some modeling task (for example, the creation of a business process diagram in some domain, for some purpose). They interact and communicate their ideas and opinions to other members. For them to reach consensus and agreement, they need to commit themselves to work as a team and abide by their collective knowledge, conventions and decisions (rules of their game). Their communication strategy sets the goals and rules (explicitly or implicitly) for a conversational dialog in which the modelers propose and argue about (negotiate) the different positions raised. This communication may result in (dis)agreement with, and acceptance/rejection of, the ideas proposed. The interplay between interactions, rules, and models, as discussed in our framework, is depicted in Fig. 2.

As mentioned, modelers are guided and restricted by modeling rules and goals. In fact, we view goals as a key type of rule ("goal rules"): from a gaming perspective, the goals are rules setting states to strive for. The rules should ideally

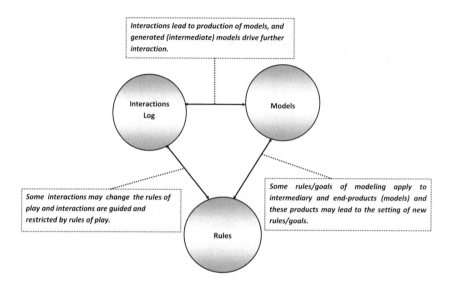

Fig. 2. A methodological approach for analyzing interactions, rules and models

guarantee process and model quality, but they also reflect existing conventions for (inter)action in modeling and conversation. We distinguish two basic types of rules in collaborative modeling: *rules set **for** the game*, i.e. setting the game as such, and *rules set **in** the game.* i.e. by the players. These rules can further be classified as either *explicit* or *implicit* rules. The combined distinctions form a simple 2x2 matrix. We consider all four resulting categories crucial in understanding "how people model" in terms of "the rules they play by", but focus on explicit rules. In our case study, the explicit rules set *in* the game outnumber the ones set *for* the game.

In order to be able to analyze a conversation in terms of specialized concepts (a form of qualitative text analysis), we need a *coding system* to be applied to the recorded interactions. In addition, we make explicit a set of rules governing the interactions and the products thereof. Finally, we can relate the product of the conversation, the model (and its consecutive versions), to the conversation, and to the rules where relevant; however, in the current paper we focus on rule setting as such.

- **Interactions** - with properties: *time and interaction number, actor(player), topic/content, and speech act type.* Table 3 gives an example of interaction coding, interpretation and the meta-data associated with its properties.
- **Rules** - with properties: *time of activation, content and number of interaction it was activated in, time of deactivation, content and number of interaction it was deactivated in, type of rule.* Interactions are identified by numbers. See Table 4.
- **Models** - These are *generated lists of propositions (statements) derived from the entire conversation up to some time t, and subject to selection criteria*

Table 3. Interaction coding, interpretation and meta-data

Time/Int#	Actor	Speech Act - [Type]	Topic
6:04 105	M	*Should we introduce a vendor, actor 9?* [Question]	Set content
6:08 106	D	*The material handler already functions as the vendor.* [Argue against 105]	Set content

Table 4. Rule coding, interpretation and meta-data

$Time_{[A]}$	$Interaction_{[A]}$	$Time_{[D]}$	$Interaction_{[D]}$	$RuleType$
14:24	*Decisions are represented by means of a diamond symbol.* [236]	-	-	Grammar goal rule

Where $Interaction_{[A/D]}$ is the interaction in which the rule is activated/de-activated. $Time_{[A/D]}$ is the activation/de-activation time of the rule. However, there were no occurrences of rule de-activation in the case study.

Table 5. Model coding, interpretation and meta-data

Time	Propositions	Selection Criteria
12:23	*Check Storage is the first activity in swim lane 6.*	Proposed and drawn, not explicitly disagreed with.
14:01	*And here the Item is finally ordered*	Explicitly agreed with by all

determining which proposals make it to the common (shared) model. Table 5 shows two example propositions and the criteria that were used in selecting them for the model.

Viewing modeling as a game requires identification of the rules under which the *modeling game* is played, including goals driving and motivating the players (i.e., modelers). Previous work has dealt with identification of modeling goals based on known aspects of quality of modeling, concerning both the process of modeling and the models themselves. Our goal types were initially derived from the QoMo framework [5,7], in turn derived from the *Semiotic Quality framework* (SEQUAL) [4], but were now tested in practice, and thus a result of this paper is partial validation of the QoMo framework. Another link with an existing approach is with the COMA approach of Peter Rittgen [3]; we will also briefly compare our findings with COMA. Such comparison is interesting as such but it also serves to demonstrate how our approach may contribute to the method and evaluation.

4   Findings

In this section we present our findings and observations; however, note that a different result is the analytical approach as such, as presented in this and the previous section.

Table 6. Duration and number of interactions of the collaborative modeling phases

Phase	Phase Activity	Duration (seconds)	No. Interactions
I	Setting of the main approach: choosing the language and sub-division of work	104	21
II	Exploring and deciding which actors play a role in the first partial process model.	414	126
III	Modeling the sub-process	527	144
	Total	**1045**	**291**

We applied the basic framework and approach shown in Fig. 2 to the case study described in Sect. 2.2. Our central aim was to discover and make explicit the "rules of the modeling game", and the dynamics of them being set in view of particular goals and situations. The whole collaborative modeling session consisted of a total of 291 interactions and took 17.25 minutes or 1045 seconds. It showed three clearly distinguishable phases (see Sect. 4.4), each with its own typical proportion of interactions types. Table 6 summarized these phases.

4.1   Categorization of the Speech-Acts

In line with [3], it can be noted from the video and the transcription that the communication among the modelers can broadly be categorized as a *negotiation*. I consists of *argumentations* (argue for/against) by the modelers which results in either *acceptance/agreement* by all modelers, or *rejection* of the proposals. Explicit agreement only occurs at some points in the negotiations, whereas "*silence means agreement*" is the convention applied most in the case conversation. Rejection may come explicitly, as a result of a *disagreement* (objection) to a proposal or as a result of an agreement to drop a proposal. For our full set of speech act categories, see Table 7, which also gives the distribution of the interactional speech acts over the three phases.

Table 7. Number and type of speech acts within the phases

Speech Act Type	Phase I		Phase II		Phase III		Total	
	#	%	#	%	#	%	#	%
Propose/Answer	7	33	30	24	39	27	76	26
Counter_propose	0	0	3	2	6	4	9	3
Question	7	33	25	20	16	11	48	16
Argue_for	2	10	3	2	7	5	12	4
Argue_against	1	5	9	7	7	5	17	6
Agree_with/Accept	4	19	17	13	23	16	44	15
Disagree_with/Reject	0	0	16	13	7	5	23	8
Non-verbal(graphical) acts	0	0	23	18	39	27	62	21
Total	**21**		**126**		**144**		**291**	

4.2   Categorization of Topics of Interactions

All interactions either contribute toward the setting of a goal or toward goal fulfillment. Interactions of one type can fulfill several goals at the same time; for example, content setting should respect grammar rules and thus fulfills *grammar* goals, but content setting also, and primarily, fulfills *creation* goals. Interactions either set some proposition, or else concern one: they ask a question about one, argue for or against it, agree with it/accept it or disagree with/reject it. Also, they may *draw* one (on the digital pad). Accepted propositions set either *rules* or *content*. Accepted content becomes part of the model (see Table 5). In Table 8 we show the interaction topics as identified. The numbers and their corresponding percentages in the column total indicate the frequency use of the interaction topics.

Table 8. Number and type of interaction topics

Phase	Interaction Topic											
	GRM		PLN		CON		CRT		COL		Total	
	#	%	#	%	#	%	#	%	#	%	#	%
I	4	25	3	43	2	1	12	100	0	0	21	7
II	2	13	1	14	120	47	0	0	3	100	126	43
III	10	63	3	43	131	52	0	0	0	0	144	49
Total	16		7		253		12		3		291	

GRM = Grammar, PLN = Planning, CON = Content, CRT = Creation, COL = Collaboration

The topics of the interactions mostly cover the categories proposed in [5], with some exceptions (see Sect. 4.5). Grammar and creation goal setting were found as expected, as was content setting (which does not concern goal setting but fulfillment of goals). Collaboration Setting is an interaction category not previously proposed. It concerns *how modelers are to collaborate with each other*: what roles, hierarchy, responsibilities; how they organize themselves. Rules and goals may well be set for collaboration, but in the case this did not happen explicitly (though collaboration was topic of conversation). Another "new" topic was found: Planning Setting, concerning options for temporal scheduling and strategies concerning the fulfillment of creation goals. One other category was found but discarded in the tables because of its odd nature but may yet be interesting: Help Setting, concerning rules for asking "external help" (for example, asking for additional domain info). Categories like collaboration setting, planning, and even help setting are noteworthy and deserve some extra study; however, in the current case study they played very minor roles in explicit conversation.

4.3   Rules and Goals

As mentioned before, some rules were set *for* the game by the researchers, some set *in* the game, by players. All rules encountered were *goal rules* (e.g. creation goal rules or grammar goal rules). A special class of goal rule is a *goal setting goal rule*: it drives the modelers to set some explicit goal(s). Below we present the three goal rules that were explicitly set *for* the game (i.e in the assignment given): a creation goal, a grammar goal setting goal, and a validation goal. Next we present all rules set *in* the game. They mainly concern the modeling language (which concepts to use: grammar goals), and in one case how to divide the main task into sub-tasks and sub-models (an agreed refinement of the assigned creation goal).

These rules were set *for* the game:

1. Goal setting rule: creation goal. Content: "Create process model". Proposed and activated in the Assignment.
2. Goal setting goal rule: grammar goal. Content: "Set grammar goals". Proposed and activated in the Assignment
3. Goal setting rule: validation goal. Content: "All participants should agree on the model". Proposed and activated in the Assignment

These rules were set *in* the game:

1. Goal setting rule: grammar goal. Content: "Use blocks and arrows to represent activities and the relations between them". Proposed at t=0:44 and activated at t=8:53
2. Goal setting rule: grammar goal. Content: "Use Swim Lanes". Proposed at t=0:59 and activated at t=2:21
3. Goal setting rule: creation goal. Content: "There should be 5 swim lane diagrams composing the process model". Proposed at t=1:15 and activated at t=1:42 (by explicit agreement)
4. Goal setting rule: grammar goal. Content: "Use numbers above the swim lanes corresponding to the actors involved in the process". Proposed at t=2:10 and activated at 2:21
5. Goal setting rule: grammar goal. Content: "Sequences of activities are started with the START symbol". Proposed at t=8:34 and activated also at t=8:34 (used without discussion, but explicitly agreed on immediately).
6. Goal setting rule: grammar goal. Content: "Use end symbol to mark end of process flow". Proposed at t=14:6 and also activated at t=14:06
7. Goal setting rule: grammar goal. Content: "Decisions are represented by means of decision diamonds". Proposed at t=14:18 and activated at 15:19 (after considerable discussion, and against UML standard; participants are aware of this).

4.4   Overall Findings and Observations

In this section we focus on answering the questions raised in Sect. 2.1. Generally, we observe that in a group modeling session, modelers indeed go through a structured and highly interactive negotiation-like process guided by goals/rules that are either set *for* the game or set *in* the game. The modelers were mainly concerned with *structuring the modeling process, modeling concept selection, and content setting*, though other topics arose. In some cases, goals set early (*for the game*, in the assignment) were later refined, in particular the creation goal. Some effort also went into setting the grammar goals, as required by the initial "goal setting goal". A relatively low number of rules set *for* the game is followed by a larger number set *in* the game. It would of course be interesting to see what happens if more rules are set in the assignment, and indeed we intend to look at this in later experiments.

As shown in Table 6, at the hand of observed distribution of interaction topics we were able to distinguish three phases in the case session: *1) Setting the main approach –choosing the language and sub-division of work, 2) Exploring and deciding which actors play a role in the partial modeling process* and *3) Modeling the subprocess.* In view of our focus on "the rules of the game", the first phase can be seen as dedicated to such rule setting, whereas in the two other (main) phases, sporadic rule setting as required by the situation occurred. We conclude that two modes of rule setting seem to occur: planned, pro-active rule setting (phase I) and ad hoc, reactive rule setting (phases II and III).

In Table 7 and Table 8 we presented the categories and patterns of *observed* interactions (speech act types and interaction topics, respectively). The speech act types observed largely fit standard speech act categorization as common in the literature, as expected. We were able to finalize a small set of speech acts that enables us to elegantly code all interactions within scope of our analysis. As for interaction topics, these can broadly be put in the following categories: *Planning, Creation, Grammar, Collaboration, and Content.* Content concerns the model as such, the other topics concern matters of process and method. As shown in Table 8, content setting has by far the biggest share in the number of interactions (253), which was to be expected.

4.5   Comparison with Existing Frameworks

In this section we compare our framework and analysis to two relevant approaches from the literature: QoMo [5,7] and COMA [3,12].

Comparison with Quality of Modeling framework (QoMo). The QoMo framework involves an analysis of aspects for quality-of-modeling based on the product-oriented SEQUAL framework [4]. Roughly speaking, QoMo rephrases the SEQUAL aspects (and some additional ones) as "goals for modeling". The QoMo Goals are theoretical in nature; our case study provides an opportunity for a reality check on QoMo. We will simply compare the QoMo goals-for-modeling from [5] (which is the most mature version) with the concerns-for-modeling that transpired from our close study of explicit interactions in an actual modeling session.

QoMo distinguishes Usage Goals, Creation Goals, Validation Goals, Argumentation Goals, Grammar Goals, Interpretation Goals, and Abstraction Goals. **Usage goals** are not explicitly encountered in our case study, as they are out of its scope, but implicitly they are part of the assigned domain description (Sect. 2.2) which provides a rough use context for which the process model is intended.

Creation goals were clearly and explicitly encountered in the case study: a rough one was set for the game, and some refinement took place in the game (agreed setting of five sub-models). A **validation goal** was also explicitly set in the assignment, but no validation goals were discussed in the game, i.e. the plain initial goal "agree on the model" appears to have been workable for the modelers. Validation goals thus seem relevant enough, but in informal or preliminary settings their finer points remained implicit. Our assumption is that the modelers fall back on generic conventions for conversation and argumentation. However, we still expect validation goals to require refinement and specification in later stages of modeling (for example, when formal commitment of stakeholders comes in); further research will have to confirm this. **Argumentation goals** as well as **interpretation goals** are specializations of validation, and they too are not made explicit in the case study, yet again seem implicitly present as part of regular conventions for interaction. Interpretation, however, does seem to play some explicit role in content setting: phase II of the case mostly concerns attempts of the modelers to get a grip on poorly understood domain terminology; differences in meaning are discussed at length, and finally resolved –up to a point. This aspect also warrants further research. **Grammar goals** are clearly and explicitly set and used in the case study, which was in fact encouraged as the assignment included a "goal setting goal" that instructed the modelers to choose modeling concepts, hence to set grammar goals. Grammar goals setting thus proves a viable concept, and it is interesting to see how gradual, incremental introduction of concepts took place. Also, in more than one respect the modelers *consciously* diverted from standard UML (their initial choice). **Abstraction goals**, an obscure category as it is, were not encountered explicitly.

In addition (as discussed in Sect. 4.2), several topics of interaction were identified that suggest extension of the theory-based QoMo goal set: Planning, Collaboration, and possibly also Help goals. However, they are arguably not directly quality-oriented, and hence this finding seems not so much to point out a gap in QoMo but rather the somewhat insufficient scope of a strict quality-oriented perspective on modeling goals.

Comparison with the Collaborative Modeling Architecture (COMA).
COMA is an interactive and collaborative modeling approach and tool which can be viewed as incorporating and thus setting various modeling goals/rules and interaction mechanisms, some of them as options, some of them "hard". Looking at the COMA tool [12] (its initial incarnation), the following rules are built into the system.

The tool is based on a standard UML editor for 5 types of diagram, including activity diagrams. This means that the *Grammar Goals* are hard-coded (though use of advanced concepts is often optional). In terms of the modeling language, therefore, our case study would probably have looked different if it had been conducted using the COMA tool: use of non-standard UML, like decision diamonds in an activity diagram, would have been impossible (which is not to say this would have presented the modelers with a problem). The other relevant goal category is that of *Validation Goals*. Rittgen built in support for validation in the form of an acceptation mechanism with decision parameters. This boils down to offering a choice out of various popular decision mechanisms observed to occur in collaborative modeling: a choice of detailed validation rules. In other words, COMA has a Goal Setting Goal underlying the validation parametrization (preceding a session). Finally, COMA is negotiation-oriented and supports *argumentation* for or against (partial) model diagrams. This is of course closely related to our speech act categories, and even amounts to the setting of an *Argumentation Goal*. All in all it seems that indeed, COMA comes close to embodying the main modeling goals as recognized in our approach and case. However, COMA is relatively restrictive in setting some main goals (so some refinement should be useful), and further ignores other aspects, like interpretation (negotiation about meaning), collaboration (team organization) and planning (delivery and task decomposition). Findings from this paper, but mostly from further research in a similar vein (Sect. 5), may well provide valuable input for evolutionary development of tools like COMA.

5   Conclusions and Further Research

We have presented and illustrated a research approach aimed at analyzing the detailed process (act) of modeling. We analyzed an actual collaborative modeling session. We presented a conceptual framework and a methodological approach. Findings were also presented, answering our research questions within scope of the case study. We also used our findings to perform a partial validation of the QoMo and COMA approaches, and thus demonstrated its applicability for evaluation purposes.

We do not claim that our approach is definitive and static. There clearly is ample room for elaboration and improvement. Similar analyzes for different (in particular, more restrictive) modeling contexts should be performed, which will no doubt require refinement of the method. Still, we hope to have shown that the sort of analysis presented can be fruitful, in particular in view of (empirical), HCI-style research into modeler-oriented, collaborative creation of models. In the near future, we plan to carry on in this line of work in a PhD project [15] that this paper is also a product of. Our main aim is to lay a foundation for the evaluation and design of advanced, modeler-oriented support tools for collaborative modeling.

References

1. Veldhuijzen van Zanten, G., Hoppenbrouwers, S.J.B.A., Proper, H.A.: System Development as a Rational Communicative Process. Journal of Systemics, Cybernetics and Informatics 2(4), 47–51 (2004)
2. Hoppenbrouwers, S.J.B.A., Proper, H.A., Weide, T.v.d.: Formal Modelling as a Grounded Conversation. In: Goldkuhl, M., Lind, G., Haraldson, S. (eds.) Proceedings of the 10th LAP Conference (LAP 2005), Kiruna, Sweden, pp. 139–155. Linkpings Universitet and Hogskolan I Boras, Linkping (2005)

3. Rittgen, P.: Negotiating Models. In: Krogstie, J., Opdahl, A.L., Sindre, G. (eds.) CAiSE 2007. LNCS, vol. 4495, pp. 561–573. Springer, Heidelberg (2007)
4. Krogstie, J., Sindre, G., Jorgensen, H.: Process Models Representing Knowledge Action: A Revised Quality Framewok. EJIS 15, 91–102 (2006)
5. van Bommel, P., Hoppenbrouwers, S.J.B.A., Proper, H.A., Roelefs, J.: Concepts and Strategies for Quality of Modeling. In: Halpin, T.A., Krogstie, J., Proper, H.A. (eds.) Innovations in Information Systems Modeling, ch. 9. IGI Publishing, Hershey (2008)
6. Becker, J., Rosemann, M., von Uthmann, C.: Guidelines of the Business Process Modeling. In: van der Aalst, W.M.P., Desel, J., Oberweis, A. (eds.) Business Process Management: Models, Techniques, and Empirical Studies, pp. 30–49. Springer, Heidelberg (2000)
7. van Bommel, P., Hoppenbrouwers, S.J.B.A., Proper, H.A.: QoMo: A Modeling Process Quality Framework Based on Sequal. In: Proper, H.A., Halpin, T., Krogstie, J. (eds.) Proceedings of EMMSAD 2007, pp. 118–127. Tapir Academic Press, Norway (2007)
8. Vreede, G.J., de Briggs, R.O.: Collaboration Engineering: Designing Repeatable Processes for High-Value Collaborative Task. In: Proceedings of the 38th HICCS Conference, p. 17c. IEEE, Los Alamitos (2005)
9. Dean, D., Orwig, R., Lee, J., Vogel, D.: Modelling with a Group Modelling Tool: Group Support, Model Quality and Validation. In: System Sciences 1994: Collaboration Technology Organizational Systems and Technology: Proceedings of the 20th HICCS Conference, vol. 4, pp. 214–223. IEEE, Los Alamitos (1994)
10. Bostrom, R.P., Clawson, V.K., Anson, R.: Group Facilitation and Group Support Systems. In: Jessup, L.M., Valacinch, J.S.M. (eds.) Group Support Systems: New Perspectives, pp. 146–168. Macmillan, New York (1993)
11. Rouwette, E., Vennix, J., Van Mullekom, T.: Group Model Building Effectiveness. A Review of Assessment Studies. Sys. Dynamics Review 18(1), 5–45 (2002)
12. Rittgen, P.: Collaborative Modelling Architecture (COMA), http://www.coma.nu/COMA_Tool.pdf (accessed on: 08/05/2009)
13. Hoppenbrouwers, S.J.B.A., van Bommel, P., Jarvinen, A.: Method Engineering as Game Design-An Emerging HCO Perspective on Methods and CASE Tools. In: Halpin, T., et al. (eds.) Workshop Proceedings of EMMSAD 2008 affiliated to CAiSE 2008, Montpellier, France, pp. 97–111 (2008)
14. Goldkuhl, G.: Conversational Analysis as a Theoretical Foundation for Language Action Approaches? In: Weigand, H., Goldkuhl, G., de Moor, A. (eds.) Proceedings of the 8th International Working Conference on LAP (LAP 2003), Tilburg, The Netherlands, July 1-2, pp. 51–69 (2003)
15. Ssebuggwawo, D.: Evaluating Collaborative Modeling Processes: Towards Understanding and Supporting Collaborative Modeling Games. In: Weigand, H., Brinkkemper, S. (eds.) Proceedings of the CAiSE Doctoral Consortium at the CAiSE 2009 Conference, Amsterdam, The Netherlands, June 8-12 (2009)

Evaluating Modeling Sessions Using the Analytic Hierarchy Process

Denis Ssebuggwawo[1], Stijn Hoppenbrouwers[1],
and Erik Proper[1,2]

[1] Institute of Computing and Information Sciences, Radboud University Nijmegen
Heyendaalseweg 135, 6525 AJ Nijmegen, The Netherlands, EU
D.Ssebuggwawo@science.ru.nl, stijnh@cs.ru.nl
[2] Capgemini Nederland B.V.,
Papendorpseweg 100, 3528 BJ Utrecht, The Netherlands, EU
e.proper@acm.org

Abstract. In this paper, which is methodological in nature, we propose to use an established method from the field of Operations Research, the Analytic Hierarchy Process (AHP), in the integrated, stakeholder-oriented evaluation of enterprise modeling sessions: their language, process, tool (medium), and products. We introduce the AHP and briefly explain its mechanics. We describe the factors we take into consideration, and demonstrate the approach at the hand of a case example we devised based on a semi-realistic collaborative modeling session. The method proposed is to be a key part of a larger setup: a "laboratory" for the study of operational (i.e. real) modeling sessions and related study and development of methods and tools deployed in them.

Keywords: Enterprise Modeling, Collaborative Modeling, Modeling Process Quality, Analytic Hierarchy Process.

1 Introduction

This paper was written in the context of the longer term goals of doing solid evidence-based study and development of operational modeling methods. This calls for an adequate way of evaluating and comparing the quality of modeling methods in their broadest sense, i.e. including modeling languages, the modeling process, the outcome of the process (the model, but also common understanding of and agreement on it), and the media used in the process (for example, some modeling tool). Also, these aspects should be viewed in terms of how good they are with respect to the actual, *operational* process. Hence we focus on specific modelling sessions, with their own specific goals and context. More general judgements concerning pros and cons of particular methods should, in our approach, be based on generalizations over data gathered from a number of individual instances of modeling sessions.

In this paper, we focus on the application of a known method from the field of Operation Research, the analytic hierarchy process (AHP) [1], for the comparative evaluation of a number of factors concerning the quality of a modeling

A. Persson and J. Stirna (Eds.): PoEM 2009, LNBIP 39, pp. 69–83, 2009.

session. This is to be a core component of what should eventually become a "modelling lab" in which methods, tools, and techniques for enterprise modelling are to be studied, evaluated, and developed within the Design Science tradition [2]. We aim to include in our eventual lab the results of sound judgements concerning the effectiveness and efficiency of particular methods, increasing (insight in) the "Return on Modelling Effort" in view of the utilitarian goals that are set for a particular session. Although our current focus is on collaborative modeling, it is our contention that if we can deal with collaboration factors, the evaluation can also cover non-collaborative (i.e. solo) sessions. While a number of approaches have been developed for the evaluation of (collaborative) modeling processes [3,4,5,6], these are limited in scope, and they do not integrate the weighting of stakeholders' (modellers', project managers', clients') priorities and preferences in view of the modelling process and its direct outcomes. We propose the AHP method as a superior tool for such goal-oriented multi-factor evaluation.

AHP is one of the most popular and widely used techniques in decision making. Its popularity stems from its ability to combine the subjective aspects and intangibles associated with human analysis of complex problems. AHP's wide use in decision making further stems from its ability to integrate the subjective and objective opinions, its ability to integrate the individual and group priorities (and/or preferences) as well as its ability to combine the deterministic and the stochastic in order to capture the interdependencies of the model [7]. Subjectivity and inconsistency are two phenomena associated with evaluation of modeling artifacts by individuals due to personal priorities and preferences. To reach consensus and reconcile their preferences, stakeholders in a collaborative modeling session undertake a negotiation and decision making process. AHP is one of the tools to control their subjectivity by bringing it within tolerable levels of inconsistency. This is achieved by aggregating individual preferences or priorities into group preferences and/or priorities, see for example [8]. To determine the most appropriate method that captures the modelers' quality goals, modelers have to weigh the attributes of the modeling artifacts by comparing them, pairwise, a-priori. It is because of this, and the desire to control modelers' subjectivity in the comparative evaluation, that we use AHP.

This paper is organized as follows. In Section 2 we present our evaluation framework in which identified quality dimensions for the artifacts are described. In Section 3 we describe a case study and the setup of the modeling session carried out. Our evaluation method as applied to the case study, using the quality dimensions, is described in Section 4. A review of some related work is given in Section 5. Finally, Section 6 closes with a brief summary of our main conclusions and future directions.

2   Modeling Process Evaluation Framework

Our evaluation framework follows and extends the approach suggested by Pleiffer and Niehaves [9] to evaluate the different artifacts used in, and produced during, the modeling process. Their approach follows a design science approach [2] to

Table 1. Modeling Language and Modeling Procedure Quality Attributes (a) and (b)

(a) Modeling Language Quality Attributes

	Quality Criterion	Explanation
Modeling Language	Understandability	Understandability refers to how adequate the model represents concepts you recognize in view of your or someone else's domain knowledge.
	Clarity	Clarity of the modeling language refers to how easily you learn and remember the concepts and notations of the modeling language through the signs, symbols, textual expressions of the modeling language.
	Syntax correctness	The syntax is the common agreed communication language for agents in a collaborative modeling process and establishes a set of signs which can be exchanged and rules (syntactical rules) governing how the signs can be combined. The syntax is related to the formal relations of signs to one another.
	Conceptual minimalism	Conceptual minimalism refers to the existence of primitive (basic) signs and symbols for representing data concepts of the domain as separate objects and assembling the objects to form composite abstractions. Conceptual minimalism relates to the simplicity of the modeling language.

(b) Modeling Procedure Quality Attributes

	Quality Criterion	Explanation
Modeling Procedure	Efficiency	Efficiency of the modeling procedure refers to the resources, e.g., time, required for reaching the solution and attaining the modeling goals and objectives; the time needed to negotiate, reach agreement and consensus.
	Effectiveness	Modeling procedure effectiveness refers to how the modeling procedure enables the modelers in using communication and negotiation to get the expected outcome and thus attain their set goals. It also includes the facilitation and the way the modeling process is carried out and/or conducted, and the decision-making process.
	Satisfaction	Satisfaction of the modeling procedure refers to the modelers' positive feeling about the achievement of the intended result using the modeling procedure. Intended results may include intermediary or end-results. Satisfaction can concern the way modelers communicated, negotiated, reached agreement and how they made modeling decisions.
	Commitment & Shared Understanding	Commitment and shared understanding refer to the modeler's stake and promise to support the goals and objectives of the modeling process, the responsibility to abide by the modeling rules and group decisions and his/her readiness to contribute to the group's shared understanding.

identifying the different IS research artifacts evaluating them. Because their framework employs the philosophical notions of structuralism, it still focuses mainly on the inner structure of the models and the evaluation of their quality. Our approach extends their framework by evaluating a wider range of modeling artifacts involved in the modeling process. The quality attributes we study for each of the modeling artifacts in the framework are given and explained in Tables 1 – 2; they are based on [4,5,6,9,10,11,12,13].

3   Research Setup: Case Study Scenario

This section of the paper describes a realistic modeling case study we carried out in one of the modeling sessions. The proposed AHP evaluation methodology is applied to this case together with the quality dimensions from Section 2.

Table 2. Products and Medium-Support System Quality Attributes (a) and (b)

(a) Modeling Products Quality Attributes

	Quality Criterion	Explanation
Modeling Products	Product Quality	Product quality refers to the accuracy of the model in depicting all the identified aspects, adequate representation of the domain concepts in the products, abstractedness, clarity and correctness.
	Understandability	Understandability of the products refers to the degree to which the modelers comprehend the language concepts represented in the products, e.g., its syntax, semantics, etc., the relationship between the different concepts which are depicted by the products, and the ease with which the modelers can explain the concepts in the products even to those who never participated in the modeling process.
	Modifiability and Maintainability	Modifiability and maintainability of the products refer to ease of changing the products to accommodate new changes and the degree to which the products can be kept up-to-date, and how easily they can be re-used in the re-engineering and re-structuring of the enterprise processes.
	Satisfaction	Product satisfaction of the modelers refers to a positive feeling about the product's quality. This could include satisfaction with respect to the product's correctness, completeness, accuracy, consistency, clarity, understandability and/or its complexity.

(b) Medium - Support System Quality Attributes

	Quality Criterion	Explanation
Medium – Support System (Tool)	Functionality	Tool functionality refers to the different functions that a tool has which support activities of the modeling process. It also refers to how the support tool executes the modeling activities and how reliable it is in executing those activities.
	Usability	Usability of a tool support refers to its effectiveness and efficiency to achieve specified goals in particular environments. It is a set of attributes which bear on the effort needed for use and on the individual assessment of such use by a stated or implied set of users. Where efficiency relates to the level of effectiveness achieved to the expenditure of resources whereas effectiveness refers to the goals or sub-goals of using the support tool to the accuracy and completeness with which these goals can be achieved.
	Satisfaction & Enjoyment	Satisfaction refers to perceived usability of the support tool by its users and the acceptability of the support tool to the people who use it and to other people affected by its use. It also refers to the degree of fun and enjoyment by the modelers in using the tool. Measures of satisfaction may relate to specific aspects of the system or may be measures of satisfaction with the overall support system.
	Collaboration & Communication Facilitation	Collaboration and communication facilitation refers to the degree to which the support system helps modelers to collaboratively achieve the set goals and objectives. It also refers to the ability of the support system to aid the communication process and decision making process to reach agreement and consensus.

Research Design and Subjects. We carried out a modeling session and applied AHP to it. Apart from the modeling process as such, we also had participants negotiate about factors for measuring the quality of the modeling process. Participants in the modeling process were drawn from an undergraduate Information Systems course. All students have skills in conceptual modeling as well as basic computer skills.

Problem Description. The assignment given to the students concerned an airline company facing a re-engineering problem. The current information systems had not kept up with information and data needs and there was therefore a need to upgrade them. To achieve this, the company wanted to come up with an information model of the system. The modeling case identified the main processes, e.g., making a booking, associated activities and tasks (e.g., air-craft inspection), business rules, (e.g., no pilot is allowed to fly a plane without undergoing a general fitness check and test), and the actors involved, (e.g., pilot, passenger, air-hostess), etc. The data model included reservations, scheduled flights, inspection, etc.

Evaluation Criteria Identification. To measure and evaluate the quality of the modeling process, especially with regard to the quality goals and satisfaction, a number of quality criteria were identified. These criteria are given in Tables 1 – 2. The modeling session experiment was aimed at evaluating the quality of modeling process.

Collaborative Modeling Session Phase. The modeling session took 1 hour 50 minutes. During this phase modelers engaged in different types of communication and negotiations to reach a shared and common understanding about the domain concepts to be modeled. The modeling process was carried out using a simple UML editor. Figure 1 is a screenshot of the model produced collaboratively using the COMA tool.

Collaborative Modeling Process Evaluation Phase. In the second part of the modeling session, which took 35 minutes, modelers were given an instrument to evaluate the modeling process. An evaluation instrument (see, Fig. 3) based

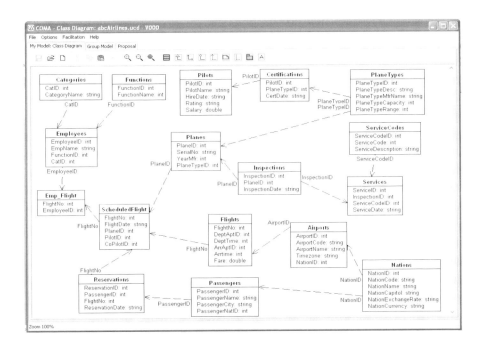

Fig. 1. Screenshot of model from the collaborative modeling session

on the analytic hierarchy process (AHP) fundamental scale was used. The same group was used to exclude their personal characteristics [14] and to track and control the degree of subjectivity in the evaluation.

4   Proposed Evaluation Method: AHP Method

In this paper we apply principles and concepts from the analytic hierarchy process (AHP) to measure and evaluate the modeling process artifacts. AHP is, essentially, a method for making complex decisions on the basis of subjective opinions by multiple stakeholders. In our case the process renders the score for an individual modeling session which can then be compared with a similarly calculated score for another session. Given that variables between the sessions are sufficiently controlled, this enables well-founded judgement about which method works best. The advantages of our evaluation framework and AHP approach lie in advanced management of subjectivity, aggregation of individual priorities, and preferences of the stakeholders about the quality of the modeling artifacts into group priorities and preferences. Also, the AHP helps the stakeholders reach consensus about their preferences and priorities.

4.1   Analytic Hierarchy Process Methodology

AHP consists of mainly three main steps: *structural decomposition, comparative judgement, and synthesizing*, broken into a number of steps, see for example [10].

4.2   Structural Decomposition Step

The decomposition step has basically two sub-steps explained below.

Problem Identification. This step involves identifying the unstructured problem to solve. It could be an evaluation, selection, or a location/allocation problem. Problem identification means also identifying the characteristics or features of the problem which can be used in decision making. These could be criteria, sub-criteria, attributes and alternatives. We decompose the modeling process evaluation problem as shown in Fig. 2 for the case scenario. This is the structural decomposition of the identified problem - *Modeling Process Evaluation (MPE)* of collaborative modeling approaches (CMAs). The different quality attributes, sub-criteria and criteria for each artifact and the overall goal are identified. By weighting these, modelers are able to assign and determine their priorities and preferences.

Hierarchy Construction. This step involves decomposing the problem into a hierarchical structural with distinctive levels. The structure can be obtained using *"decision-tree like diagrams"*. The topmost level, in the hierarchy, is the goal level followed by the criteria level, which is followed by the sub-criteria (if any) up to the lowest level which consists of alternatives.

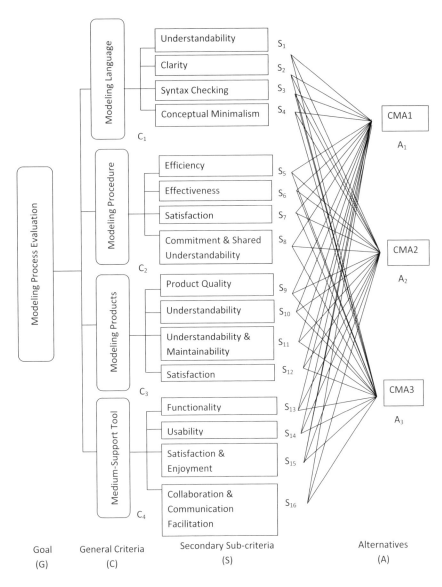

Fig. 2. AHP hierarchy for modeling process evaluation

4.3 Pairwise Comparison - Comparison Scale

The comparative step consists of pairwise comparison, formation of a comparative matrix and priority vector, and checking consistency. The comparative judgment step is aimed at establishing (local) priorities at each level by comparing, pair-wise, each criterion, sub criterion, etc., in the low hierarchy levels to determine the priority of each. Therefore, if we have n evaluation criteria

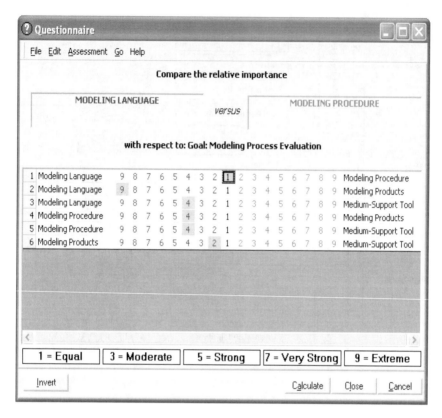

Fig. 3. Expert Choice questionnaire form

(sub criteria or attributes) we will have to carry out a total of $n(n-1)/2$ pairwise comparisons. In the comparison step, each of the elements is assigned and ranked using a nine (1 - 9) point scale in a questionnaire-like instrument in order to determine their relative importance to each other.

To answer the question: *"Of the two elements, which one is more important with respect to a higher level criterion and what is the strength of its dominance?"*, we ask judges (collaborative modelers) to compare, pairwise, the elements at each level in the AHP hierarchy given in Fig. 2. This is aided by using, for example, ExpertChoice [15], a software tool for multi-criteria decision analysis. Figure 3 shows how the relative importance of elements is determined by comparing them, pairwise, with respect to their parent element. In this case, two criteria: *modeling language* and *modeling procedure* are pairwise compared with respect to their parent criterion: *Modeling Process Evaluation*. A judgement (relative scale), e.g., 9, is given in the left half of the questionnaire meaning that *"modeling language is relatively strongly more important than modeling procedure"* in measuring or assessing modeling process quality. A reciprocal, (1/9), means that *" modeling procedure is strongly more important than modeling language"*.

4.4 Pairwise Comparison - Forming a Comparative Matrix

The outcome of the comparative judgment step is a comparative matrix the entries of which are the comparison values between the ith row and the jth column indicating the relative importance (from scale 1-9) of one criterion over another. This comparison value gives the importance of the row's criterion relative to the column's criterion. Let $\mathbf{A} = (a_{ij})$ be an $n \times n$ comparative (judgement) matrix and let a_{ij} be its entries. Then $\mathbf{A} = (a_{ij}) = 1/a_{ji} = 1, i = j$. This means that the elements, a_{ii}, for all i, on the principal diagonal are all equal to 1. The purpose of the pair-wise comparison is to determine the (priority) vector, w, with weights $w_1, w_2, ..., w_n$ which represent the expert's relative opinion/judgement for the criteria, sub-criteria or attributes, i.e.,

$$w = (w_1, w_2, ..., w_n)^T, \quad where \quad w_i > 0, \quad \sum_{i=1}^{n} w_i = 1 . \tag{1}$$

The relation of the weights w_i to the entries of the matrix A is:

$$a_{ij} = w_i/w_j, \qquad 1 \leqslant i, j \leqslant n . \tag{2}$$

The matrix $\mathbf{A} = (a_{ij})$, where $a_{ij} = w_i/w_j$, for $i, j \in \{1, ..., n\}$, has all its entries positive and is called a *reciprocal matrix* since it satisfies the property:

$$a_{ji} = 1/a_{ij} . \tag{3}$$

Matrix $\mathbf{A}$ is said to be *consistent* if the following condition holds:

$$a_{jk} = a_{ik}/a_{ij}, \quad i, j, k \in \{1, ..., n\} . \tag{4}$$

The judgements given by the modelers are put in a comparative (judgement) matrix, using Eq. 2, and the reciprocal condition in Eq. 3. The criteria, sub-criteria, etc., are put along and on top of the matrix. Table 3 is an example of a comparative matrix which, pairwise, compares the relative importance of the general criteria $(C_1 - C_4)$: with respect to the goal, G. When an element is compared to itself, we give it a relative scale of 1 (equal importance) and this explains these values on the principal diagonal of the comparative matrix. The reciprocal property in Eq. 3 requires that if an element (criterion comparative

Table 3. Comparative matrix of general criteria $C_1 - C_4$ w.r.t goal G

	Modeling Language	Modeling Procedure	Modeling Products	Medium Support Sys.	Priorities vector
Modeling Language	1	1	9	4	0.469
Modeling Procedure	1	1	4	4	0.093
Modeling Products	1/9	1/4	1	2	0.079
Medium (Support Sys.)	1/4	1/4	1/2	1	0.041

λ_{max} = 4.220   C.I = 0.073   C.R = 0.082

judgement intensity), say, 9 is entered in the first row, third column, i.e., $a_{13} = 9$, its reciprocal is entered in third row, first column, i.e., $a_{31} = 1/9$.

The matrix in Table 3 is a 4×4 positive reciprocal matrix (see Eq. 3), a necessary though not a sufficient condition for consistency. A necessary and sufficient condition for a consistent matrix (see for example, [16]) is that the principal eigenvalue, λ_{max}, in Eq. 7 be equal to the order, n, of the matrix in Eq. 5.

4.5   Relative Weight Estimation - Eigenvector Method

There are a number of methods for computing the (priority) vector of the relative weights and aggregating individual and group judgements or priorities. The most popular aggregation methods are *aggregation of individual judgements (AIJ)* and *aggregation of individual priorities (AIP)* [8]. For prioritization, the *right eigenvector method (EGVM)* and the *row geometric mean method (RGMM)* are the most popular. We prefer to use EGVM to show how the relative weights are computed because of its simplicity and transparency. The relative weights of all the attributes are computed from the eigenvalue problem of the form:

$$\mathbf{A}w = nw \quad or \quad (\mathbf{A} - n\mathbf{I})w = 0 . \tag{5}$$

which is a system of homogeneous linear equations and $\mathbf{I}$ is the identity or unit matrix. This system has a non-trivial solution if and only if the determinant of $\mathbf{A}$ vanishes, i.e.,

$$det(n\mathbf{I} - \mathbf{A}) = |n\mathbf{I} - \mathbf{A}| = 0 . \tag{6}$$

In this case n is the eigenvalue of $\mathbf{A}$. In order to facilitate the computation, the eigenvalue problem in Eq. 5 can be expanded as:

$$\mathbf{A}'w = \lambda_{max}w \quad or \quad (\lambda_{max}\mathbf{I} - \mathbf{A}')w = 0 . \tag{7}$$

where λ_{max} is the largest eigenvalue of $\mathbf{A}$, called the *principal eigenvalue of $\mathbf{A}'$*, which is used as an estimator of n in Eq. 5 and $w = (w_1, w_2, ..., w_n)^T$. The importance of this largest eigenvalue is its use in controlling the inconsistency and subjectivity in the evaluators' judgements. Equation 7 is a system of homogeneous linear equations having a non-trivial solution if and only if the determinant of $\mathbf{A}'$ vanishes, i.e.,

$$det(\lambda_{max}\mathbf{I} - \mathbf{A}') = |\lambda_{max}\mathbf{I} - \mathbf{A}'| = 0 . \tag{8}$$

• *Normalization.* Normalization is a process that shows relative importance of the criteria when compared with respect to each other. If R_i is the row-sum for the ith row, i = 1, 2, ..., n, and T_R is the total of all row-sums of matrix $\mathbf{A}$ then we have:

$$R_i = \sum_{j=1}^{n} \frac{w_i}{w_j}, \quad i \in \{1, ..., n\}. \quad T_R = \sum_{i=1}^{n} R_i . \tag{9}$$

Table 4. Modeling language and procedure comparative matrices (a) and (b)

(a) Comparative matrix of subcriteria $S_1 - S_4$ w.r.t subcriterion C_1

	Understandability	Clarity	Syntax Checking	Conceptual Minimalism	Priorities vector
Understandability	1	1/4	3	1	0.178
Clarity	4	1	5	6	0.607
Syntax Checking	1/3	1/5	1	1	0.096
Conceptual Minimalism	1	1/6	1	1	0.119

λ_{max} = 4.139   C.I = 0.046   C.R = 0.052

(b) Comparative matrix of subcriteria $S_5 - S_8$ w.r.t subcriterion C_2

	Efficiency	Effectiveness	Satisfaction	Communication & Shared Understand	Priorities vector
Efficiency	1	2	6	3	0.464
Effectiveness	½	1	5	6	0.368
Satisfaction	1/6	1/5	1	1	0.077
Communication & Shared Understanding	1/3	1/6	1	1	0.092

λ_{max} = 4.174   C.I = 0.058   C.R = 0.065

Therefore, the normalized entries, w'_i, of the principal eigenvector (local priorities), $w' = (w'_1, w'_2, ..., w'_n)^T$, are given by:

$$w'_i = R_i/T_R, \quad where \quad w'_i > 0, \quad \sum_{i=1}^{n} w'_i = 1 . \tag{10}$$

which is the solution to Eq. 5. The principal eigenvector (vector of priorities), $w = (w_1, w_2, ..., w_n)^T$ is given by Eq. 7. Concepts from this section were applied to the case study and the results are given in Tables 4 and 5. The priorities given in these tables are normalized as can easily be checked by Eq. 10. From Table 4(b), efficiency has the highest priority, followed by effectiveness and communication and shared understanding, whereas satisfaction has the least priority. This means that while determining the quality of the modeling process with respect to the modeling procedure, modelers' priority and preference is on modeling procedure's efficiency and effectiveness. Results in Table 5 are similarly interpreted.

4.6 Consistency Check

To check whether matrix judgments (decisions) are consistent, we need to check the consistency of the comparative matrices at each level of the hierarchy. This is done via the *Consistency Index (C.I)* and the *(Consistency Ratio (C.R)*, calculated, respectively, by:

$$C.I = (\lambda_{max} - n)/(n - 1) \quad C.R = C.I/R.I . \tag{11}$$

Table 5. Modeling products and medium comparative matrices (a) and (b)

(a) Comparative matrix of subcriteria $S_9 - S_{12}$ w.r.t subcriterion C_3

	Product Quality	Understandability	Modifiability & Maintainability	Satisfaction	Priorities vector
Product Quality	1	1/9	1/5	1	0.064
Understandability	9	1	2	8	0.559
Modifiability & Maintainability	5	1/2	1	6	0.318
Satisfaction	1	1/8	1/6	1	0.061

λ_{max} = 4.014   C.I = 0.047   C.R = 0.053

(b) Comparative matrix of subcriteria $S_{13} - S_{16}$ w.r.t subcriterion C_4

	Functionality	Usability	Satisfaction &Enjoyment	Collaboration & Comm. Facilitation	Priorities vector
Functionality	1	1/2	3	5	0.309
Usability	2	1	6	4	0.505
Satisfaction & Enjoyment	1/3	1/6	1	2	0.109
Collaboration & Comm. Facilitation	1/5	1/4	1/2	1	0.077

λ_{max} = 4.133   C.I = 0.044   C.R = 0.049

where, as noted in [16], R.I is a *Random Index* (the average consistency index) calculated as an average of a randomly generated pair-wise matrix of the same order. It is noted, in [17] that the acceptable upper threshold for C.R is:

$$C.R = \begin{cases} 0.05, & n = 3 \\ 0.08, & n = 4 \\ 0.10, & n > 4 \ . \end{cases} \qquad (12)$$

Therefore, if C.R is less than or equal to the given upper bound, matrix **A** is of sufficient consistency and the judgment/decision is acceptable. To check for consistency, we use Eq. 8 and Eq. 11 to compute the principal eigenvalue (λ_{max}), consistency index (C.I) and the consistency ratio (C.R). The random index (R.I) for an n = 4 order matrix (the order in our case) is 0.89, [17]. These values are given at the bottom of the comparative matrix tables. The comparative matrices in Tables 4 - 5 are all of order n = 4 (4×4 square matrices). Equation 12 confirms consistency except for 0.082 (in Table 3) which is slightly above the upper-bound indicating some small degree of inconsistency.

4.7   Synthesizing - Overall Rating and Ranking

This step consists of determining overall rating and ranking of alternatives whose priorities may be given as normalized or idealized priorities. It determines the overall priority (preference) rating of the alternatives by aggregating the relative weights of the criteria. Suppose we have got m alternatives. Let w'_{ik} be the local priority for the kth alternative, A_k, for $k \in \{1, 2, ..., m\}$, with respect to the ith criterion, C_i. Let w'_i be the local priority of C_i with respect to the goal, G. Then the global priority, w'_{A_k}, of alternative A_k with respect to all local priorities of the criteria is given by:

$$w'_{A_k} = \sum_{i=1}^{n} w'_{ik} w'_i, \quad w'_{A_k} > 0, \quad \sum_{k=1}^{m} w'_{A_k} = 1 . \qquad (13)$$

Idealized Priorities. An alternative way of expressing overall (global) priorities for alternatives is to use an idealized form [18]. Priorities for the ideal mode are obtained by dividing each priority by the *largest one*. Let w''_{A_k} be the idealized overall priority for alternative k, $k \in \{1, 2, ..., m\}$. Then

$$w''_{A_k} = w'_{A_k} / \max\{w'_{A_k}\}, \qquad k \in \{1, 2, ..., m\} . \qquad (14)$$

Note that from this point, CMA1 reflects our case whereas CMA2 and CMA3 are fictional, i.e. would require further cases. To synthesize the priorities of alternatives, we make use of the local priorities of the alternatives with respect to each criterion and compute the composite or the global priorities using Eq. 13. Synthesized results, are shown in Table 6.

Table 6. Synthesized results for alternatives with respect to goal

	Modeling Language (0.469)	Modeling Procedure (0.359)	Products (0.093)	Medium (0.079)	Priorities (Normalized)	(Idealized)
CMA 1	0.705	0.637	0.573	0.683	0.667	1.000
CMA2	0.181	0.274	0.330	0.205	0.230	0.345
CMA3	0.141	0.089	0.098	0.112	0.116	0.174

Interpretation

The overall priority values indicate that the first collaborative modeling approach: CMA1 has the highest priority followed by CMA2 and CMA3 has the least priority. The normalized priorities in Table 6 can also be given in an idealized form (last column) using Eq. 14, meaning: CMA2 is 35% as good as CMA1 in meeting the evaluation goals and criteria whereas CMA3 is 17% as good.

5   Related Work

The first work to counteract criticisms for lack of methodology for the evaluation process of (process) modeling is [11]. The methodology developed therein provides an initial understanding of process model quality and is used as a generic approach for deriving theoretically grounded measurements and empirically-based strategies for evaluating quality. There are a number of methods and frameworks that have been proposed for the evaluation of the *"quality"* of the models produced from the *"modeling process"*. In [12], for example, a process -oriented framework for quality of modeling (*QoMo*) is proposed based on the SEQUAL [13] framework. QoMo is one of the first process-oriented quality frameworks. The QoMo framework extends the SEQUAL framework by incorporating the *rules* and *goals* of modeling as a way of describing the processes for modeling. There are, however, very few methods for performing a comprehensive evaluation of all the modeling artifacts used in and produced during the modeling process, more particularly in collaborative modeling [19]. Evaluation of the modeling process, including its "return on modeling effort", through cost-benefit analysis is a key part of the evaluation phase in the design cycle of the collaborative modeling game analysis [20].

6   Conclusion and Future Work

This paper has presented an evaluation approach for modeling processes. Driven by the aim of trying to understand modeling process, the paper has put emphasis on the quality of four artifacts that are used or produced during the modeling process. Analysing the quality of these artifacts by identifying the different attributes and criteria gives us a way to gauge the quality of the modeling process. By using the AHP we can deal with the important phenomenon that modelers and evaluators, in general, may be biased towards evaluation criteria. We do this by using an approach in which every one's judgement and evaluation is put into consideration and the overall priority is aggregated as a group decision. The developed approach serves as a basis for deriving adequate as well as theoretically sound and quantified quality criteria for the modeling process using the AHP method. Further research activities will be geared towards tracing judgements pertaining to the end state of the process to tangible flaws within the communication and negotiation process as such, i.e. interactions and rules governing the modeling process stemming either from the method and tools (media) used, or from particular actions taken by participants within boundaries set by tool or method. Studying interdependencies (sort of "cause-effect" relationships) between the modeling artifacts forms part of our future work.

References

1. Saaty, T.L.: The Analytic Hierarchy Process. McGraw-Hill, New York (1980)
2. Hevner, A.R., March, S.T., Park, J., Ram, S.: Design Science in Information Systems Research. MIS Quarterly 28(1), 75–105 (2004)
3. Barjis, J., Kolfschoten, G.L., Verbraeck, A.: Collaborative Enterprise Modeling. In: Proper, E., Harmsen, F., Dietz, J.L.G. (eds.) PRET 2009. LNBIP, vol. 28, pp. 50–62. Springer, Heidelberg (2009)
4. Briggs, R.O., de Vreede, G.J., Reinig, B.A.: A Theory and Measurement of Meeting Satisfaction. In: Proccedings of the 26th HICCS Conference, p. 25c. IEEE, Los Alamitos (2003)
5. den Hengst, M., Dean, D.L., Kolfschoten, G.L., Chakrapani, A.: Assessing the Quality of Collaborative Processes. In: Proceedings of the 39th Annual HICCS Conference (HICCS 2006), vol. 1, p. 16b. IEEE Computer Society, Los Alamitos (2006)

6. Duivenvoorde, G.P.J., Kolfschoten, G.L., Briggs, R.O., de Vreede, G.J.: Towards an Instrument to Measure the Successfulness of Collaborative Effort from the Participant Perspective. In: Proceedings of the 42nd HICCS Conference (HICCS 2009), pp. 1–9. IEEE Computer Society, Los Alamitos (2009)
7. Altuzarra, A., Moreno-Jiménez, J.M., Salvador, M.: Searching for Consensus in AHP Group Decision Making. In: A Bayesian Perspective. CODAWORK 2005. La Universitat, Girona (2005), http://hdl.handle.net/10256/698 (accessed on: August 17, 2009)
8. Escobar, M.T., Moreno-Jiménez, J.M.: Aggregation of Individual Preference Structures in AHP-Group Decsion Making. Group Decision and Negotiation 16, 287–301 (2007)
9. Pfeiffer, D., Niehaves, B.: Evaluation of Conceptual Models - A Structuralist Approach. In: Proceedings of the 13th ECIS Conference: Information Systems in a Rapidly Changing Economy, ECIS 2005, Regensburg, Germany, May 26-28 (2005)
10. Ngai, E.W.T., Chan, E.W.C.: Evaluation of Knowledge Management Tools using AHP. Expert Sys. with Appl. 29, 889–899 (2005)
11. Recker, J.: Towards Understanding of Process Quality. Methodological Considerations. In: Ljungberg, J., Anderson, M. (eds.) Proceedings of the 14th ECIS Conference, Goetenborg, Sweden, pp. 12–14 (2006)
12. van Bommel, P., Hoppenbrouwers, S.J.B.A., Proper, H.A.: QoMo: A Modeling Process Quality Framework Based on Sequal. In: Proper, H.A., Halpin, T., Krogstie, J. (eds.) Proceedings of EMMSAD 2007, pp. 118–127. Tapir Academic Press, Norway (2007)
13. Krogstie, J., Sindre, G., Jorgensen, H.: Process Models Representing Knowledge Action: A Revised Quality Framewok. EJIS 15, 91–102 (2006)
14. Rittgen, P.: Collaborative Modeling of Business Processes-A Comparative Case Study. In: Proceedings of the 24th Annual ACM Symposium on Applied Computing, Waikiki Beach, Honolulu, Hawaii, March 9-12, pp. 225–230. ACM, New York (2009)
15. Expert Choice Inc. (2009), http://www.expertchoice.com (accessed on: 08/06/2009)
16. Saaty, T.L.: How to Make a Decision: The Analytic Hierarchy Process. European J. of Ops. Res. 48, 9–26 (1990)
17. Saaty, T.L.: The Analytic Hierarchy and Analytic Network Measurement Processes: Applications to Decisions under Risk. Honorary invited paper. Eur. J. Pure & Appl. Math. 1, 122–196 (2008b)
18. Saaty, T.L.: Decision Making with the Analytic Hierarchy Process. Int. J. Services Sciences 1(1), 83–98 (2008a)
19. Rittgen, P.: Collaborative Modelling Architecture (COMA), http://www.coma.nu/COMA_Tool.pdf (accessed on: 08/05/2009)
20. Ssebuggwawo, D., Hoppenbrouwers, S.J.B.A., Proper, H.A.: Analysizing a Collaborative Modeling Game. In: Yu, E., Eder, J., Roland, C. (eds.) Proceedings of the Forum at the CAiSE 2009 Conference, Amsterdam, The Netherlands, June 8-12, vol. 453, pp. 73–78 (2009)

A Goal–Oriented Approach for Business Process Improvement Using Process Warehouse Data

Khurram Shahzad and Jelena Zdravkovic

Department of Computer and Systems Science (DSV),
Royal Institute of Technology (KTH)/ Stockholm University (SU),
Stockholm, Sweden
{mks,jelenaz}@dsv.su.se

Abstract. In a process-oriented enterprise management, process optimization focuses on studying and evaluating existing processes, such as utilization of resources and identification of problems in the process flow and functionality, for facilitating potential improvements. Conventional data warehouses do not provide information necessary for studying processes, such as executed process activities, utilized resources, or control-flow. Thereby, decisions on process improvements either cannot be taken, or they are taken without complete information. Additionally, process improvements methods commonly suffer from a number of limitations with respect to their complexity, efficiency and degree of automation. In this study, we consider process-oriented data warehouses and thereby we identify the information required from such awarehouse, to facilitate a semi-automatic method for improving processes, starting from established business goals toward concrete decisions. A case study from the Swedish health care sector is used to ground and illustrate the presented method.

Keywords: Business Process Management, Business process optimization, Process warehouse, Goal analysis, Decision making.

1 Introduction

Enterprises are continuously looking for ways to improve their business processes. This activity is no longer a luxury – in order to stay competitive, or to achieve a level of quality, effective methods for process improvements need to be employed.

In enterprise practices, any process improvement analysis requires profound information about the running processes. Conventional data warehouses cannot provide an adequate basis for an in-depth analysis of business processes, because data from transactional systems (OLTP) [1] is extracted, transformed and loaded in data warehouse [3] i.e. the data about ongoing activities is not captured. As a consequence, credible decisions on potential process improvements by using data-oriented warehouses as information sources cannot be taken at all [2].

The second problem concerns the amount of information that needs to be considered when analyzing the data from the execution logs. Process warehouse is a large database and the magnitude of data needed for a decision is very small as compared to

A. Persson and J. Stirna (Eds.): PoEM 2009, LNBIP 39, pp. 84–98, 2009.

the total size of a process warehouse. Therefore, identification of information that should be consulted for decision making is a pre requisite of the decision making process and it is a complex task. Thereby, there is a significant need for structuring a process warehouse in a way that will enable a fast extraction of the process data relevant for improvement decisions.

The third problem in the process improvement effort concerns a lack of automation in the analysis methods. In this task, business experts, envisaged for making improvement decisions, heavily depend on IT personnel to get the information about running systems. The major obstacle in this context is that the business process data is widely un-automated for analyses.

Following the outlined, in the effort to evaluate quality of existing business processes, it is of a great importance to consolidate methods for enabling an efficient insight to process-related data. To achieve that, in this study, we present a goal-based Decision Relationship Model for process analysis and improvement. Starting from business goals, we explore a Decision Relationship Model based on using data from a well-structured process warehouse. In addition to the proposed model, we define a semi-automated procedure including a set of guidelines for managing the analysis of processes with the use of the proposed Decision Relationship Model.

The rest of the paper is organized as follows. Section 2 of the paper discusses the related work. Section 3 contains the Process Design Framework based on four perspectives. A case study from Swedish health care sector is presented in section 4. Our Decision Relationship Model is presented in section 5. A method of using the Decision Relationship Model for process improvement is given in 6. The case study from Swedish healthcare sector is used to exemplify the use of the method for process improvement in section 7.

2   Related Work

Process analysis is a "feedback" phase in the process lifecycle, in which evaluation of executed processes, diagnosis of bottlenecks and optimization of processes takes place [5, 6]. Business Process Management Systems (BPMS) enable process analysis by logging process data and later on querying it with built-in and third part reporting tools [2]. The acquired reports are used for analyzing executions of operations, identifying bottlenecks and detecting deficiencies. However, the use of reports with current BPMSs presents performance, data quality and semantic limitations [2, 7, 8]. Processes Warehousing [4, 9] and Process Mining [10] have been presented as the techniques to overcome these limitations.

Process mining is used to reveal hidden patterns in process logs for analysis and optimization of process models [11]. In addition to that, it has been used for business alignment (i.e. for comparison of expected and real behavior of an information system or its users [12]) and re-discovering process models from event logs [13]. In general, data miners are the technical experts who are engaged in discovering potential relationships between data elements [14].

The Process Warehousing technique is significant because it works as a data source for process mining [15, 16] and provides a foundation for process-oriented decision support systems [17]. Additionally, it supports various analytical tools (like OLAP) for *what-if* analysis and it is also recognized as a tool for analysis of process execution, identifying bottlenecks and other decision supporting analysis [5, 9]. In general, process warehouse users (PW users) are the technical experts who answer the questions or provide historical data for answering questions of business experts. A number of efforts have been made to design and develop process warehouses [18, 19, 20] which are user driven, goal driven or data driven [21]. Also, some studies (such as [22]) have been conducted to evaluate the design quality of different process warehouses.

Application of process warehouse has been discussed in several areas such as healthcare [23], engineering [24] and businesses. However, these studies discuss the use of process warehouse on a high level and therefore concrete guidelines on using process warehouse and methods for identification of information for analysis are missing.

A few studies have been conducted on the use of goals for data warehousing and process warehouse [25, 26]. These studies have at least one of the following limitations, a) the study scope is restricted to data-orientated information systems, b) the decision-relevant information are elicited purely manually, c) the focus is on the identification of requirements for data warehouse, d) DW design requirements are based on a set of queries, whereas all the queries cannot be identified at the design time.

Our approach focuses on the utilization of process warehouses for analysis and optimization of business processes. The approach differs from the outlined related studies as we: a) rely on a process-oriented (i.e. not data-oriented) warehouse when analyzing collected execution data; b) structure process-execution data from several perspectives to be able to decrease the amount of data relevant for different analysis and c) outline a goal-oriented approach for process improvement, that is in a semi-automatic method for obtaining the relevant information from a process warehouse.

3   Process Design Framework

A business process has been defined in various ways [27, 28]; however the core of all definitions is that, a process has a set of activities that are executed in an ordered way. In order to design a process, Curtis has proposed four design perspectives of a process model [29]: *functional, informational, organizational,* and *behavioral*. The main purpose of Curtis process design framework is to enable the obtainment of a complete, i.e. explorative process model.

a) Functional perspective: The perspective considers how a process is decomposed, i.e. what *activities* are to be executed. Activities can be either *atomic,* or *composite*, which are recursively refined to atomic ones. Functionality of an activity is defined by its name, which uniquely identifies the goal of the activity.

b) Informational perspective: The perspective regards the *resources* manipulated in a process. A resource can be either *traditional*, such as a product, or service, or *informational*, such as data and artifacts. A resource is consumed or produced by an atomic process activity.

c) Organizational perspective: This perspective describes the distribution of the responsibility for executing process activities. The main focus here is on the *notion of the actor*. An actor can be an organization unit, a human or a software system.

Actors are commonly modeled as roles, that is, as the set of the functions that an actor is responsible for performing. Using the organizational perspective, it is possible to dedicate and control responsibilities of parties engaged in a process.

d) Behavioral perspective: This perspective concerns the flows of data and activities within a process. The *data flow* describes the flow of information resource from one activity to another. The second flow aspect describes the *control flow*, i.e. when an activity is to be executed in relation to others. For specification of coordination rules among activities, process specifications rely on three basic control flow constructs: sequence, parallel execution and conditional branching. The basic and the advanced control flows, such as synchronization, looping and advance branching, make possible to specify decisions made according to certain *business rules*.

In this study, we use the described process design framework for defining the organization of the data of a process warehouse and to identify the information required for decision making. Additionally, we extend the framework with a temporal aspect that we found as also relevant when analyzing executed processes:

e) Time perspective: It describes the occurrence of events, status of resources, notion of actors and control flow from *temporal* perspective. The perspective is meaningful together with at least one of the four perspectives. Temporal perspective for organizational perspective could be about the availability timing of actors and time utilized by actors etc.

4   Case Study

In this section we introduce a real world case from the Swedish health care sector. Figure 1 shows a process model of an eye-care referral case that is used in this paper as an example study for illustrating the applicability of the proposed approach. The healthcare process is modeled using the Business Process Modeling Notation (BPMN) [30].

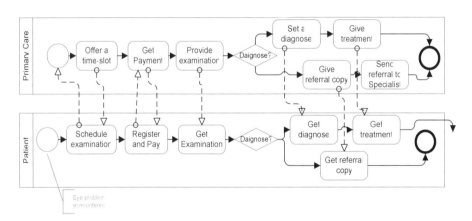

Fig. 1. The base eye-care referral process

The referral process given below belongs to a primary eye-care centre at the commune level. On facing an eye health problem, the patient calls hospital, and a time-slot is offered to him/her. This is followed by a payment and registration, and patient visits a doctor during the allocated time-slot. A primary diagnoses investigates the nature of the disease and a treatment is given in case more investigation is not required. However, if the diagnose needs an expert's treatment, a copy of the referral is forwarded to a specialist.

Activities of the referral process give the functional perspective of the process i.e. *offer a time-slot*, *get payment* etc. The relationship between activities of the referral process gives the behavioral perspective i.e. *get payment* follows *offer a timeslot* and *provide examination* (activity) can either be followed by *set a diagnose* (activity) or *give referral copy* (activity). *Payment amount* and *referral copy* gives the informational perspective (data) related to the eye care process. The *doctors* and the *phone attendant* give the organizational perspective of the referral process. Finally, time perspective is related to all the perspective when the process is executed i.e. the *call-time*, *offered time-slot*, *doctor's availability slots* etc.

5   A Decision Relationship Model for Process Improvement

The purpose of this section is to present and describe a Decision Relationship Model (DRM). For that, each component of the DRM is explained with examples, and a semi-structured definition for representing the components.

Various types of users may be involved in process analysis and improvement. These are, *business experts* who define desired goals regarding process analysis, *decision makers* who take concrete improvement decisions and *technical experts* who interact with process warehouse.

The overall aim of our Decision Relationship Model (DRM) is to reduce the gap between business experts, decision makers and technical experts by providing a structured way of using process warehouse for identifying data related to decision making. For using our approach the business expert should define a process goal and decompose it to one or more leaf goals. By using the given process-related leaf-goals, PW experts can identify the information that is necessary for decision maker to take decision.

The Decision Relationship Model (DRM) (presented in Figure 2) consists of the following elements: Business Process, Leaf Goal, Decision-Associated-Information (DAI), Decision and Action. Below, we describe the elements of our model,

a) Business Process: Process is defined as a set of activities. Primarily, a process includes the activities which are performed in a specific order, the actors who perform the activities, the resources involved in the process and the data or messages transferred between actors or activities.

b) Leaf Goal: Leaf Goal is *'a desired state on any of the four process elements'* of a business process: resources, actors, activities and flow (see Section 3). An example of a leaf goal is, "avoid more than 8 hours workload of doctors". A semi structured formulation of goals is defined as follows

(*Condition* on *process element*)

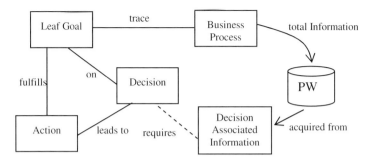

Fig. 2. Decision Relationship Model for Process Improvement

Condition is a desired state and it could be anything related to a process element. A leaf goal defines the targeted element (resource, actor, activity or flow) of a process for process improvement. For example if goal is *optimal use of doctor's availability*, the doctor (actor) is the targeted area (of the process), in which improvement is desired. Leaf goal is defined by business experts and it is fulfilled by the actions which are identified through decision making.

c) Decision Associated Information: The *'information that must be consulted to take a decision'* is called Decision Associated Information (DAI). It is the information that can be used for evaluation of the available alternative decisions which leads to selection of an alternative (decision). Based on the five perspectives of the Process Design Framework (given in Section 3), the data in the process warehouse can be organized into four primary categories and a secondary category. The primary categories are: functional, informational, organizational and behavioral information whereas the time (the secondary information) is a part of each primary-category of information, because it doesn't give any meaningful information independently.

The data in process warehouse that is related as: actors are called organizational information, activities are called functional information, resources are called resource-related information and ordering is called control information. This classification is used for identifying which information should be consulted for which kinds of decisions. For example, in order to take a decision on ordering of activities, behavioral information should be consulted. It is important to identify DAI, because a PW typically involves a large amount of data and thereby the technical expert may not identify the necessary information that must be consulted for decision making.

In what follows, we define the keywords that are used for identifying which data element in the process warehouse is related to which category of information.

- o *Organizational Information,* The information that is related to actors, workload of actors, activities associated with actors, completed activities by the actor, failed activities, pending activities and temporal information on actor.
- o *Functional Information,* The information that is related to activities, start-time, end-time (expected and real), output, deadlock, frequency, cycle-time, activities failed due to resource unavailability and activities failed due to actors non availability and temporal information on activities.
- o *Resource-related Information,* The information that is related to resource, activities related to resource, consumed, produced, transferred, utilized/usage,

required, available, deficient, condition of resource, affect of absence of resource, minimum level and temporal information on resources.

o *Control Information,* The information that is related to outcome of sequence,
frequency, deadlock, alternative paths and temporal information on ordering.

d) Decision: Decision is *'a directive of a course of action'* on resource, actor, activity
or flow. A decision can be formulated as

(*Directive* on *element*) e.g. (*add* more *actors*).

Direction is the course of action and element is the element of process model on
which the directive is applied. Decision is result of a decision-making activity performed by management and it is done in consultation with Decision-Associated-
information (DAI) that is provided by data warehouse expert. The possible directives
to achieve a goal could be on an element or on a set of elements.

e) Action: An Action is a *'realization or implementation of a decision'* taken by the
management. As a result of realization the goal is achieved. In the process improvement life cycle this is related to the implementation of the solution.

In the remaining part of this paper, we present a method for using the Decision Relationship Model and exemplify the use of the Decision Relationship Model to discuss
the applicability of the Model.

6   Using DRM for Process Improvement

In this section we describe how the presented Decision Relationship Model (DRM) can
be used for improving business processes in an organization. For that, we present a
four-step method for guiding the use of the model. For each step we define input, output, involved actors (users) and high-level guidelines (wherever possible) for the users.
   Figure 3 shows the possible use cases and the actors of the Decision Relationship
Model. For process improvement, business users' model business goals. The goals
serve as an input for technical users (PW experts) for identification of Decision Associated Information (DAI). Decision maker uses DAI for decision making to produce
directives (called decisions) for improvement of processes that are realized by business and technical users.

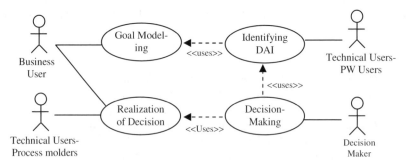

Fig. 3. Use cases of Decision Relationship Model for Process Improvement

Step 1: Define Goal Models

In the first step, a goal model is developed by business experts in such a way that it is broken down to one or more leaf goals (see Figure 4). As stated earlier, a leaf goal is a desired state on any of the four process element of business process: resource, actor, activity and flow. A goal can be broken down into several sub-goals and each sub-goal can further be broken down into sub-goals of its own. The process continues until the leaf goals are reached. Figure 4 shows the meta-model for the goal model in which self-loop on sub-goal can be used to build a hierarchy of goals. The goals at the same level can have AND, OR or XOR operator between them. The goal model is used to: a) identify the targeted elements of the process model for process improvement, and b) identify a desired state of the element.

Fig. 4. Metamodel for Modeling Goals

There are some goal modeling languages (like i*, KAOS) however they are not used in order to a) keep the solution generic i.e. independent of any goal modeling language, b) keep the focus on DRM, without going deep into any specific language.

Step 2: Identifying Decision Associated Information

Inputs to this step are leaf-goals (*condition* on *process element*), whereas the output is decision associated information (DAI). Typically, this step is performed by technical experts (PW experts).

A process warehouse is a non-volatile database with a large amount of data; however, not all the information required for decision making. Therefore, PW experts are supposed to provide only the information that is related to a decision-making. By using the guidelines (presented in this section) together with the keywords, presented in decision associated information, PW experts can provide the information sufficient for the decision making.

> **Guideline 1.** If goal is a *condition* of *actor,* the decision-associated-information is organizational, functional information.

Justification. If the leaf goal regards the actor, then the organizational information should be consulted for the decision(s) that fulfills the goal. However, the actors are related to the activities for which they are responsible, and therefore some decisions may need for consultation of the functional information. For example, if goal is to optimally utilize doctors' working hour, it may only require information on doctor, their working hours, and the activities on which they are involved. However, the decision maker may go deeper to analyze which activities are performed by doctors in order to reschedule doctors' involvement in valuable activities only.

Based on the guidelines it is suggested that PW expert should primarily provide actors' information and secondarily functional information about the process on which the goal is defined, to decision makers.

Guideline 2. If goal is a *condition* of *resource*, the decision-associated-information is resource, functional information

Justification. If the goal is on resource the resource-related information should be consulted for the decision(s) that fulfills the goal. However, the resources are produced, consumed or transferred as a result of activities therefore some decisions may need functional information. For example, if goal is to consume a resource it may only require information on the total resources, consumed resources and available resources. However, the decision maker may go deeper to analyze the affect of presence and absence of each resource on activities and time slots of activities in which the resources are consumed.

Based on the guidelines it is suggested that, PW expert should primarily provide resource related information and secondarily functional information about the process on which the goal is defined, to decision makers.

Guideline 3. If goal is a *condition* of *activities*, the decision-associated-information is organizational, functional, resource related, control information.

Justification. If the goal is on activities functional information should be consulted for the decision(s) that fulfills the goal. However, actives play a central role in the process and changes in activities may affect the resource involved in the activities, the actors who perform the activities and the ordering of the activities. Therefore organizational, functional, resource-related and control information should be consulted for decision making. For example, if goal is to perform activities at some specific order and at specific time the decision maker should consult the information on the activities. However, before deciding a specific time for an activity the availability of related resources and related participants should also be consulted.

Based on the guidelines it is suggested that, PW expert should primarily provide functional information and secondarily control, participant and resource-related information about the process on which the goal is defined.

Guideline 4. If goal is a *condition* of *flow*, the decision-associated-information is control, function perspective.

Justification. If the goal is on flow control information should be consulted for the decision(s) that fulfills the goal. However, the flow is between activities therefore some decisions may need functional information.

Based on the guidelines it is suggested that, PW expert should primarily provide information related to control and secondarily functional information about the process on which the goal is defined, to decision makers.

Step 3: Decision Elicitation

Inputs to this phase are goals and their Decision-Associated-Information whereas the output is a directive of course of action. It is a manual activity that is performed by domain experts (also called decision makers).

Domain experts have sufficient knowledge in their area and they are aware of the critical information that should be consulted for decision making. However, the decision makers may or may not have substantial knowledge to interact with process warehouse. Therefore, they rely on process warehouse experts (PW experts) for

Decision-Associated Information. On the other hand, PW users may have substantial knowledge of process warehousing but they may not be aware of the critical issue of the domain therefore they may not know the information that must be consulted.

Decision elicitation is a three phase process, including: *identification*, *evaluation* and *selection* of an alternative. In the *Identification* phase the possible alternatives of the decision are identified by the decision maker. In the *Evaluation* phase the possible alternatives are evaluated by using the DAI. Finally, in the *Selection*, the best suitable decision is selected based on the evaluation of alternatives.

Step 4: Realization of Decision

Input to this phase is a directive (decision) selected by the decision-maker which is of the form (*directive* on *element*). As a result of this phase the action is completed and goal is fulfilled.

In this step, the directives can be realized at two levels, business level and process level. At *business level*, the directives are realized from organizational aspects for example hiring new doctors, assigning new duties to doctors etc. Business users contribute to realization of directives for fulfillment of goals. At *process level* the directives are realized from process modeling perspective for example, changes to duties (activities) of doctor (actor), if new duties (activities) are assigned to doctors (actor). Technical users (process modeling experts) contribute to realization of directives for fulfillment of goals.

7   Application of DRM for Process Improvement: A Case Study

In this section we exemplify the use of our Decision Relationship Model with the help of a four-step method (presented in Section 6). For that, we use the eye-care referral process (presented in Section 4 of the paper) to in a step-wised manner describe the use of the Decision-Relationship-Model.

To apply the method, first business experts need to create a goal model for the Eye-Care Referral process. From leaf goals, decision associated information is collected further used for decision-making to select a directive, whose realization fulfills the top-goal. The method can be summarized as:

o   By using goal modeling we identify the targeted element of the process model and its desired states.
o   With the help of the guidelines presented in step 2 in the preceding section, DAI is collected.
o   Alternative directives are identified (manually), and evaluated with the help of DAI for selection of a decision.
o   The directives are realized by business and technical experts (i.e process modeling experts).

Below we explore the method steps in details:

Step 1: Define Goal Model

In this step the goals are modeled (by business users) and broken down to leaf goals. Figure 5 shows a segment of a goal model for the eye-care referral process. Consider that the top goal is to provide *'fast eye-care service'* to patients. As described in Step 1 (in Section 6), the goal is broken down to obtain leaf goals. The sub-goals becomes *'waiting time should be short'* and *'doctors will be skilled'*. These are further divided to leaf goals that are shown below, in figure 5.

In addition to the goal modeling, in this step, target element of process model (for optimization) and desired state of the element is identified. In semi-structured form it can be written as (condition on process element). For the goal model,

> Leaf goal = *'doctors availability will be used optimally'*
> Target element = *'Doctor'* (actor)
> Desired state = *'Optimal use'*
> Semi-structured goal formulation becomes (*Optimal use of doctors*)

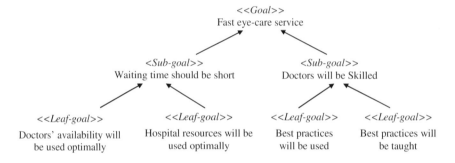

Fig. 5. Goal Model for the eye care referral process

Step 2: Identifying Decision Associated Information

Once the target element and a desired state are defined by business experts, the next step is to identify decision-associated information. However, technical experts may not be able to easily identify the information that must be consulted in decision making. To overcome this problem, we presented the keywords for each process perspective as outlined in Section 5 and the guidelines for choosing the perspective (information) described in Section 6.

According to Guideline 1, if a goal is condition on actor the DAI is organizational and functional information which can be acquired with the help of keywords given in functional and organizational perspective (in section 5). Therefore, for the goal (*Optimal use of doctors*) the keywords lead to:

o   *Organizational Information,* The information that is related to doctors, doctor's workload, tasks performed by doctors, completed tasks by the doctors, failed tasks, pending tasks and temporal information on doctors.

    o   *Functional Information,* The information that is related to activities, output, deadlock, frequency, cycle-time, tasks failed due to resource unavailability and activities failed due to doctors un- availability and temporal information on tasks related to the doctors (expected and real start-time, end-time of tasks).

Step 3: Decision Elicitation

Once the target element and a desired state are defined by the business expert, the next step is a manual identification of the decision alternatives. This step takes place by domain experts having sufficient and in-depth knowledge of the domain. The identified alternatives are evaluated by using decision-associated-information and an alternative is selected.

    In the eye-care referral process, the possible directives can be identified in the form of the means that could fulfill a leaf-goal. For (*optimal use of doctors*) the identified alternatives are:

> a) Reschedule doctors availability timings (office timings),
> b) Spare doctors from irrelevant activities,
> c) Involve doctors in diagnosis activities only,
> c) Allocation of time slots to patients in doctor's availability timings.

In order to evaluate the suitability of every alternative DAI should be consulted. The information required for evaluation has already been acquired by step 2. For example, the possibility of rescheduling doctors' availability timings, the temporal aspects of organizational information should be consulted i.e. arrival time of doctors, department time of doctors etc.

    From the functional and the organizational information it can be elicited what are the activities in which doctors are participating, how many of them are succeeding, on average how much time each activity takes etc. For example, if doctors' are involved in checking of blood-pressure before examination and because of that doctor attends the patient for an extended period of time. In this case, the decision could be to save the time of doctors by handing over the blood-pressure checking activity to nurses. Similarly, based on the information provided by process warehouse, the alternatives can be evaluated and suitable decision(s) can be made. The decision (i.e. a directive on a process element) for the eye-care referral process can be formulated as:

> *(doctor should not check blood pressure) AND/OR*
> *(nurse should check blood pressure)*

Step 4: Realization of Decision

Once a directive is defined, the final step is the realization of decision. As described in step 4 in Section 6, the realization of directive can be at two levels, business level and process level.

    For the directives *doctor should not check blood pressure AND/OR nurse should check blood pressure* the realization should be at two levels. At the *business level*, the nurses would be asked to check the blood pressure whereas the doctors will be stopped from doing it. At the *process level*, the process model will be re-designed in such a way that the blood pressure activity will be disassociated from the doctor (actor) and associated with a new actor (nurse). In this way, the goal *'doctor's avail-ability will be used optimally'* can be fulfilled.

8 Conclusion

Process models are highly important for designing and structuring the activities of an enterprise. Therefore, it is important to constantly improve those models in such a way to align them with long term enterprise goals, and thereby justify the process evolution from a strategic perspective.

In this paper, we have proposed a model-based approach for analyzing enterprise processes, using the information from a process warehouse to facilitate correct decisions for process improvements. In our approach, we have considered a process consisting of four design perspectives: organizational, functional, informational and behavioral. Furthermore, the proposed model has involved several components: goals, a process warehouse, information retrieved from the warehouse, and directives. Firstly, in a hierarchy-based goal model, the top-level goals are defined upon desired high-level improvements and decomposed to the leaf goals describing the necessary conditions on one of the four process perspectives (such as actors, activities, resources, etc). The use of leaf-goals is twofold. Firstly, they are used for eliciting a number of means that are considered as the candidates for realizing top-level goals. Secondly, the leaf goals are used as a basis for acquiring data from the process warehouse, which is also structured using the mentioned process perspectives; this enables retrieving of only the relevant information from the bulky warehouse, and in addition, in a semi-automated way. Finally, the business expert uses the obtained information to choose among the means-alternatives to make an appropriate directives about the process improvement. We have illustrated the use of our approach on a eye-care process from the Swedish health.

Regarding directions of a future work, we see the augmentation of the automation of the proposed approach, in particular guidelines, as the major issue. Another interesting topic involves the exploration of possibilities for mapping created directives into process-related parts and elements.

References

[1] Paulraj, P.: Data Warehousing Fundamentals: A Comprehensive Guide for IT Professionals. John & Wiley Sons, Chichester (2001)

[2] Casati, F., Shan, M.C.: Semantic analysis of business process executions. In: Jensen, C.S., Jeffery, K., Pokorný, J., Šaltenis, S., Bertino, E., Böhm, K., Jarke, M. (eds.) EDBT 2002. LNCS, vol. 2287, p. 287. Springer, Heidelberg (2002)

[3] Inmon, W.H.: Building the Data Warehouse, 4th edn. John & Wiley Sons, Chichester (2005)

[4] Casati, F., Castellanos, M., Dayal, U., Salazar, N.: A Generic Solution for Warehousing Business Process Data. In: Proceedings of the VLDB 2007, Vienna, Austria (2007)

[5] Castellanos, M., Casati, F., Shan, M.C.: A Comprehensive and Automated Approach to Intelligent Business Processes Execution Analysis. Distributed and Parallel Databases 16(3), 239–273 (2004)

[6] Biazzo, S.: Approaches to Business Process Analysis: A Review. Business Process Management Journal 6(2), 99–112 (2000)

[7] Jin, L., Casati, F., Moorsel, A.: Design of A Business Process Analyzer. Technical Report Software Technology Laboratory, HPL-2002-145, HP Laboratories Palo Alto, USA (2002)

[8] List, B., Schiefer, J., Tjoa, A.M., Quirchmayr, G.: Multidimensional Business Process Analysis with the Process Warehouse. In: Selected Aspects of Knowledge Discovery for Business Information Systems. Kluwer Academic Publishers, Boston (2000)

[9] Kueng, P., Wettstein, T., List, B.: A Holistic Process Performance Anlaysis thourhg a Performance Data Warehouse. In: Proceedings of the American Cofnerence on Information Systems (AMCIS 2001), Boston, USA, pp. 69–76 (2001)

[10] Weijters, A., Alast, W.M.P.: Process mining: A Research Agenda. Computers in Industry 53(3), 231–244 (2004)

[11] Dubouloz, B., Toklu, C.: Discovering the Most Frequent Patterns of Executions in Business Processes Described in BPEL. In: Ngu, A.H.H., Kitsuregawa, M., Neuhold, E.J., Chung, J.-Y., Sheng, Q.Z. (eds.) WISE 2005. LNCS, vol. 3806, pp. 701–710. Springer, Heidelberg (2005)

[12] Aalst, W.M.P.: Business Alignment: Using Process Mining as a Tool for Delta Analysis and Conformance Testing. In: Proceedings of the 5th Workshop on Business Process Modeling, Development and support (BPMDS 2004), in conjunction with CAiSE 2004, Riga, Latvia, vol. 2, pp. 138–145 (2004)

[13] Weijters, A.J.M.M., Aalst, W.M.P.: Rediscovering Workflow Models from Event-Based Data using Little Thumb. Integrated Computer Aided Engineering 10(2), 151–162 (2003)

[14] `http://www.b-eye-network.com/view/1276`

[15] Casati, F., Dayal, U., Sayal, M., Shan, M.C.: Business Process Intelligence. Technical report, HPL-2002-119, HP Laboratory Palo Alto, USA (2002)

[16] Bae, J., Liu, L., Rouse, W.B.: Process Mining, Discovery, and Integration using Distance Measures. In: Proceedings of the IEEE International Conference on Web Services, Chicago, USA, pp. 479–488 (2006)

[17] Sayal, M., Casati, F., Dayal, U., Shan, M.C.: Business Process Cockpit. In: Proceedings of the 28th International Conference on VLDB, Hong Kong, China (2002)

[18] Eder, J., Olivotto, G.E., Gruber, W.: A data warehouse for workflow logs. In: Han, Y., Tai, S., Wikarski, D. (eds.) EDCIS 2002. LNCS, vol. 2480, pp. 1–15. Springer, Heidelberg (2002)

[19] Mansmann, S., Neumuth, T., Scholl, M.H.: Multidimensional data modeling for business process analysis. In: Parent, C., Schewe, K.-D., Storey, V.C., Thalheim, B. (eds.) ER 2007. LNCS, vol. 4801, pp. 23–38. Springer, Heidelberg (2007)

[20] Schiefer, J., List, B., Bruckner, R.M.: Process data store: A real-time data store for monitoring business processes. In: Mařík, V., Štěpánková, O., Retschitzegger, W. (eds.) DEXA 2003. LNCS, vol. 2736, pp. 760–770. Springer, Heidelberg (2003)

[21] List, B., Bruckner, R.M., Machaczek, K., Schiefer, J.: A Comparison of Data Warehouse Development Methodologies Case Study of the Process Warehouse. In: Hameurlain, A., Cicchetti, R., Traunmüller, R. (eds.) DEXA 2002. LNCS, vol. 2453, pp. 203–215. Springer, Heidelberg (2002)

[22] Shahzad, K., Johannesson, P.: An Evaluation of Process Warehousing Approaches for Business Process Analysis. In: Proceedings of the 5th EOMAS in CAiSE 2009, Amsterdam, Netherland. CEUR-WS proceedings, vol. 458, pp. 1–14 (2009)

[23] Neumuth, T., Mansmann, S., Scholl, M.H., Burgert, O.: Data warehouse technology for surgical workflow analysis. In: 21st IEEE International Symposium on Computer-based Medical Systems, pp. 230–235 (2008)

[24] Brandt, S.C., Schluter, M., Jarke, M.: A Process Data Warehouse for Tracing and Reuse of Engineering Design Processes. International Journal of Intelligent Information Technologies 2(4), 18–36 (2006)

[25] Prakash, N., Singh, Y., Gosain, A.: Informational Scenarios for Data Warehouse Requirements Elicitation. In: Atzeni, P., Chu, W., Lu, H., Zhou, S., Ling, T.-W. (eds.) ER 2004. LNCS, vol. 3288, pp. 205–216. Springer, Heidelberg (2004)

[26] Giorgini, P., Rizzi, S., Garzetti, M.: Goal-oriented requirement analysis for data warehouse design. In: Proceedings of 8th ACM International Workshop on Data warehousing and OLAP (DOLAP 2005), pp. 47–56 (2005)

[27] Business Process Definition,
`http://www.cecausa.com/business_process_glossary.htm`

[28] Johannesson, P., Andersson, B., Bergholtx, M., Weigand, H.: Enterprise Modelling for Value Based Service Analysis. In: Proceedings of the 1st IFIP WG 8.1 Working Conference on The Practice of Enterprise Modeling, Stockholm, Sweden. LNBIP, vol. 15, pp. 153–167. Springer, Heidelberg (2008)

[29] Curtis, B., Kellner, M.I., Over, J.: Process Modeling. Communications of ACM 35(9), 75–90 (1992)

[30] BPMN Specification Release, Object Management Group (OMG),
`http://www.omg.org/spec/BPMN/1.2/` (last accessed on June 30, 2009)

From i* Requirements Models to Conceptual Models of a Model Driven Development Process

Fernanda Alencar[1,2], Beatriz Marín[1], Giovanni Giachetti[1], Oscar Pastor[1], Jaelson Castro[2], and João Henrique Pimentel[2]

[1] Universidad Politécnica de Valencia, Camino de Vera s/n, CP:46022, Valencia, Spain
{fribeiro,bmarin,ggiachetti,opastor}@dsic.upv.es
[2] Universidade Federal de Pernambuco, Av. Prof. Luiz Freire s/n, 50740-540, Recife, Brazil
fmra@ufpe.br, {jbc,jhcp}@cin.ufpe.br

Abstract. A good understanding of the systems requirements has a high impact in the successful development of software products. Therefore, an appropriate requirements model must provide a comprehensive structure for what must be elicited, evaluated, specified, consolidated, and modified, instead of just providing facilities for software specifications. Since there is a well-known gap between requirements specifications and final software products, we propose the integration of Goal-Oriented Requirements Engineering (GORE) and Model-Driven Development (MDD) to solve this gap. The core of our proposal is comprised by a set of guidelines to automate the process of going from an initial i* model to a final software product by means of a precise model transformation process. Finally, we use a case study that is based on a photographic agency system in order to illustrate our approach.

Keywords: Goal-Oriented Requirements Engineering, i*, Requirements Integration, Object Oriented Method, Model-Driven Development.

1 Introduction

The success of computer applications increasingly depends on a good understanding of the system requirements. Currently, a requirements specification should include, in addition to software specifications, business models, domain models and other kinds of information that describe the context in which the intended system will operate. During early stages of requirements engineering, it is necessary to identify and specify how the intended system meets the organizational goals, why the system is needed, what alternatives were considered, what the implications of the alternatives are for the stakeholders, and how the stakeholders' interests and concerns might be addressed.

Hence, Goal-Oriented Requirements Engineering (GORE) stood out because it is mainly concerned with the stakeholders intentions and their rationales. Several works on GORE have being proposed: KAOS [6], i* framework [18], MAPS [15], Non-Functional Requirements (NFR) framework [5]. In all of them, requirements modeling appears to be a core process. However, how to go from requirements models to

A. Persson and J. Stirna (Eds.): PoEM 2009, LNBIP 39, pp. 99–114, 2009.
© IFIP International Federation for Information Processing 2009

the corresponding software product is still an open question. To answer this question, we advocate the use of GORE with Model-Driven Development (MDD) [17], two complementary model-based approaches.

Thus, we need a requirements model with such a structure that facilitates the specification of model transformations for the automatic generation of conceptual models used in MDD approaches. In this context, since present-day technologies (such as ATL or QVT) propose the specification of model transformations driven by metamodels, the use of GORE approaches is a suitable alternative, given that they have an abstract syntax formalized by a metamodel specification [3][11]. Among these GORE approaches, we selected the *i framework [18] because it is a consolidated modeling technique [8] with good tools support [10].

In this paper we propose guidelines to generate, from an i* requirements model, a conceptual model that is used as input of a MDD process for software products generation. This MDD process is based on the OO-Method approach [14]. We have chosen OO-Method as a reference MDD technology because it allows the complete generation of the final application from a conceptual model, and it has been successfully applied to industrial software development by means of the OlivaNova tools [4].

Therefore, this work proposes the generation of an OO-Method conceptual model from an i* requirements model based on a set of transformation guidelines, aiming to improve the quality of the models used on the development of information systems, and consequently to obtain better software products. To illustrate these guidelines, we have selected a real problem that was solved in the context of the PROS Research Center [12]: a Photography Agency. The main contribution of our work is to present an approach that provides a solution for filling the gap between GORE proposals and MDD proposals. The approach presented in this paper is part of a wider effort, which investigates the use of MDD techniques to define a full software process that covers the long path that goes from requirements modeling to the corresponding final software product.

This paper is organized as follows: Section 2 briefly describes the background considered in our proposal. Section 3 outlines the transformation process and a set of guidelines to perform it. Section 4 describes some relevant related works. Finally, Section 5 summarizes our work and points out open issues.

2 Background

This section starts with the presentation of an illustrative case study used as example across the paper to clarify the involved concepts. Later, the main features of the participant technologies (i* and OO-Method) are presented.

2.1 The Case Study

The photography agency is dedicated to the management of photo reports and their distribution to publishing houses. This agency operates with freelance photographers, which must present a request to the production department of the photography agency. This request contains: the photographer personal information, a description about the owned equipment, a brief curriculum, and a book with the performed photographic reports. An accepted photographer is classified in one of three possible levels for which minimum photography equipment is required. For this, the technical department creates a new record for the photographer, and saves it in the photographer's file. For each photo report presented by a photographer a new record with a sequential code is created. This record has the price that the publishing houses must pay to the agency, which is established according to the number of photos and level of the photographer. Furthermore, this record has a descriptive annotation about the content of the report. The commercial department establishes according to the level of photographers, the price that will be paid to the photographers and the price that will be charged to the publishing house for each photo.

2.2   The i* Goal-Oriented Requirements Framework Overview

The goal-oriented modeling has proved to be an efficient means of capturing the 'Whys' and establishing a close relationship with the 'Whats' [10][16]. GORE is concerned with the use of goals for eliciting, elaborating, structuring, specifying, analyzing, negotiating, documenting, and modifying requirements.

The i* framework [18] captures the intentional requirements using strategic relationships among actors. The term actor is used to generically refer to any unit for which intentional dependencies can be ascribed. Actors are intentional, in a sense that they do not simply carry out activities and produce entities, but also they have desires and needs. Actors are also strategic, since they are not merely focused on meet their immediate goals, but also they are concerned about longer-term implications of their structural relationships with other actors, for instance, opportunities and vulnerabilities.

The i* framework offers two congruous models: the *Strategic Dependency* (SD) model and *Strategic Rationale* (SR) model. The SD model is focused on external relationships among actors. It includes a set of nodes and connecting links, where nodes represent actors (*depender* and *dependee*) and each link indicates a dependency (*dependum*) between two actors. In the SD model, the internal goals, knowhow, and resources of an actor are not explicitly modeled. In this model, we distinguish among four types of dependency links, based on the type of *dependum*: *goal*, *resource*, *task*, and *softgoal* dependencies. A *goal* in the i* context is a condition or state of concerns that the actor would like to obtain. A *resource* is a physical or informational entity that must be available for an actor. A *task* specifies a particular way of doing something, which can be decomposed in small sub-tasks. Finally, a *softgoal* is a condition that the actor would like to achieve, but some criteria are not well-defined. In general, the *softgoal* is associated to non-functional requirements.

The SR model (such as the example i* model presented in Fig. 1) expands the description of a given actor and all rationales involved on its intentions, providing support for modeling the reasoning of each actor about its intentional relationships. In addition to the dependencies present in the SD model, three new type of relationships are incorporated in the SR model: (i) *task-decomposition links*, which describe what should be done to perform a certain task (e.g. *To process a work request* task); (ii) *means-end links*, which suggest that a task (e.g. *To process a work request* task) is a means to achieve a goal (*A photographer´s work request be processed* goal); (iii) *contributions links*, which suggest how a model element can contribute to satisfy a *softgoal*. In particular, in our example, we do not have this last link. With the SR model (Fig. 1), we capture some of the rationales involved in a photographer´s work request approval. For instance, a photographer must present a work request to the Production Department in order to have a work opportunity. In Fig. 1, this is represented by the resource dependency link between the *Photographer* actor and the *Production Dep* actor. To achieve this goal, the photographer must compose a work request that contains: a description of his/her equipment, a brief curriculum, and a book with his/her photographic reports. Finally, this request is processed by the *Production Dep.* actor.

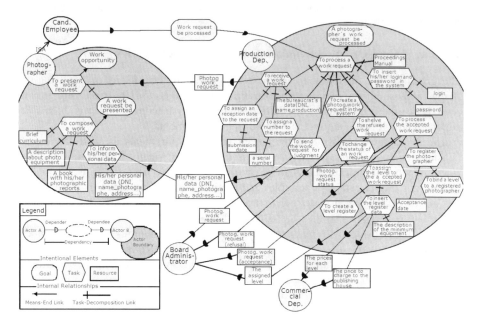

Fig. 1. The SR model of the Photographer work request

Despite an empirical evaluation has indicated that there are some problems with the i* framework [7], this framework is considered to be efficient enough to deal with complex actors, their organizational environment, and all rationales involved in their relationships. It allows the clear and simple statement of actors, their goals and the dependencies among them. Therefore, with the i* intentional views, we can obtain a rich model. However, the problem still remains: from the requirements model, how can we obtain the corresponding software product? For this, we propose the use of models transformations to integrate i* and Model-Driven Development approaches.

2.3   The OO-Method Model-Driven Development Approach Overview

Models help to understand a complex problem and its potential solutions through abstraction [17]. Thus, MDD methods have been created to take advantage of models in development processes, by using concepts that are much less bound to the underlying

Fig. 2. The OO-Method Software Production Process with i*

implementation technology and are much closer to the problem domain. This makes it easier to specify, understand, and maintain software systems. Besides, with MDD methods it is possible to achieve the automatic generation of the final products by means of models transformations. Among different MDD approaches, we have selected the OO-Method approach as the reference MDD approach for our proposal.

The OO-Method MDD approach separates the application and business logic from the platform technology, allowing the automatic code generation from the conceptual representation of the software systems [14]. The OO-Method production process (Fig.2) is comprised of four models: the *Requirements Model*, the *Conceptual Model*, the *Execution Model*, and the *Implementation Model*.

In our proposal, we consider to use the i* framework as the OO-Method Requirement Model in order to capture the organizational context and the actors intentions. Next, from the defined i* model, an initial OO-Method Conceptual Model is inferred, which is used for the generation of the final software product. At this point, it is important to mention that the main modeling constructs provided by OO-Method Conceptual Model are the same as UML provides [17]. This situation also occurs in several object-oriented MDD approaches. Therefore, the results presented in this paper can be generalized to other MDD approaches based on the use of UML-like models.

The OO-Method Conceptual Model captures the static and dynamic properties of the functional requirements of the system in a *Class Model*, a *Dynamic Model*, and a *Functional Model*. The conceptual model also allows the specification of the user interfaces in an abstract way through the *Presentation Model*. These four models represent the different views of the whole conceptual model that has all the details needed for the generation of the corresponding software application. The complete definition of the elements of the OO-Method Conceptual Model is described in detail in [14]. From the models that comprise the OO-Method conceptual model, the class model is the most important, and the other models are defined (or derived) from this central model. Fig. 3 shows the original class model of the case study presented in section 2.1. In this model, the classes with their respective attributes and relationships, including all the necessary details, are introduced.

In the OO-Method Conceptual Model, certain classes can access properties and invoke services provided by other classes (or by the same class). The permissions that a class has over other classes are defined by *agent relationships* (see dashed lines in Fig. 3). In OO-Method, the associations are binary, i.e., they only have one or two participant classes (one class in the case of recursive associations).

With the OO-Method Execution Model, it is possible to perform the transition from the problem space (represented by the conceptual model) to the solution space (the corresponding software product).

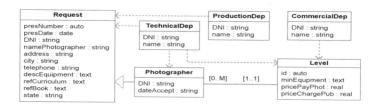

Fig. 3. The conceptual class model of the Photographic Agency System

Finally, the Implementation Model fixes the mappings between the conceptual constructs and their corresponding software representations in a target implementation platform, for instance C# or Java. The OO-Method approach has been successfully applied to the software industry with a MDD tool created by the enterprise CARE-Technologies [4]: *OlivaNova The Programming Machine*.

3   From i* Requirements Models to Conceptual Models

We propose a transformation process to make it possible the transformation of the i* models into a preliminary conceptual model for the OO-Method approach, presented in Fig. 4 with the Business Process Modeling Notation (BPMN). For lack of space, we only use the i* SR model.

Initially, we analyze the goals defined in the SR model (see Fig.1) to capture the organizational processes that we want to automate. Then, we highlight the intentional elements that are related to these processes (goals and tasks in the i* model). Those elements will be related with the information and/or entities to be stored by the intended system. From the list of identified intentional elements we obtain an initial conceptual model through model transformation rules, based on nine guidelines.

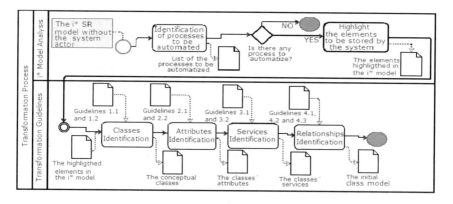

Fig. 4. The transformation process modeled with BPMN

3.1   The i* Model´s Analysis

According to the transformation process (Fig. 4), this phase is comprised by the following activities: (i) identification of processes to be automated in the intended information system from the i* SR model; and (ii) highlighting of the essential issues that must be stored at the intended system.

Identification of the process to be automated. In this activity, we deal with the goals in the i* SR model. We seek for processes (tasks in a means-end link) that operationalize the intended goal, making it reachable. Therefore, in our case study, we recognize the following goals: *Work opportunity* for the *Photographer* actor; and, *A photographer´s work request be processed* by the *Production Dep.* actor. There are processes as means to reach those ends, respectively: *To present a work request*; and *To process a work request*. From these, we decided to automate the last process,

Highlighting the essential elements. For each process to be automated, we analyze the respective task-decomposition tree inside the actor boundary(e.g. the task – *To process a work request*). Through this analysis we highlight all essential elements that must be stored in the intended system, at the considered process (see Fig. 5). These selected elements are all those related with the process to be automated. Then, the selected elements from the i* model will be translated to elements of the Class Model using the transformation guidelines presented below.

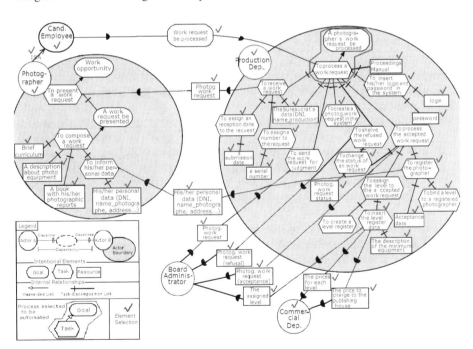

Fig. 5. The highlighted SR model of the Photographer work request

3.2 The Transformation Guidelines

In this phase, the guidelines to construct the OO-Method Conceptual Model from the i* model are presented. These guidelines are grouped in four activities: (i) the class identification; (ii) the attributes identification; (iii) the services identification; and (iv) the relationships identification. We have selected the class model as target because it is the core model of the OO-Method Conceptual Model.

Identification of classes. This activity deals with the identification of the main classes that should be in the class model. Indeed, in this step we are looking for the actors and the resource elements at the i* models. We do this because, by definition [18], an actor is an active entity that carries out actions to achieve goals by using its capabilities, while a resource is an entity (physical or informational), a finished product of some deliberation-action process. Therefore, both are related with the class concept.

Guideline 1.1: Related to actors of the i* model
We have two options to make the transformation from the i* actors to the class model.

(i)   Looking for the *actors* whose data must be captured and maintained at the intended system. In this case, the actor is transformed into a *class* in the class model. For instance, in Fig. 5 we found *Cand. Employee* (Candidate Employee), *Photographer, Production Dep.* and *Commercial Dep.* actors, which are transformed in classes (see Fig. 6).
(ii) Actors that do not satisfy the previous statements are not transformed into elements of the class model. For instance, there is no need to save any information of the *Board Administrator* actor (see Fig. 5).

Guideline 1.2: Related to resources of the i* model
In relation to the resources elements, and considering the dependencies between actors, we propose the following transformation:
(i)   Resources representing a physical entity that must be maintained in the system. In this case, the resource is transformed into a class. For instance, in our case study we have the following resources: *Photog. work request, Photog. work request (refusal), Photog. work request (Acceptance), Proceedings Manual* and *Assigned level*. These elements are transformed in the classes *WorkReqPhoto, ReqRefused, ReqAccepted, ProcManual* and *Level*, respectively (see Fig. 6).

The identification of attributes of classes. For each class obtained by the transformation of an i* actor or resource, their attributes must be identified. To do this, the main branch related to the process to be automated is analyzed. Usually, this branch corresponds to the means task that satisfies the intended goal (means-end link at i* models). Therefore, the resources that represent an informational entity will be our main target because they represent the attributes of the related class. These resources are transformed into attributes of the previously generated classes. To do this, we analyze the actor boundary. For instance, in the case study (see Fig. 5) we select the class *ProductionDep* using the Guideline 1.1 (item i) and the class *WorkReqPhoto* (Guideline 1.2). To ask for a job (means task for the goal *Work opportunity*) the photographer must compose the corresponding work request. Thus, in order to define the attributes of a class obtained by a resource mapping, we must also look for the task related with this resource.

Guideline 2.1: Related to classes generated from actors of the i* model
The following elements must be analyzed to obtain the attributes of the classes generated from actors of the i* model:

(i)   A resource (informational entity) inside of the transformed actor. If this resource expresses information about the actor, then it is transformed into an attribute of the class. For instance, in Fig. 5, the actor *Photographer* (transformed into the class *Photographer*) must inform his/her personal data. Therefore, the resource *personal data* will be transformed into attributes of the class *Photographer*. Finally, the details of *personal data* are the attributes of the target class: *DNI*, *name photographer*, *address*, *city*, *telephone*, and *brief curriculum*.

(ii) A resource outside the transformed actor (a resource dependency where the mapped actor is the *dependee* actor). This resource is transformed into an attribute of the mapped dependee actor. For instance, the dependency resource *personal data (DNI, name_photographer, address, etc.)* that will be available by the actor *Photographer* (the *dependee* actor in this dependency).

Guideline 2.2: Related to classes generated from resources of the i* model
For each resource that was transformed into a class, it must be considered if the resource is an internal element (it is inside of the actor boundary) or if the resource is related to a resource dependency link.

(i)   If the resource is inside of an actor boundary (see in Fig. 5), then the attributes are inferred (according to the analyst experience) from the task that produces this resource or a sub-task (of another task) that produces informational entities related to the state of the analyzed class. In our case study (Fig. 5) we have the resource *Proceedings Manual* as an example for this case.

(ii) If the resource is a *dependum* element (it is outside of the actor boundary, in a resource dependency link), then both sides of this dependency must be analyzed to capture any informational entity (attribute) about the involved resource. This will be done by analyzing the tasks inside of the graphs of the *depender* and *dependee* actors. The task that produces the resource (inside of the *dependee* actor) and the tasks that need the resource (inside of the *depender* actor). For instance, in the case study, the class *WorkReqPhoto* (Fig. 6) is related with a resource dependency between the actors *Photographer* and *Production Dep.* (see Fig. 5). From the side of the *dependee* actor (*Photographer*), the graph with the task *To present a work request* as root is analyzed. A deep search is performed to find resources (leafs of the searched graph) related with the analyzed resource. From this search, we find the resources *Brief curriculum, a description about photo equipment* and *a book with his/her photographic reports* which will be transformed into attributes of the class *WorkReqPhoto* (the dependum element at Fig. 5). From the side of the *depender* actor (*Production Dep.*), we do the same. Thus, by analyzing the task *To receive a work request*, the resources *submission date* and a *serial number* are found. These resources are also transformed into attributes of the class *WorkReqPhoto*. However, the task *To receive a work request* is a sub-task of another task. Therefore, we must rise a level in our quest, and make the deep search in other branches of the graph. By the analysis of the task *To change the status of a work request* the resource *Photog. work request status* is found. This resource is also transformed into an attribute of the class *WorkReqPhoto*.

Fig. 6 shows all the attributes obtained after applying these transformation guidelines on all the classes that were derived from resources of the i* model (Fig. 5).

The identification of services of classes. At this point, the tasks of the i* SR model and their possible decompositions are inspected (deep search). In the i* framework, a task specify a particular way of doing something. When a task is described as a sub-component of a (higher) task, in a hierarchy of tasks, this restricts the higher task to that particular course of action (a task-decomposition link at the SR model). Moreover, from the practical experience, a task in the i* model generally is responsible for a goal's satisfaction and/or for the resource's production. We must remember that a service describes a specific behavior of the objects of a class, and, in the OO-Method approach, a service can be atomic (*Event*) or a composition of other services (*Transaction*). The events related to creation, deletion, and modification of class instances are always created by default in the Olivanova tool. Thus, to identify the other services of a class, we propose the following guidelines:

Guideline 3.1: Identification of services of a class generated from an actor
The internal sub-graphs must be analyzed, which generally are a routine responsible for the satisfaction of a goal of the corresponding actor. From these sub-graphs, only must be considered the tasks that must be stored at the intended information system.

(i)   If the task represents a change in the state of an object that occurs instantly, then this task is transformed into an event of the generated class. In Fig. 5, we do not find this situation because atomic services are not represented according to the considered abstraction level in the i* model.

(ii) If the task represents a service that groups other services, then this task is transformed into a transaction of the generated class.

Guideline 3.2: Identification of services of a class generated from a resource
In this case, we are looking for tasks that are used or produced by the transformed resource, and identifying if the resource is inside or outside an actor.

(i)   If the task represents an instantaneous change in the state of an object, then this task is transformed into an event of the generated class. For instance, for the resource *Photog. work request*, inside of the *depender* actor (see *Production Dep.* in Fig. 5), there is a task called *To create a work request in the system*. This task is transformed into an event of the class *WorkReqPhoto*. In addition, the generated event allows the generation of new instances of the class. On the other side, at the *dependee* actor (*Photographer*), the task *To present a work request* is also transformed into an event of the class *WorkReqPhoto*.

(ii) If the task represents a service that groups other services, then this task is transformed into a transaction of the generated class. For instance, in the Photographic Agency example (see Fig. 1), an accepted work request must be processed according to the task *To process the accepted work request*. This task is decomposed on three sub-tasks: *To register the photographer*, *To assign the level to the accepted work request*, and *To change the status of a work request*. Therefore, a new transaction must be created in the class *WorkReqPhoto* to represent the execution of these three tasks.

These two guidelines must be applied to all classes generated from the i* model.

The identification of relationships between classes. In this point, the three basics relationships of object-oriented approaches are considered: generalization / specialization, association, and aggregation. However, it is important to remark that i* mainly focuses on representing strategic concerns by means of intentional elements and their relationships. Therefore, the information of each relationship of the i* model must be analyzed to derivate the kind of relationships among the generated classes.

Guideline 4.1: Identification of Generalization/Specialization relationships among generated classes

We must considerer two possibilities:

(i) If the class is derived from an actor and there is an inheritance relationship between actors of the i* model (the *is-a* relationship), then this relationship is automatically transformed into a generalization in the class model. For instance (see Fig.5), we found the *is-a* relationship between the actors *Candidate Employee* and *Photographer*. This relationship is represented as a generalization between the corresponding generated classes of the class model (Fig. 6).

(ii) If the class is derived from a resource and the inheritance relationship is not explicit at the i* models, then we must analyze the processes (tasks) involved in the production of this resource. For instance, from the resource dependencies between the actors *Production Dep.* and *Board Administrator*, we can observe that a work request may be accepted or refused. These work requests were transformed into the classes *WorkReqPhoto, ReqRefused* and *ReqAccepted*. Since *ReqRefused* (refused photographer's work request) and *ReqAccepted* (accepted photographer's work request are a *WorkReqPhoto*, then we generate an inheritance relationship between these classes (see Fig. 6).

Guideline 4.2: Identification of Association relationships among generated classes

We must considerer the following possibilities:

(i) For two classes generated from i* actors, if there is any dependency link between the two transformed actors, then an association between the corresponding classes is automatically generated in the class diagram. For instance, the actor *ProductionDep* was transformed into a *class* and it must also be associated with the service of other class. The *Photographers* present their request to the production department (class *ProductionDep*). Therefore, an association is generated between these two classes (Fig. 6).

(ii) If there exists a resource dependency link where the *dependum*, the *depender* and *dependee* actors were transformed into classes, then associations are automatically generated between these classes. However, if there is any generalization relationship between one of these classes (resulting from the actors transformations), then the association is defined with the corresponding father class. For instance, for the class *Photographer* (from the actor *Photographer*) it must be defined an association to the class *WorkReqPhot* (from the *dependum* resource *Photog work request*). However, since there is a generalization between the classes *Photographer* and *CandidateEmp*, then the involved association is defined between *CandidateEmp* and *WorkReqPhoto* (Fig. 6). The same occurs for the association defined between the classes *WorkReqPhoto* and *ProductionDept*.

(iii) For a resource dependency link where the *dependum* is transformed into a class attribute and the *depender* and *dependee* actors are transformed into classes, an association is generated among the classes generated from actors and the class that has the attribute generated from the involved resource. For instance, in the Fig. 5 there is a resource dependency link (*The prices for each level* resource) between the actors *Production Dep.* and *Commercial Dep.* The respective resource was transformed into an attribute of the class *Level*. Thus, an association is generated between the classes *CommercialDep* and *Level*, and between the classes *Level* and *ProductionDep* (Fig. 6).

(iv) For a class resulting from the transformation of an internal resource, an association is created between this resource class and the class resulting from the transformation of the respective actor boundary (the one that contains the resource). For instance in Fig. 5, inside the actor *Production Dep.* there is a resource (*Proceedings Manual*) that was transformed into a class. Therefore, an association is generated between the respective classes into the class diagram (Fig. 6).

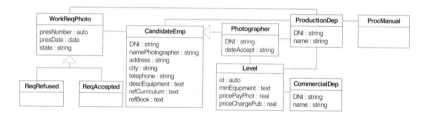

Fig. 6. The class model obtained from the application of the proposed guidelines

Guideline 4.3: Aggregation relationship between generated classes
We must considerer two possibilities:

(i) If the class is generated from an actor and there is an aggregation relationship between actors of the i* model (the *is-part-of* relationship), then this relationship is automatically transformed into an aggregation in the class model.

(ii) If the class is generated from a resource and the aggregation relationship is not explicit at the i* models, then the internal behavior of the actor that is directly associated with a resource that was transformed into a class must be analyzed.

3.3 Discussion

In this paper, we have presented nine guidelines that are used to go from i* requirement models to the class model of a MDD approach. These guidelines were systematically designed in accordance with the i* framework [10]. To illustrate the application of the guidelines, we have manually applied the guidelines to a Photography Agency case study. Even though the guidelines have been designed in the OO-Method MDD context, many conceptual constructs of the OO-Method class model are similar to the constructs of the other object-oriented methods. For this reason, the proposed guidelines can be generalized to allow the application to other MDD methods.

With respect to the automation of the guidelines, we classified the guidelines as *automatic* (it is not necessary any intervention of the analyst), *semi-automatic* (some decisions of the analyst are required), and *manual* (they application completely depends of the analyst expertise). Thus, the guidelines *1.1*, *4.1i*, *4.2*, and *4.3i* are automatic, the guidelines *1.2*, *2.1*, *2.2*, *3.1* and *3.2* are semi-automatics, and finally, the guidelines *4.1ii* and *4.3.ii* are manuals.

Analyzing the Photography Agency case study, we can state, through a comparison between the class model originally constructed for the case study (Fig. 3) and the class model generated by the application of the proposed guidelines (Fig. 6), that some elements were incorrectly represented in the original class model (Fig. 3). For example, a *photographer* was considered as a *request*, which is incorrect because these are different objects. Furthermore, the class *TechnicalDep* (Fig. 3) was merged with the class *ProductionDep* because during the specification of the i* model (Fig.1) we identify that both roles have common tasks from the organizational viewpoint, so that we decide to merge all the tasks in the actor *Production Dep.* (*ProductionDep* in the generated class model – Fig. 6). A new generalization/specialization relationship with two new classes (*ReqRefused* and *ReqAccepted* classes) was created for the class *WorkReqPhoto*. While in the original class model, there was only one attribute in the class *WorkReqPhoto* to indicate whether the proposal was rejected or accepted. With the representation obtained in the generated class model, it is possible to define specific attributes related to accepted and refused requests, which is not possible in the original class model. Hence, we may conclude that GORE approaches, as the i* framework, are very rich in terms of intentions and their rationales, which must be reflected in later development stages. Thus, taking GORE approaches as starting point of the software development process, and using MDD techniques to reach the final software product, an improved solution for software development is obtained.

It is important to note that in our proposal the quality of the GORE models directly affects the generation of correct conceptual models of the MDD approach. This quality mainly depends of the experience of the analyst in the problem domain and in the usage of the modeling technique. The abstraction level is also dependant of the viewpoints and the focus of the analyst. In this proposal, we assume that the i* models are correct, complete, and that do not present defects (omissions, inconsistency, erroneous facts, ambiguous, etc.). Therefore, applying the proposed guidelines, we can infer the basis of the conceptual model without introducing any modeling defect. We know that this assumption is unrealistic. For this reason, we are also working in proposals to evaluate the quality of the i* models in order to improve the application of our proposal in MDD environments.

Despite of the positive and important aspect of our work that concludes that it is possible to incorporate goal concepts in a MDD approach we also highlighted some other points which are being investigated: (i) the i* framework is more expressive at a high abstraction level than the OO-Method conceptual model, consequently, the guidelines only consider a subset of the i* framework; (ii) some important concepts for the OO-Method Conceptual Model are not captured by the i* models, since the abstraction levels are different into these approaches (for instance, additional relationships information such as roles or cardinality), therefore, additional information is required to correctly infer the corresponding OO-Method concepts; (iii) since certain guidelines are not automatic, the transformation cannot be fully automated; (iv) the traceability between requirements and conceptual models is not considered in the transformations; (v) the guidelines only provide a partial generation of the class model and additional formalization is required for a correct software product generation.

4 Related Works

Some strategies based on i* have been proposed with the aim of reducing the gap between requirements phase and the software development phase.

The proposal presented in [13] is a methodological approach that enables the generation of conceptual and requirements models from organizational descriptions. To do this, two strategies were considered: (1) to extend the organizational model with monitoring plans and concerned objects, and (2) to define guidelines to establishing correspondences among business requirements and the conceptual model of the system. This proposal uses the particular version of i* defined in *Tropos* [9] and defines a set of complex steps to obtain a partial conceptual model definition. By contrast, we use the i* version disposable at *i* Guide* [10] to define guidelines for the direct inference of OO-Method conceptual constructs from i* models. This provides a more straightforward way for the generation of an initial conceptual model, which facilitates the application of our proposal to MDD processes.

In previous works ([1][2][16]) we have proposed a process to derive late requirements specifications specified in *pUML* (precise Unified Modeling Language) from early requirements model represented in *i** framework. In [1], we proposed a set of guidelines to go from i* models to class diagrams in order to obtain the conceptual model of the business model, which differs from the approach presented in this paper, that generates the conceptual model of the information system. In [2] and [16] we intended to generate scenarios and use cases represented with UML from i* models. To do this, a set of guidelines that helps the requirements engineer to determine the existence of potential use cases from the business model specification were proposed. However, the use case generation is not our goal in this paper, since we intend to directly transform an i* model into a conceptual model of the OO-Method MDD approach.

5 Conclusions and Future Works

In this work we consider the combination of a specific GORE approach (i*) and a specific MDD approach (OO-Method) to go from the requirements models to the corresponding software product. Both GORE and MDD are based in the use of models, and we believe that they can complement each other. This proposal is part of a wider work that is related to the use of MDD techniques to define a full software process that covers the long path that goes from goal-oriented requirements modeling to a final high-quality software product.

In this paper, we presented a set of transformation guidelines that are applied to the industrial MDD approach OO-Method, in order to facilitate the transformation of an initial i* intentional requirement model into an automatically generated software product. In addition, since OO-Method is an object-oriented MDD approach many of the concepts analyzed can be reused by other object-oriented MDD approaches.

The automatic generation of the complete final software products is performed by means of a precise model transformation process. Therefore, as future work, we plan to apply the guidelines to other case studies in order to evaluate the correctness and completeness of our proposal. In addition, we plan to formalize the guidelines using metamodeling techniques and models transformations technologies in order to be automatically applied and to preserve the requirements traceability through the models. Finally, we also consider the definition of extensions for the i* framework in order to facilitate the capture of new features.

Acknowledgments. This work has been developed with the support of CNPq and CAPES research grants, BIT initiative, and MEC under the project SESAMO TIN2007-62894.

References

1. Alencar, F.: Mapping an Organizational Model in Precise Specification. Ph.D. Dissertation, Department of Informatics from University of Pernambuco. Recife, Brazil (1999)
2. Alencar, F., Pedroza, F., Castro, J., Amorim, R.: New Mechanism for the Integration of Organizational Requirements and Object Oriented Modeling. In: Proc. of the VI Workshop on Requirements Engineering (WER 2003), Piracicaba, Brazil, pp. 109–123 (2003)
3. Ayala, C., Cares, C., Carvallo, J.P., Grau, G., Haya, M., Salazar, G., Franch, X., Mayol, E., Quer, C.: A Comparative Analysis of i*-Based Agent-Oriented Modeling Languages. In: Proceedings of the 17th SEKE, pp. 657–663 (2006)
4. Care Technologies Company: OlivaNova Suite, http://www.care-t.com (last access: July 2009)
5. Chung, L., Nixon, B., Yu, E., Mylopoulos, J.: Non-Functional Requirements in Software Engineering. Kluwer Academic Publishers, Dordrecht (2000)
6. Dardenne, A., van Lamsweerde, A., Fickas, S.: Goal-Directed Requirements Acquisition. Science of Computer Programming 20(3) (1993)
7. Estrada, H., Rebollar, A.M., Pastor, O., Mylopoulos, J.: An Empirical Evaluation of the i* Framework in a Model-Based Software Generation Environment. In: Dubois, E., Pohl, K. (eds.) CAiSE 2006. LNCS, vol. 4001, pp. 513–527. Springer, Heidelberg (2006)
8. Grau, G., Franch, X., Ávila, S.: J-PRiM: A Java Tool for a Process Reengineering i* Methodology. In: RE 2006, pp. 352–353 (2006)
9. Giorgini, P., Mylopoulos, J., Sebastiani, R.: Goal-Oriented Requirements Analysis and Reasoning in the Tropos Methodology. Engineering Applications of Artificial Intelligence 18(2) (March 2005)
10. Abdulhadi, S.:i* Guide v.3 (August 2007), http://istar.rwth-aachen.de/tiki-view_articles.php (last access: July 2009)
11. Lucena, M., Santos, E., Silva, M.J., Silva, C., Alencar, F., Castro, J.F.B.: Towards a Unified Metamodel for i*. In: 2nd IEEE Int. Conference on Research Challenges in Information Science (RCIS 2008), Marrakech. Proceedings of the RCIS 2008, pp. 237–246 (2008)
12. Marín, B., Giagchetti, G., Pastor, O.: The Photography Agency: A case study of the OO-Method Approach. Technical Report DSIC-II/13/08, Universidad Politécnica de Valencia, Valencia, Spain (2008)

13. Martínez, A.: Conceptual Schemas Generation from Organizational Models in an Automatic Software Production Process, PhD Thesis, Universidad Politécnica de Valencia, Valencia, Spain (2008)
14. Pastor, O., Molina, J.C.: Model-Driven Architecture in Practice: A Software Production Environment Based on Conceptual Modeling, 1st edn. Springer, New York (2007)
15. Rolland, C., Prakash, N., Benjamen, A.: A multi-model view of process modeling. Requirements Engineering 4(4), 169–187 (1999)
16. Santander, V., Castro, J.: Deriving Use Cases from Organizational Modeling. In: 10th Anniversary IEEE Joint International Conference on Requirements Engineering (RE 2002), Essen, Germany, September 2002, pp. 32–42 (2002)
17. Selic, B.: The Pragmatics of Model-Driven Development. IEEE Software 20, 19–25 (2003)
18. Yu, E.: Modelling Strategic Relationships for Process Reengineering, PhD Thesis, University of Toronto, Toronto, Canada (1995)
19. BPMI.org: Business Process Modeling Notation; OMG Available Specification. Object Management Group, version 1.1 (2008), http://www.bpmn.org/ (last access September 2009)

A Combined Framework for Development of Business Process Support Systems

Shang Gao and John Krogstie

Norwegian University of Science and Technology (NTNU), Trondheim, Norway
shanggao@idi.ntnu.no, krogstie@idi.ntnu.no

Abstract. In this paper, a combined modeling framework consisting of goal modeling, process modeling and business process characterizing modeling is presented. The framework is made to guide both business experts and model developers during the life cycle of a modeling-based project development. We consider a business process characterizing model (BPCM) as a starting point for developing an IT system. Then, the start of goal models and process models can be derived from a BPCM model. Process models are then used as inputs for deriving a candidate IT system. A development methodology to guide the development of process models from business process characterizing model is proposed. Furthermore, the development methodology is illustrated by an exemplar in the field of scientific conference organization.

Keywords: Business Process Characterizing Model, Process Modeling.

1 Introduction

Information system development often starts with development of process models. However, being focused on processes from the start might be premature. The process model tends to primarily focus on process-oriented aspect, and might not address some business requirements properly. Some industry projects and case studies [19], indicates that process models are not a good starting point for identifying stakeholder requirements. Many business people want to start a modeling-based project with the development of a business oriented model addressing essential business aspects (i.e. what are the essential requirements of the project, what is offered by whom to whom etc), rather than look at a relative complicated business process model showing how things are executed operationally. Furthermore, when using for instance BPMN [46] the process model might too quickly turn into a diagrammatic representation of the executable solution with implementation attributes added because of technical considerations, which is quite difficult for business experts to understand.

As illustrated in [14], one of the main ways of utilizing models is to describe some essential information of a business case as informal support in order to facilitate communication among stakeholders. In [15], by taking inspiration from this idea, we proposed a business process characterizing model (BPCM), which can be seen as an important early, business-oriented model in a modeling-based project. BPCM aims to provide an enhanced ability to understand and communicate business processes to all

A. Persson and J. Stirna (Eds.): PoEM 2009, LNBIP 39, pp. 115–129, 2009.

stakeholders involved in the development lifecycle. Such a model shows some essential elements of the business solution to be developed, anchored to business –oriented terminology. Business experts not being familiar with traditional modeling should be able to produce a BPCM model that can capture the knowledge of an organization and of major business processes. Such an approach allows all stakeholders involved in a modeling-based project to have a holistic perspective integrating human and organizational aspects to gain better understanding of business scenario to ease constructing of other relevant models (i.e. goal model, business process model, etc). Furthermore, BPCM can help to bridge the gaps between business experts and technical model developers towards a better construction of business process models.

Developers of technically oriented models must first understand a business case and explore the business context in which the IT system will function before they can build effective systems to support it. This means a proper understanding of a BPCM model in the earliest stage of an IT project is important for technical model developers to design the IT systems. However, having a good BPCM model does not mean that the IT system can be generated automatically, since this is informal. Thus, the next problem is how a BPCM model can be utilized to facilitate a model-based IT system development. The main objective of this paper is to create a combined modeling framework consisting of goal modeling, process modeling, and business process characterizing modeling.

In this paper, we will illustrate the relation between BPCM, and process models and goal models in a combined framework. In this manner, relevant information from a high level BPCM model on an organizational or business perspective can be integrated into goal and process models. We will provide a development methodology to guide the development of goal models and process models from business process characterizing model. Our primary support is on modeling lifecycle support for both business experts and model developers. We aim at a new approach which can reduce misinterpretations between the stakeholders during development.

The remainder of this paper is organized as follows. Section 2 discusses related work. Section 3 briefly describes BPCM, which in this work is extended with improved links to relevant business ontologies compared to [14]. Section 4 illustrates a combined framework for BPCM, goal and business process modeling. Guidelines for mapping from a BPCM to a BPMN process model are provided in section 5. In Section 6, these preliminary guidelines are illustrated by an exemplar describing a conference arrangement process. The use of exemplars is widely recognized as a technique for early evaluation of modeling approaches [12]. Due to page limitations, only parts of the exemplar and approach are illustrated in the paper. Finally, section 7 discusses some related issues and further work to our approach.

2   Related Work

The notations of a modeling language used for business process management can be classified in several categories, based on their conceptual features [34] [24] [25]. For example, business modeling languages such as the e³value [18] aims at identifying exchanges of value objects between the actors in a business case; actor-oriented modeling language such as i* [47], is mainly used for describing the situation as networks of strategic dependencies among actors. In general, it is recognized by analysts that some notations or models are more appropriate towards specific user's types (e.g. technical users / non-technical users).

In recent years, the problem of relating process models, value models, goal models and IT system prototype models has been extensively studied. Many modeling perspective and notations focus on specific aspects, with limited relation to some important aspects in constructing business process models. This leads to the need for a new modeling perspective integrating various aspects to support the development of business process support system.

Some have considered the business value perspective as a foundation to relate or map to other enterprise models. There exist a number of approaches, and languages for business modeling [4] [11]. E^{3}value is one example. The e^{3}value methodology models a network of enterprises creating, distributing, and consuming things of economic value [17]. The basic concepts in the e^{3}value are actor, market segment, value object, value port, value interface, value activity and value exchange. In [41], they offer guidelines for producing an i* model from an e^{3}value model and vice versa. In [5], they addressed the problems of aligning business models with goal models and a method for this has been proposed. Also, an approach for deriving a process model from a business model is proposed in [3]. Resource, Events, Agents (REA) [38] is another relevant approach. The REA framework has been designed for representing and reasoning about economic exchanges. The basic REA pattern models an exchange by three components: the events of the exchange, the resources that are exchanged, and the participating agents.

Some studies consider goal oriented analysis as a starting point. In [32], they have presented a design method for modeling business processes in which the concept of the 'goal' is fundamental. This approach can be characterized as being, in the main, concerned with the construction of a process from its functional goals. In [26], they have proposed a method which is called GoalBPM, to support the controlled evolution of business processes. Control is supported through the explicit modeling of stakeholder goals, their relationship, and their evolution traceable to related business processes. GoalBPM is used to couple an existing and well-developed, formal goal modeling and reasoning methodology, i.e. KAOS [33], and a business process modeling notation, i.e. BPMN.

Business process modeling plays a vital role in the business process life cycle. BPMN, Petri nets [40], and EPC [1] are examples of process modeling languages. A business process is a set of one or more linked procedure or activity, which collectively realize a business objective or policy goal, normally within the context of an organizational structure defining functional roles and relationships [7]. Many process models are intended to describe what goes on in a process from the model developers' view, but not why those activities occur or why processes are to be carried out. Therefore, being only focused on process modeling might be insufficient for redesign purposes. As a result, it leaves the model developers at risk for meeting the logistic of the process, but not satisfying the strategic intention of business people. This is also one of the motivations behind BPCM: to ease the communication and collaborate among different stakeholders in a modeling-based project [15].

Enterprise knowledge development (EKD) [36] is another modeling methodology used for modeling different aspects of organizations. EKD describes an enterprise as a network of related business processes which collaboratively realize business goals. This is achieved by several sub-models: enterprise goal submodel, enterprise process submodel, and information system component submodel [36]. Extended Enterprise Modeling Language (EEML) [29] is another approach resembling EKD used for business process modeling according to five main categories of usage areas of process modeling sketched in [31]. EEML includes four modeling domains: process modeling, resource modeling, goal modeling, and data modeling. In addition to capturing the various tasks and their interdependencies, models show which roles perform each task, and the tools, services and information they apply. In particular EEML combines goal modeling and process modeling in a novel way [30].

Actor oriented approaches emphasize the analysis and specification of the role of actors that participate in the process [25]. The i* modeling framework [47] has been proposed for business process modeling and engineering. Much work has been carried out on supporting guided transformation of i* into other modeling languages [27, 28]. In [9], some preliminary ideas have been proposed for developing a process model given the existence of an i* model. Furthermore, [37] describes how i*, use case, and human activity modeling (HTA) were applied and integrated using synchronization checks to model requirements in an air traffic management case study. The use of HTA in this case resembles the role we see for BPCM, as an informal early model to be used among the stakeholders, potentially in a distributed fashion.

Our argument for creating a BPCM is that we need to base the development of business process models on high level models of the enterprise which can bridge the gap between model developer and business experts, In our work, BPCM is primarily focused on supporting sense-making and communication whereby the concern is for constructing a characterizing model on a sketch level to facilitate the development of detailed business process design. The BPCM modeling methodology can be seen as a business-oriented modeling approach with a consideration of context. Continuous changes of various requirements such as technical and economic, are becoming the nature of business environments. In [15], we have illustrated the capability of BPCM to capture and reflect changes in order to realize a better representation of the knowledge in a sales example. Our aim here is anchor BPCM in relevant business ontologies and describes a model based development framework and design guidelines that can lead from a BPCM model into an implementable IT system.

3   Business Process Characterizing Model (BPCM)

The business process characterizing model is intended not only to facilitate the communication between business experts and model developers, but also to guide and support the development of business process modeling and goal modeling. In particular the model is meant to be applicable in a mobile and multi-channel work environment setting.

The elements of the BPCM are defined as follows:
BPCM= (P, R, A, C, D, G, T)

P: Process: The business process people want to characterize. This element can be related to a common business process ontology such as SCOR [8]. SCOR is a process reference model which has been developed and endorsed by the supply chain council as the cross-industry standard diagnostic tool for supply-chain management. However, SCOR has a limited scope mainly focusing on the supply chain. We will also look to extend the scope of SCOR to cover a wider set of process-types.

R: Resource: This element is inspired by the resource concept in the REA framework [38]. In order to acquire a resource, an actor has to give up some other resource. The events in REA model have the duality relationship. One of these events usually represents a resource being given away or lost, while the other represents a resource being received or gained. For example, in a purchase process the buyer has to give up money to gain some goods. This element can clearly address what are consumed and what are gained in a business process.

A: Actor: This element describes the people and organizations with different roles involve in a business process. Actor can be at different levels (e.g. individual level, group level, organizational level). This element can illustrate who are important to which business process.

C: Context: Context is a broad concept. [10] describes context as "typically the location, identity, and state of people, groups and computational and physical objects". It is not always relevant to cover all context information in this element. In this work, we focus the channel aspect of the context and working environment information (e.g. mobile working environment over WLAN or over GPRS, fixed working environment). This element can depict the channels that could be supported in the different working environment. Today, mobile workers have increasing demands for better multi channel support model on a variety of mobile computing device. The needs of multi channel support from end users can be expressed in this element. In addition, the multi channel support framework proposed in [16] can be adopted to bridge the gap between the BPCM and business process modeling related to context. Furthermore, [2] discusses the usage of i*/Tropos [6, 47] goal-oriented framework for representing the variable behaviors of a mobile information systems can switch to depending on location properties, and presents location-based goal modeling. When a more detailed characterization of this area is needed, one can use for example the proposed delivery context ontology (see http://www.w3.org/TR/2009/WD-dcontology-20090616/)

D: Business Domain: This element classifies the business domain. We attempt to link to NAICS. The North American Industry Classification System (NAICS) is a standard for the collection, tabulation, presentation, and analysis of statistical data describing the U.S. economy. NAICS is based on a production-oriented concept, meaning that it groups establishments into industries according to similarity in the processes used to produce goods or services. Each business process is labeled with a business domain. This is of help for model users to search or retrieve business processes within specific business domain.

G: Goal: This element can address what kinds of goals need to be fulfilled in the business process. The process items will interconnect to correspondent goals. In this way, the business experts will see how the business process model can contribute to the organizational goals. We would like to describe both hard goal and soft goal in this element. According to [29, 44], some attempts to incorporate goals into process modeling have been made in the past, both addressing the operational goals and strategic goals. Operational goals can be related to hard-goals, forming the basis for functional requirements; while strategic goals are related to soft-goals, which set the basis for non-functional requirement. The intention for us to incorporate the goal element into BPCM is to make it easier to relate BPCM to goal modeling and process modeling.

T: Process Type: According to REA [22], REA does not model only exchanges but also conversions. Exchange and conversion can be seen as two typical process types. An exchange occurs when an actor receive resource from another actor and give other resources back to that actor. A conversion occurs when an actor consumes resources in order to produce other resources. Unlike an exchange that models the exchanges of resources by agents, a conversion models the creation or maintenance of resources by agents.

As we described above, the key attributes and elements involve in the business process development can be reflected in the BPCM. We aim to manage all the business processes in a universal way in the characterizing model. On the one hand, this model is intended to help business experts to browse and describe the business process for different purposes. On the other hand, since the BPCM model can be organized in the textual table (as illustrated in chapter 6); it is easier for the business experts, most of whom are non-modeling experts, to understand than BPMN or EPC. As a result, the BPCM can lessen the modeling competence gap between model developers and business experts. In other words, it means the BPCM has the potential to help the model developer to build and develop process models and goal models in a more efficient and effective way. Therefore, both business experts and model developers can benefit from this business process charactering model.

4 The Combined Framework

In this section, the combined modeling framework, as presented in Figure 1, is discussed. In this framework, we consider a BPCM Model as a starting point for developing an IT system. It is possible to have other approaches, e.g. starting with a goal model and then deriving use cases from a goal model [43], but we will not pursue this here. In our framework, we will start with a relatively informal model, more specifically BPCM here, which can ease the communication and cooperation between business experts and technical model developers, and then will derive and develop the BPCM into the visual models and executable models. In [37], they also argued that it is often beneficial to start a modeling-based project with an informal model and then develop the visual models.

In our combined framework, as a first step, data about all components of BPCM are gathered and recorded in a textual table according to the elements presented in the last section. Some early stage requirement engineering techniques [23] can be used to gather this information. Then, we will try to derive the start of goal models and process models from the BPCM model. The goal model will typically need to be extended, and this will also provide input to the process model. Lastly, those models can be used as inputs for deriving a candidate IT system.

4.1 Business Process Characterizing Model

While process execution is crucial from the technical developers' point of view, it is equally important to have models that can express characteristics of business processes in their organizational context, which can ultimately be able to support the development of the executable business process models. In today's fast paced changing world, understanding characteristics of business processes and impacts of proposed or underlying changes is a must. Previous experience from large and complex business process projects indicated that many of them fail to achieve desired results because of overlooked organizational issues. Therefore, identifying the important business process characteristics in the early phase is as important as building the executable process models. At this level, the BPCM is used as a sketch to describe the key attributes and elements involve in the business domain or problem description in order to facilitate the communication between business experts and model developers. Although the BPCM does not directly address the construction of business process models and goal models, the elements in the BPCM are close to the concepts of process models and goal models , e.g. actor, resource, hard goal etc.

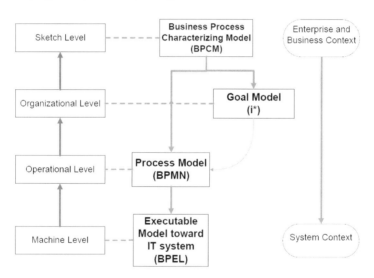

Fig. 1. The Combined Modeling Framework

4.2 Goal Model

According to [35], goals express intentions and capture the reasons of the system to be built. Goal models are used to elicit and make the goals of an enterprise. Goals are essentially optative as they refer to what an organization or its desired IT system is to ensure [48]. Goals may be formulated at different levels of abstraction for different purposes, from high level strategic concerns to low level technical concerns, by using different modeling notations (e.g. i*, KAOS). Goals are also useful in validating system requirements in the context of business or enterprise objectives.

A clear understanding of goals is essential to guide the design of process models and evaluate the operational quality of the solution. Goals can be used to systematically guide the development and refinement of processes during the design. In our framework, the goal model is defined at the organizational level based on information in the BPCM. In this context, goals are defined as statements to declare the states to be achieved. In connection to the process model at the operational level, goals are used to state what has to be achieved in the context of process modeling.

i* supports modeling rich organizational contexts by offering high-level social abstraction (such as goals, soft goals and dependencies) as modeling constructs for reasoning support during business process redesign [24] [47]. Furthermore, there has been some work on translating i* to process models. i* has also recently been standardized by ITU. For those reasons, we use i* for goal modeling. Goal modeling is not discussed in detail in this paper due to space limitations.

4.3 Process Model

According to [20], a business process can be seen as a set of partially ordered activities intended to reach a goal. Since BPMN has relatively higher expressiveness and ability to map directly to executable process languages such as business process execution language (BPEL) [21] and XPDL [13] compared to other process modeling notations, it has been widely accepted by the BPM community [42] for the purpose of business process modeling. In [39], an analysis of BPMN also stated its high maturity in representing concepts required for modeling business process. Therefore, we have chosen BPMN for the construction of process models derived from BPCM.

As presented in Figure 1, process models can be constructed based on the BPCM and goal models. In our framework, the process model is defined at the operational level. The operational requirements derived from BPCM should be reflected in the process models including: involved participant (who), functional goals (what), coordination and cooperation (when). The model developer is supposed to design and develop the business process models based on models from the upper two levels (sketch level and organizational level) as a blueprint for the IT systems to be implemented. In order to build the IT system, these models should be understandable by the system developers and IT experts. If necessary, XML scheme will be defined and embedded into business process models to make them executable.

4.4 Executable Model

In recent years, some initiatives have emphasized process models which can be directly executed. Business process execution and deployment can be achieved by using BPEL. Since model developers are able to convert some resources into XML schema before annotating the associations between tasks with XML type in BPMN, it is possible to design an executable model directly. For instance, the Intalio designer, which is a tool used for BPMN modeling, allows the developers to open the XML schema in the process navigator and design and drag XML types into the associations between pools in the process models.

Some formal models are executable. In an ideal case, the executable system can be generated automatically, which will facilitate developing IT systems. Otherwise, some manual steps will be involved in developing and realizing the final IT systems. In particular, aspects relating to supporting multi-channel solutions must typically be addressed manually.

5 Ideas to Guide Process Modeling Based on a BPCM

In this section, we describe some preliminary ideas to guide the development of process modeling given the availability of a set of BPCMs. Our methodology relies on establishing relationships between the meta-models of BPCM, goal models and process models similar to the approach in [32].

The intent of our methodology for the process model extraction is to derive as many cues for these models from BPCM as possible. Once the BPCM has been established and agreed upon, the translation from BPCM to process models and goal models can be started. A BPCM can be obtained by collecting relevant information from business stakeholders in terms of filling a BPCM table (as shown in Table 2).

The following describes guidelines to map a BPCM model to a BPMN model:

1.   Identify the actors in a BPCM. Each actor within BPCM is a candidate to be a pool in a BPMN process model.
2.   Map actors. First of all, we need to identify internal and external actors from the actors identified from a BPCM. This is required because BPMN separates internal organizational actors by representing them as lanes within pools whereas external actors are assigned their own pool. Then, the relevant lanes and pools can be labeled in a BPMN process model.
3.   Identify the resources in a BPCM. For each resource in a BPCM, it should include a message flow which links two associated tasks in a BPMN process model, whereby the source of the message flow connected to the dependee's task and the destination of the message flow connected to the depender's task. Since we do not have element in a BPCM to address the relevant tasks in the business process domain, some additional efforts need to be put into tasks discovery in process modeling. Therefore, we proposed the complementary requirement table in Table 1. The complementary requirement table is a table specifying the related tasks in a source pool (lane) or a destination pool (lane), associated to various resources in a BPCM. A complementary requirement table can be filled by model developers with their understanding of a BPCM model.
4.   Map tasks and resources. After getting the defined tasks name from the last step, those tasks can be labeled in a BPMN process model. An association flow link is also used to represent the dependencies going from a source pool (lane) to a destination pool (lane), as shown in the complementary requirement table. In the meantime, the message flow between the associated tasks can be labeled with the resource names.
5.   Sequence the labeled tasks. The intention of this step is to make sure the clear placement of tasks and messages in a BPMN process model. The sequence of tasks needs to be consistent with routine requirement specified in the specification. The model developer can sequence tasks guided by the process element

(e.g. SCOR) in a BPCM. Furthermore, a start event and an end event must be placed to the correspondent actor's pool or lane.

6. Revisit the BPMN process model. This is intended to rearrange the layout of the already represented tasks to improve the empirical quality of the model.

Table 1. Complementary Requirement Table

Resource	Source Pool or Lane	Destination Pool or Lane	Related Task in Source Pool	Related Task in Destination Pool

6 Exemplar

In this section, we apply our preliminary guidelines to a conference organization exemplar. The exemplar is an extension of the original conference case used e.g. in the IFIP CRIS conferences in the eighties. Whereas the CRIS-case primarily looked upon the paper handling process, the extended exemplar also includes the interaction between different actors needing to arrange the practical parts of the conference. Parts of the overall case are presented here: *Prior to holding a conference, an organization committee and a program committee are established. All services involved in a conference cost money, which have to be balanced by the income from registration fee from participants and sponsors. In order to get funds from sponsors, a call for sponsor is sent out by the organization committee. The program committee consists of a number of researchers working within the theme of the conference, whom are normally distributed across the world. In order to get good papers, on the behalf of the program committee of the conference, the organization committee announces a Call for Papers. Potential researchers receive this, and some of them decide to submit one or more papers for review. The paper is distributed to between 3 to 4 members of the program committee for review. Then, based on the review made by the program committee members within an announced deadline, the program chair makes and distributes paper acceptance decisions of the submitted papers. Researchers of accepted papers are requested to make a final version of their papers, a so called camera ready copy (CRC) and a copyright form to a professional conference proceeding publisher within a predefined deadline. Next, the program chair makes the conference program. In addition, the social program of the conference is also important to attract larger number of participants. In order to have a well-organized social program, the organization committee sends a social program request to a local tourist office. When both of programs are ready, the organization committee announces the conference program and registration method. Then, researchers make registration and payment to the organization committee. The conference proceeding is published by a professional publisher a couple of days before the conference.* Whereas most services are provided over internet, some services (e.g. entering of reviews, registration, information services) is planned to be possible to do using a mobile device. After characterizing this conference organization case using the characterizing model proposed in section 3, we summarize the derived BPCMs in Table 2. Note that this actually is a summary of a number of BPCMs, but it is here described in one table due to size limitations of the paper.

Table 2. Conference Organization Case in a BPCM Model

BPCM Elements \\ BPCM Name	Conference Organization Case
Process	Plan conference (P1 Plan supply chain, P2 Plan Source, P4 Plan Deliver) Source Conference (S2 Source make-to-order Product (Proceedings) Deliver Conference (D2 Deliver Make-to-order Product), Enable (Manage Capital Assets)
Resource	Call for Sponsor, Funds, Social Program Request Form, Social Program, Call for Paper, Paper, Review Form, Acceptance Result, Paper Presentation Program, CRC & Copyright Form, Conference Program, Registration Information, Registration Payment, Conference Proceeding
Actors	Organizational Committee, Sponsor, Local Tourist Office, Researcher, Program Committee, Program Chair
Context	Multi-channel (PC over LAN/WLAN/UMTS/GPRS). Some services PDA over WLAN/UMTS/GPRS
Business Domain	561920 Convention and Trade Show Organizers (some of the suppliers are in other business domains e.g. 561591 Convention and Visitors Bureaus, 51113 Book Publishers)
Goal	Soft Goal: A conference is well-arranged Hard Goals: Attendance at a conference, higher; Balance positive Paper Reviewing Process, Acceptance rate 15-20%.
Process Type	Conversion

Table 3. Complementary Requirement Table: the conference organization case

Resource	Source Pool or Lane	Destination Pool or Lane	Related Task in Source Pool	Related Task in Destination Pool
Call for Sponsor	Organizational Committee	Sponsor	Publish Call for Sponsor	Receive Call for Sponsor
Fund	Sponsor	Organizational Committee	Sponsor Conference	Receive funds
Social Program Request Form	Organizational Committee	Local Tourist Office	Inquiry Social Program	Receive request form
Social Program	Local Tourist Office	Organizational Committee	Make a social Program	Receive a social program

Figure 2 is a part of the BPMN process model thus extracted from the BPCM of the scientific conference organization case (depicted in Table 2) (a derived goal model is not shown, due to page limitations).

As presented in the BPCM, there are seven actors in this conference organization process. The seven actors can directly map to seven pools in the BPMN process model. More than ten resources are identified in the BPCM. In order to discover the tasks related to the resources, the complementary requirement table is filled as shown in Table 3 (due to space limitation, only part of the table is presented here). Then, both resources and related tasks can be mapped to the BPMN process model, and flow links are placed to associate tasks between pools. In the next step, the already labeled

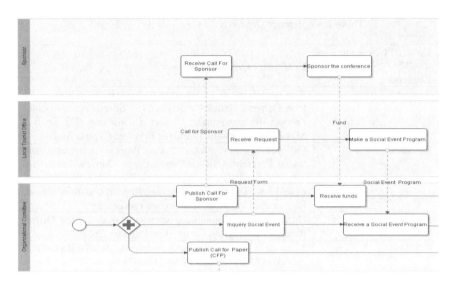

Fig. 2. The BPMN process model[1]

tasks are sequenced in a logical manner guided by process element in the BPCM (e.g. the link to SCOR) and a start event and an end event are added to the BPMN process model. Lastly, the BPMN process model is revisited to enhance the layout.

7   Discussion

In this paper, we have described how to utilize a BPCM as shown in the combined framework to guide the design and construction of business process models in the life cycle of business process modeling development. However, it must be admitted that the evaluation and validation of the BPCM in the combined framework is currently quite limited since we only illustrated the usage of the BPCM in an exemplar. In this section, we discuss some problems we found from the exemplar study and propose some future research directions.

7.1   Lessons Learnt from the Exemplar

In applying our preliminary ideas on mapping a BPCM to a BPMN process model in the case, we found that the projection process is straightforward. However, in practice, the case might be more complicated than what we proposed in the last section. We also recognized some potential limitations to the preliminary ideas we described in section 4. First, we do not address the issue on control flow. Second, we do not set up the criteria to evaluate how well a BPMN process model can meet hard goals or soft goals proposed in a BPCM. Third, we need to have a better solution to deal with the consistency check between a BPCM and a BPMN process

---

[1] Full Size Image of the whole BPMN process model is available at:
http://www.idi.ntnu.no/~shanggao/BPMN/Conference.jpg

model. From the exemplar it appears that we basically capture high level activities. On the other hand, if we performed a further drill-down according to the identified processes in SCOR, more detailed processes would have been identified.

7.2   From a BPMN Process Model to IT System

BPMN is often used when designing and improving the business process, whereas BPEL is used when implementing it. The main approach for execution of a BPMN process model is a translation from BPMN to BPEL. If BPMN can be transformed into BPEL, the BPEL process can be executed on BPEL engines. There are many tools on the market that transforms BPMN into BPEL, which makes implementing IT system from a BPMN process model possible. In [45], the authors present an approach for combining process modeling notations such as BPMN and user interface modeling. Here it is identified a need to translate analysis level BPMN models to a design time BPMN model. Since BPCM in our framework can take care of the analysis level, we map directly to the design level BPMN and can add aspects relevant for user interfaces that can take the multi-channel aspects into account.

7.3   BPCM Related Issues and Future Work

You might find that some of the elements in the BPCM are not used in mapping from a BPCM to a BPMN process models. You may question that those elements are useful? The answer is yes, but for other purposes. For instance, the context element can help the model developer to develop the models with a consideration of the mobile working environment and multi channel supports issues. Different processes might be needed for the provision of services over different channels. Moreover, some elements of the BPCM can be used as a key for querying purposes. For instance, the element business domain can be used to identify solutions from similar areas.

Future research will address the problems we proposed in this section. In addition, we will validate and evaluate our combined framework in case studies. In particular we will use the approach in connection to supporting a loosely organized conference series with a firmer framework. Also further comparisons with related approaches for multi-model integration (e.g. [36]) will be performed.

References

1. Aalst, W.v.d.: Formalization and Verification of Event-driven Process Chains. Information and Software Technology 41(10), 639–650 (1999)
2. Ali, R., Dalpiaz, F., Giorgini, P.: Location-Based Variability for Mobile Information Systems. In: Bellahsène, Z., Léonard, M. (eds.) CAiSE 2008. LNCS, vol. 5074, pp. 575–578. Springer, Heidelberg (2008)
3. Andersson, B., Bergholtz, M., Edirisuriya, A., Ilayperuma, T., Johannesson, P.: A Declarative Foundation of Process Models. In: Pastor, Ó., Falcão e Cunha, J. (eds.) CAiSE 2005. LNCS, vol. 3520, pp. 233–247. Springer, Heidelberg (2005)
4. Andersson, B., Bergholtz, M., Edirisuriya, A., Ilayperuma, T., Johannesson, P., Gordijn, J., Grégoire, B., Schmitt, M., Dubois, E., Abels, S., Hahn, A., Wangler, B., Weigand, H.: Towards a Reference Ontology for Business Models. In: Embley, D.W., Olivé, A., Ram, S. (eds.) ER 2006. LNCS, vol. 4215, pp. 482–496. Springer, Heidelberg (2006)

5. Andersson, B., Bergholtz, M., Edirisuriya, A., et al.: Aligning Goal Models and Business Models - extended abstract. In: CAiSE Forum 2008, pp. 13–16. CEUR Proceedings (2008)
6. Bresciani, P., Perini, A., Giorgini, P., et al.: Tropos: An Agent-Oriented Software Development Methodology. Autonomous Agents and Multi-Agent Systems 8(3), 203–236 (2004)
7. Coalition, T.W.M. Terminology & Glossary (1999)
8. Council, S.-c. SCOR Model 8.0 Quick Reference Guide (2006)
9. Cysneiros, L.M., Yu, E.: Addressing agent autonomy in business process management- with case studies on the patient discharge process. In: 2004 Information Resources Management Association Conference (2004)
10. Dey, A.K., Abowd, G.D., Salber, D.: A conceptual framework and a toolkit for supporting the rapid prototyping of context-aware applications. Human-Computer Interaction 16(2), 97–166 (2001)
11. Dietz, J.L.G.: Enterprise Ontology: Theory and Methodology. Springer, New York (2006)
12. Feather, M.S., Fickas, S., Finkelstein, A., et al.: Requirements and Specification Exemplars. Automated Software Engineering 4(4), 419–438 (1997)
13. Fischer, L.: Workflow handbook 2005. Workflow Management Coalition, WfMC (2005)
14. Fowler, M.: UML Distilled: A Brief Guide to the Standard Object Modeling Language. Addison-Wesley, Reading (2003)
15. Gao, S., Krogstie, J.: Facilitating Business Process Development via a Process Characterizing Model. In: International Symposium on Knowledge Acquisition and Modeling 2008. IEEE CS, Los Alamitos (2008)
16. Gao, S., Krogstie, J.: Multi-channel support framework for mobile workers. In: International conference SITIS 2007. IEEE CS, Los Alamitos (2007)
17. Gordijn, J., Akkermans, H.: E3-value: Design and Evaluation of e-Business Models. IEEE Intelligent Systems 16(4), 11–17 (2001)
18. Gordijn, J., Akkermans, H.: Value based requirements engineering: Exploring innovative e-commerce ideas. Requirements Engineering Journal 8, 114–134 (2003)
19. Gordijn, J., Akkermans, H., Vliet, H.V.: Value Based Requirements Creation for Electronic Commerce Applications. In: HICSS 2000. IEEE CS, Los Alamitos (2000)
20. Hammer, M., Champy, J.: Reengineering the Corporation: A Manifesto for Business Revolution. Nicholas Brealey Publishing, London (1994)
21. Havey, M.: Essential Business Process Modeling. O'Reilly Media, CA (2005)
22. Hruby, P.: Model-Driven Design Using Business Patterns. Springer, New York (2006)
23. Hull, E., Jackson, K., Dick, J.: Requirements Engineering. Springer, New York (2004)
24. Katzenstein, G., Lerch, F.J.: Beneath the surface of organizational processes: a social representation framework for business process redesign. ACM Trans. Inf. Syst. 18(4), 383–422 (2000)
25. Kavakli, V., Loucopoulos, P.: Goal-Driven Business Process Analysis Application in Electricity Deregulation. In: Pernici, B., Thanos, C. (eds.) CAiSE 1998. LNCS, vol. 1413, pp. 305–324. Springer, Heidelberg (1998)
26. Koliadis, G., Ghose, A.: Relating Business Process Models to Goal-Oriented Requirements Models in KAOS. In: Hoffmann, A., Kang, B.-h., Richards, D., Tsumoto, S. (eds.) PKAW 2006. LNCS (LNAI), vol. 4303, pp. 25–39. Springer, Heidelberg (2006)
27. Krishna, A., Ghose, A.K., Vranesevic, A.: Agent-oriented conceptual models to UML sequence diagrams via effect annotations. Multiagent and Grid Systems 2(4) (2006)
28. Krishna, A., Guan, Y., Sombattheera, C., Ghose, A.K.: Agent-Based Prototyping of Web-Based Systems. In: Ali, M., Dapoigny, R. (eds.) IEA/AIE 2006. LNCS (LNAI), vol. 4031, pp. 780–789. Springer, Heidelberg (2006)

29. Krogstie, J.: Integrated Goal, Data and Process modeling: From TEMPORA to Model-Generated Work-Places. In: Johannesson, P., Soderstrom, E. (eds.) Information Systems Engineering: From Data Analysis to Process Networks, pp. 43–65. IGI Publishing (2008)
30. Krogstie, J.: Using EEML for Combined Goal and Process Oriented Modeling: A Case Study. In: EMMSAD 2008. CEUR-WS (2008)
31. Krogstie, J., Dalberg, V., Jensen, S.M.: Process Modeling Value Framework. In: Manolopoulos, Y., Filipe, J., Constantopoulos, P., et al. (eds.) ICEIS 2006. LNBIP, vol. 3, pp. 309–321. Springer, Heidelberg (2006)
32. Kueng, P., Kawalek, P.: Goal-based business process models: creation and evaluation. Business Process Management Journal 3(1), 17–38 (1997)
33. Lamsweerde, A.V.: Goal-Oriented Requirements Engineering: A Guided Tour. In: Requirements Engineering (RE 2001). IEEE CS, Los Alamitos (2001)
34. Lillehagen, F., Krogstie, J.: Active Knowledge Modeling of Enterprises. Springer, Heidelberg (2008)
35. Loucopoulos, P., Karakostas, V.: System Requirements Engineering. McGraw-Hill, Inc., New York (1995)
36. Loucopoulos, P., Kavakli, V.: Enterprise Knowledge Management and Conceptual Modelling. In: Chen, P.P., Akoka, J., Kangassalu, H., Thalheim, B. (eds.) Conceptual Modeling. LNCS, vol. 1565, pp. 123–143. Springer, Heidelberg (1999)
37. Maiden, N.A.M., Jones, S.V., Manning, S., Greenwood, J., Renou, L.: Model-Driven Requirements Engineering: Synchronising Models in an Air Traffic Management Case Study. In: Persson, A., Stirna, J. (eds.) CAiSE 2004. LNCS, vol. 3084, pp. 368–383. Springer, Heidelberg (2004)
38. McCarthy, W.E.: The REA accounting model: a generalized framework for accounting systems in a shared data environment 57, 554–578 (1982)
39. Muehlen, M.Z., Recker, J.: How Much Language Is Enough? Theoretical and Practical Use of the Business Process Modeling Notation. In: Bellahsène, Z., Léonard, M. (eds.) CAiSE 2008. LNCS, vol. 5074, pp. 465–479. Springer, Heidelberg (2008)
40. Murata, T.: Petri nets: Properties, analysis and applications. IEEE 77(4), 541–580 (1989)
41. Raadt, B.v.d., Gordijn, J., Yu, E.: Exploring Web Services from a Business Value Perspective. In: Requirements Engineering (RE 2005). IEEE CS, Los Alamitos (2005)
42. Recker, J.C., Indulska, M., Rosemann, M., et al.: Do Process Modelling Techniques Get Better? A Comparative Ontological Analysis of BPMN. In: Campbell, B., Underwood, J., Bunker, D. (eds.) Australasian Chapter of the Association for Information Systems (2005)
43. Santander, V.F.A., Castro, J.: Deriving Use Cases from Organizational Modeling. In: RE 2002, pp. 32–42. IEEE CS, Los Alamitos (2002)
44. Soffer, P., Wand, Y.: On the notion of soft-goals in business process modeling. Business Process Management Journal 11(6), 663–679 (2005)
45. Trætteberg, H., Krogstie, J.: Enhancing the Usability of BPM-Solutions by Combining Process and User-Interface Modelling. In: Stirna, J., Persson, A. (eds.) POEM 2008. LNBIP, vol. 15, pp. 86–97. Springer, Heidelberg (2008)
46. White, S.A.: Introduction to BPMN (2005)
47. Yu, E.: Modelling strategic relationships for process reengineering. PhD Thesis, University of Toronto (1996)
48. Zave, P., Jackson, M.: Four dark corners of requirements engineering. ACM Transactions on Software Engineering and Methodology 6(1), 1–30 (1997)

Towards Better Fitting Data Warehouse Systems

Naveen Prakash, Deepika Prakash, and Y.K. Sharma

MRCE Faridabad, IIIT Banglore, NIC, New Delhi, INDIA
praknav@hotmail.com, dpka.prakash@gmail.com, yks@nic.in

Abstract. In order to produce data warehouse systems that reflect organizational decisional needs, development should be rooted in the goals and decisions of organizations. The goal-decision-information model and associated information elicitation techniques for decision making are presented. There are four main techniques, Ends analysis, Means analysis, Critical Success Factor analysis, and Outcome Feedback analysis. Using these, the requirements engineer is able to elicit the required information as well as the sub decisions of a given decision. The elicitation techniques are then applied to these sub decisions. The elicitation process ends when all decisions/sub decisions have been thus processed. A comparison of this approach is made with data base driven and ER driven development approaches to data warehouse development to show that it produces systems that fit well with decisional requirements.

Keywords: Data Warehouse system, requirement engineering.

1 Introduction

Enterprise information systems come to us in many forms ranging from early 'packages' like payroll systems to those addressing application domains like hotel reservation systems, full enterprises like ERP systems and through to systems supporting cross organization operations like supply chain management. Notice that this evolution considers the class of functional/transactional systems. However, there is another way of looking at enterprises, not in terms of what they do but in terms of the decisions that they have to make. In this approach, information generated as a trace of functions/transactions carried out is not interesting per se. Rather it is the management decisions that need to be taken to change enterprise operation that comes to the fore. Therefore, now information is a record of what happened and it can be analysed to reveal trends, patterns, associations etc. that can be used to take decisions. This is the area of enterprise information systems as supported by Data Warehouse (DW) technology and we shall refer to these as decisional enterprise systems in contrast to the other functional enterprise systems.

Decisional enterprise systems share a number of common problems with the functional class. An important one is the issue of fitment: can we ensure that the decisions made in organizations are indeed supported by the information contained in the data warehouse? Is the Data warehouse a faithful representation of the information that is to be kept in the warehouse? In other words, the problem is of building data warehouses whose content fits well with information needed for decision making.

A. Persson and J. Stirna (Eds.): PoEM 2009, LNBIP 39, pp. 130–144, 2009.
© IFIP International Federation for Information Processing 2009

In this paper, we will show that the Goal-Decision-Information or GDI approach [Pra04, Pra08] when supported by appropriate information elicitation technique promote a direct relationship between DW information contents and the decisions of interest. We propose four elicitation techniques, Ends analysis, Means analysis, Outcome Feedback analysis, and Critical Success Factor analysis. These techniques are applied to an initial, given set of decisions to determine decision parameters. An analysis of these parameters is then carried out to determine those which are sub decisions of the initial decision, and those which are information to be kept in the Warehouse. Elicitation is done for each sub decision so discovered. The elicitation process ends when no further decisions are to be processed.

This paper is organized in three main sections. The next section, Section II, considers the DW in the organizational context. It presents the GDI approach and the manner in which it can be supported to arrive at the information contents of the data warehouse to-be. Section III contains a comparison of the proposed technique with conventional data warehouse development life cycles. This comparison is based on experience of developing a data warehouse using database driven, ER driven, and GDI driven techniques respectively.

2   DW in the Organizational Context

In this section, we present a technique that arrives at DW information contents through an exploration of organizational goals, associated decisions to meet these, and information relevant to decision making.

2.1   The Goal-Decision-Information (GDI) Model

The basic assumption of the GDI model is that since a data warehouse system is used for decision-making, any model that is developed must be rooted in the essential nature of decision-making. According to [Mon86] the decision-making process consists of three phases, (a) intelligence, that involves searching for conditions that call for decisions, (b) design, which involves inventing, developing, and analyzing possible courses of actions, and (c) choice, which implies the selection of a course of action from those available.

We model [Pra08] the notion of 'conditions that call for decisions' through the concept of a goal. We view a goal as an aim or objective that is to be met. A goal is a passive concept and it cannot perform or cause any action to be performed; it is non-operational. As shown in Fig.1, a goal can be either simple or complex. A simple goal cannot be decomposed into simpler one. A complex goal is built out of other goals which may itself be simple or complex. The component goals of a complex one may be in an AND/OR relationship with one another. This is in accordance with goal modelling approaches of traditional Requirements engineering.

The Requirements engineering view [Pra08] suggests that goals 'guide decisions'. So, we naturally get the second concept of the GDI model, that of a Decision. For us, a decision is a specification of an active component that causes goal fulfillment. As shown in Fig.1, a decision can be either simple or complex. A simple decision cannot

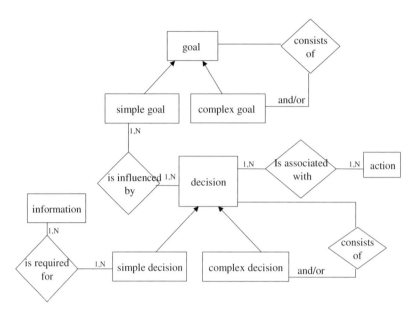

Fig. 1. The GDI Model (taken from [Pra08])

be decomposed into simpler ones whereas a complex decision is built out of other simple or complex decisions. Fig. 1 also shows that there is a relationship between goals and decisions through the association *'is influenced by'* between goals and decisions. This association identifies the decisions which when taken can lead to goal satisfaction.

According to [Mar91] information is the critical resource for decision-making. This is captured, in Fig. 1, by the association *is required for* between decisions and decisional information. The *is required for* ensures that only relevant information is associated with decisions.

Notice the strong embedding of the GDI diagram in the larger decision making environment of an organization. For a decision-maker the primary task is to take the appropriate decision and obtaining information is the means to do it. Thus, the GDI diagram-decision-maker interaction is done in terms of the goals, decisions, and information that the decision makers see and work with. The decisions and information here are necessarily high level and a number of details remain hidden. For example, one may only identify Market Profile as the information needed without making it precise, what comprises it? How does it translate to the data structure to be kept in the Data Warehouse? How shall it be physically organized? This is in consonance with our desire to establish a broad alignment between organizational needs for decision making information and a specification of what shall be kept in the DW.

The GDI diagram is obtained by instantiating the GDI model with the relevant goals, decisions, information and relationships between these. As an example, consider a vehicle manufacturing company that has one of its goals as Provide Responsible After Sales Service. Now, an important decision that influences this goal is to Recall Product and requires information about the suppliers of the company, the material supplied by them, customer complaints, customer data, inspection reports of faulty products etc. This goal-decision-information data is used to instantiate the GDI model.

2.2 Eliciting Information

The GDI diagram suggests a three stage elicitation process for goals, decisions and information respectively as shown in Fig. 2.

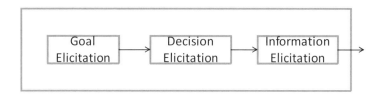

Fig. 2. The Three Stage Goal-Decision-Information Process

Our interest in this paper is in the information elicitation stage that addresses the problem, given a set of decisions elicit information relevant to these.

We introduce our elicitation technique by describing a tool called Raju whose architecture is shown in Fig. 3. There are four main components, Decision Parameter Guide, Information Identifier, Decision Identifier and the Verifier. All these interact with the repository of Raju. Conceptually, this repository is organized in three parts. The first part contains the goals of the organization, the second contains the set of decisions, and the third contains the parameters of the decisions. These parts are related to one another. The Goal and Decision parts are linked together by the Goal-Decision relationship to keep track of which goal is satisfied by which decision. Similarly, the Decision and Parameter parts are linked together to keep a record of which parameter is relevant to which decision.

The four main components of Raju carry out specific functions as follows:

Decision Parameter Guide (DPG): This component is organized in four parts corresponding to the elicitation strategies of Critical Success Factor, Ends, Means and Outcome Feedback analysis respectively. The engineer is offered a menu of these and is thereafter guided to enter the material required by the selected strategy. As we shall see later, each strategy culminates in identifying the parameters of relevance to the decision being explored. Decision parameters can be interpreted either as sub decisions of the decision or as information relevant to the decision. Once the parameter of decision is identified then this distinction can be made by going to the Information Identifier.

Information Identifier: This component supports the application of heuristics that determine whether a given parameter is to be interpreted as information or not. These heuristics identify a number of properties of parameters and if the parameter possesses any one or more of these, then the parameter is treated as information otherwise not.

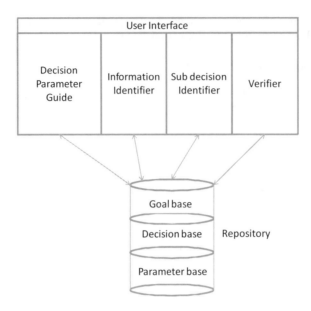

Fig. 3. The Architecture of Raju

Sub Decision Identifier: As its name implies, the Decision Identifier processes parameters to identify which of these are to be treated as sub decisions.

Verifier: The verifier looks to see that

- All initial decisions and those produced by the Decision Identifier have gone through the requirements engineering process,
- All parameters of all decisions have been identified as either information or decisions.

We briefly review the elicitation techniques available in Raju. These are Critical Success Factor (CSF) Analysis, Ends Analysis, Means Analysis, and Outcome Feedback Analysis.

2.2.1 CSF Analysis

According to (Wet91) most managers have a portfolio of 4-8 critical factors on which their success or failure depends. The essential question here is to identify the parameters that must be monitored to ensure that these factors remain in control. This control is carried out by appropriate decision making. Therefore, CSF analysis provides structure (Mon86) to the decision-maker/requirements engineer interaction thereby reducing the chance of including irrelevant data in the decisional system.

CSF Analysis is a three step process consisting of (a) CSF determination, (b) determination of CSF parameters, and (c) determination of properties of parameters. CSF analysis for a decision is complete when all its CSFs have been determined and steps (b) and (c) have been carried out for each of these

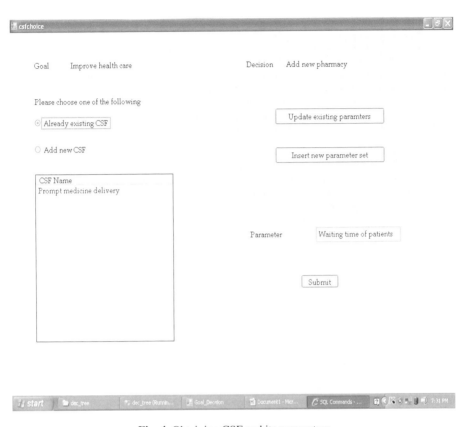

Fig. 4. Obtaining CSF and its parameters

Raju provides the user interface shown in Fig. 4 for CSF elicitation. The top of the screen of Fig. 3, shows that requirements engineering for the decision Add new Pharmacy for the goal Improve health care is being done. The left hand side of the screen allows the requirements engineer to either enter the CSF affected by the decision or to select an existing CSF for modification. In the latter case, selection can be made from the list displayed.

The screen shows that a new CSF, Prompt medicine delivery, has been entered and that its parameter is waiting time of patient. In general, these may be more than one parameter for a given CSF.

2.2.2 End Analysis
The second elicitation process in Raju is Ends Analysis. 'Ends' refers to the result achieved by a decision. It identifies a concrete change in the organization that is a consequence of the decision. Ends analysis, is the identification of information needed to evaluate the effectiveness of the end to be achieved. The decision-maker/requirements engineer interaction is centred round determining the parameters of interest in estimating this effectiveness. As shown by (Wet91) for an order processing system, parameters

required to evaluate the end "provide customer service" are, for example, customer credit status and payment history.

The needed parameters are again obtained in Raju by following a three step elicitation process. These steps are (i) determining Ends, (ii) determining the effectiveness measures of the Ends, and (iii) determining the parameters pertaining to evaluating the effectiveness. The relevant screen of Raju is shown in Fig. 5. Similar to the CSF analysis screen, on the left hand side of Fig. 4 Raju elicits the Ends of the decision. As before, an option exists to modify existing Ends. The right hand side of the screen contains boxes for entering the effectiveness measure as well as the parameters that help to evaluate the effectiveness measure.

The example shown in Fig.5 is for the same decision, Add new pharmacy, as before. An End of this decision is Full utilization of the new pharmacy, the effectiveness measure of this end is Service provided and one of the parameters of this measure is Amount of medicine distributed.

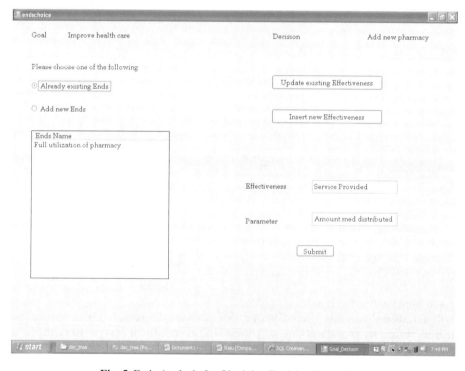

Fig. 5. Ends Analysis for Obtaining Decision Parameters

2.2.3 Means Analysis

Means analysis, is the identification of parameters needed to evaluate the efficiency of the means adopted to produce the ends. Thus, the requirements engineer/stakeholder interaction is now centered round eliciting parameters that provide information on the efficiency of the means adopted for each decision.

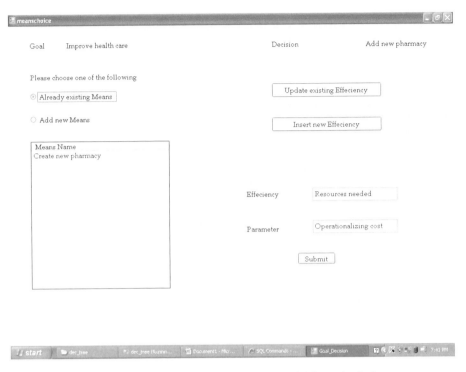

Fig 6. Obtaining Decision Parameters through Means Analysis

Fig. 6 shows an example of means analysis for the decision Add new pharmacy. It is possible to cerate the new pharmacy by splitting the existing pharmacy into two or by creating an altogether new pharmacy. The figure shows the second of these means to add a new pharmacy. The efficiency of the means can be evaluated by the efficiency criteria, resources needed and a parameter for this efficiency measure is operational zing cost.

2.2.4 Outcome Feedback Analysis

Sterman (Ste89) noted the crucial role played by outcome feedback and changes in the environment in management behaviour. Once a decision is taken, it produces an outcome. This outcome changes the environment and eventually feeds back into the outcome of the decision forming a feedback cycle. It follows that outcome feedback can help in discovering decision parameters by considering the environmental effects that a decision produces.

We illustrate the manner in which Raju supports outcome feedback analysis. Consider the decision Add new pharmacy once again. Addition of a new pharmacy shall affect the perception and behavior of the dispensary in which it is added. For example, there may be an increase in the registered members of the health service, which may lead to requirement of additional medical staff which in turn affects the pharmacies of the dispensary. Thus, we find a feedback cycle which starts off from the outcome of the decision, goes through the organization and returns back to the outcome. The screen of Fig. 7 shows this situation.

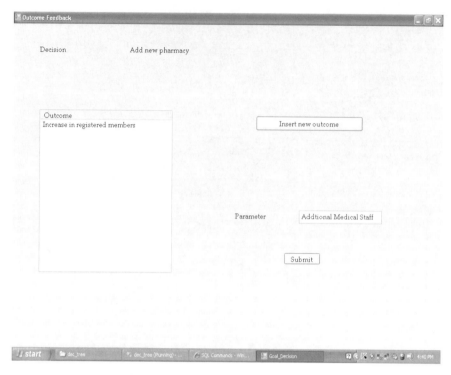

Fig. 7. Eliciting Parameters through Outcome Feedback Analysis

In the foregoing example we have one outcome that causes the feedback loop to close by reaching Add new pharmacy. In general, it is possible that a number of outcomes may be gone through before the starting decision is reached. Raju allows for this by allowing a number of outcomes to be entered. The one whose parameters are to be defined is selected and the parameters entered in the box on the screen. The closure of the feedback loop, that is, the outcome Add new pharmacy, in our example, is not entered in the outcome list.

2.3 Information Identifier

Raju uses heuristics to determine whether a parameter obtained through the Decision Parameter Guide is information or decision. These are as follows.

1. A parameter whose history is to be maintained. For example, registered members for the last five years. The history of the parameter registered members must be available for the last 5 years.
2. A parameter expressed category-wise. This category can be formed on temporal basis, for example, month-wise or on some semantic criterion like age wise, designation-wise etc.
3. A parameter that is a report or document.
4. A parameter that is obtained by applying a function like Count of, Average etc.

5. A parameter involving comparison. For example, comparison of our performance against others.

The example in Fig. 8 is for the parameter, number of patients serviced. It is seen that it is a report, its history is to be maintained, and the function max is to be applied. That is the report should contain a five year history of the maximum number patients serviced per year. Since this parameter satisfies more than one heuristic, it is information that is relevant to the decision with which the parameter, number of patients, is associated.

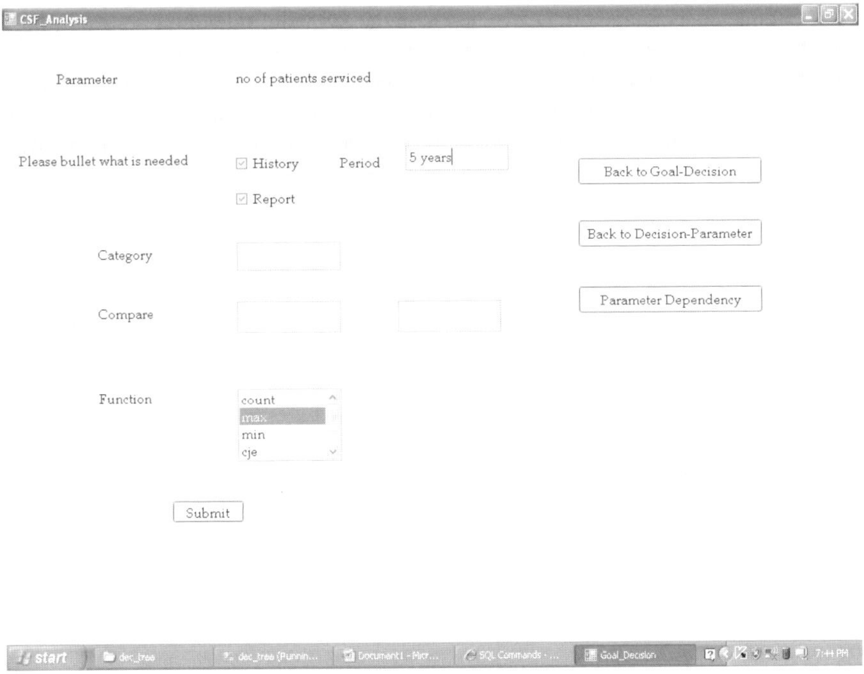

Fig. 8. Identifying Parameters as Information

2.4 Sub Decision Identifier

The sub decision identifier is charged with (a) determining which parameters are decisions, (b) determining the interrelationships between these newly postulated decisions and (c) applying our requirements engineering process of parameter elicitation etc. to each of these decisions.

Assume that P parameters were elicited for a decision and out of these I parameters are identified as information. Then (P-I) parameters are decision candidates. These (P-I) decisions may be related to one another. The requirements engineer elicits these relationships through a dependency graph. The dependency graph represents which decision is dependent upon which other one. As an example consider the Add new pharmacy decision once again. Let the parameters P for this decision be

P = { waiting time of patients, operationalizing time, operationalizing cost, change in patients serviced, additional medical staff, change in registration, amount of medicine disbursed, patient serving capacity, average waiting time}

Let the parameters I identified as information be

I = {waiting time of patients serviced, operationalizing time, operationalizing cost, change in patients serviced, change in registration, amount of medicine disbursed, average waiting time}

Therefore, the parameters that are decisions, D, are

D = {additional medical staff, patient serving capacity}

The parameters contained in D are shown on the left hand side of the screen of Fig. 9. Now, the requirements engineer draws a dependency graph on the right hand side of the screen by dragging and dropping the parameters. This dependency graph shows the decisions that are dependent on one another. Thus, starting from Add new pharmacy a hierarchy of decisions is constructed by the Sub Decision Identifier that shows which decision is the sub decision of which one. This hierarchy is stored in the repository. The newly discovered decisions are now sent through the requirements engineering process recursively till no new decisions are left.

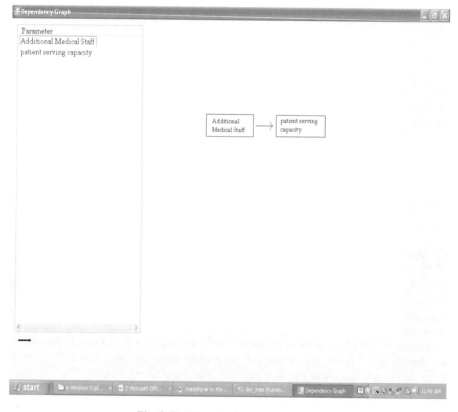

Fig. 9. Building the dependency graph

3 Impact: Comparison

A comparison of our approach with goal oriented techniques in requirements engineering has been made in (Pra08). Here we compare our approach to DW development with other prevalent approaches. A detailed description of this is available in (Pra09).

An operational database for a health organization was available to us. This organization runs a number of dispensaries all over the country. The database maintains data about each dispensary of the health scheme. To avail of health services in a dispensary, one must be registered in the health scheme and then opt for the most convenient dispensary. Information about the registered members in the health scheme as well as in the dispensary is maintained in the database. Additionally, the database keeps track of the doctors, pharmacies, laboratories and other facilities of the dispensary. Each visit of the registered member, the disease, diagnosis, prescriptions, recommended tests and their results etc. are also kept track of. Inventory information of medicines, X-ray films and other consumable and non-consumable items is maintained. When any of these gets depleted, it is indented from recognized chemists and the central store of the health scheme.

1. The Golfarelli (Gol99) life cycle: Start development with database schema.

This scheme assumes that the data contents of the operational databases more or less define the information contents of the data warehouse system to be built. Thus, a conversion of these into star/snowflake schemas is the major activity to be carried out. The basic idea is to examine each relation defined in the database(s) and identify whether it is a fact or a dimension. We believe that due to this, the technique is limited to the information in the database and identification of external sources and any other internal sources is difficult.

We used Oracle SQL Developer and Data Modeling tool Version: 1.5.1 (Ora) for developing the star schema of the health schema. The tool asked us to manually identify the relations that are facts and those that are dimensions. The dimension hierarchies and hierarchy levels were also to be specified manually. Based on this input, the tool created a snowflake schema. In applying this technique, we were not able to find any significant guidance on how to decide which relation is a fact or a dimension. Experience in applying the basic definitions of facts and dimensions available in the area of data warehousing, is essential.

Now consider deciding what historical data is to be maintained. Again, where temporal information is available in the operational database, one can assume that historical information shall also be needed in the data warehouse environment. For example, in our database, the date when a patient was examined is available. However, such temporal data was not available for indenting of depleted material. We needed to know if this is to be included in the data warehouse for projecting inventory requirements or not. Again this is ad-hoc and experience based and no guidance was available to us. Similarly, we found the definition of aggregates to be ad-hoc and experience based.

Involving stakeholders to look at every relation to identify facts is certainly possible but, in the absence of guidance, it is very ad-hoc and unsystematic. Stakeholders who are decision makers in an organization are not used to thinking in terms of relations and their mappings to data warehouse structures.

Finally, there is no articulation of the decision capability supported. Thus, if a decision maker wants to know what decisions are supported or whether a given decision is supported then it is not possible to do so. This is because no relationship is established between the data and the decision for which it might be relevant.

2. The Hüseman life cycle (Hüs00) that uses the ER schema

The ER diagram of our health schema was not available to us. Therefore, we developed it from the documentation of the health scheme and the relational schema of the operational database. The requirements engineering problem is centered round the conversion of the ER schema into star/snowflake schemas.

Again, as for the database oriented approach, the assumption is that data warehouse contents are more or less available in the ER diagrams. Again, due to this, the technique is limited to the information in the ER schemas and identification of external sources and any other internal sources is difficult.

Regarding maintaining history it is to be noted that the ER schema does not specifically cater to temporal information and the real focus is on entities, relationships and attributes. This was true about our health scheme ER diagram as well which does not contain any temporal information. Therefore, deciding on whether or not historical data is to be kept was difficult in the absence of any guideline. Again deciding on aggregation of data from the ER diagram is hard in the absence of any guidelines to do so. There is no provision in the ER technique that makes its developer examine aggregates. Though one can define derived attributes, summarized information as required in data warehouses is not systematically investigated in this approach.

Lastly, there is no effort made in relating the ER diagram to the decision making capability to be provided. Therefore, it is not possible to know whether information for a given decision could be found in the data warehouse or not. In other words, it is not possible to know the decision capability supported by the data warehouse.

3. The Goal-Decision-Information Approach

Now, let us consider the approach adopted in this paper and the use of Raju. This approach distinguishes between transactions/functions that are required for operational systems and the managerial decisions to be taken. Identification of these managerial decisions is outside the scope of the work reported here. In terms of Fig. 2, this identification refers to the upstream activities of decision and goal elicitation respectively.

For the health scheme example, we arrived at goals and decisions through an informal interview process and from the health scheme documentation available with us. Our experience is that this is a non-trivial exercise and appropriate elicitation techniques for this have to be developed.

The initial set of goals and decisions were entered into Raju. Clearly, the identified information is obtained in an unstructured form. No effort is made to determine facts and dimensions or to move to the star/snowflake schema. The focus in Raju is on information elicitation rather than on information structuring. As a result, the thought process of the requirements engineer is channeled and the requirements engineering team is made to focus on the task at hand.

There is a close relationship between decisions and the information relevant to these. Additionally, since Raju starts off with an initial set of decisions, the decision making capability is well defined and it is possible to know what is and what is not supported by a data warehouse.

The information obtained may be unstructured but it is possible to identify its properties through Raju. Thus, it is possible to identify historical data and the number of years of history required as well as aggregates. This became quite evident in the health scheme example and only reinforced the use of heuristics of Fig. 8.

4   Conclusion

There is marked difference between the fitment issue in data warehouse systems and traditional information systems. This difference arises because the former are oriented towards decision making done by managers whereas the latter support transactions/functions performed by 'end users'. To do rational decision making, managers need information about the state of the organization and expectations of various stakeholders. The identification of this information is therefore a crucial issue. Poorly identified information leads to data warehouses that do not meet the requirements of managers. In contrast, when support is to be provided for transactions/functions then the identification of these functions is crucial. Additionally, the process model should fit well with that of the organization.

We have shown in this paper that the focus of database driven and ER driven life cycles seems to be not so much on information identification as on determination of facts and dimensions. Indeed this focus is very pronounced and even the determination of historical and aggregated information is not easily supported by these life cycles. In other words, interest is in determining the structure of the star/snowflake schemata from given information. This begs the issue of identification of needed information.

The support provided by Raju for the GDI approach elicits information relevant to decisions of interest to managers. This information is broad, top-level but has the property that aggregates and historical information can be identified. An additional step of conversion to data warehouse schemata is necessary. Our assumption is that this can be done using the notions of information scenarios and SSQL reported in [Pra08].

This leaves us with investigating the upstream activities, decision elicitation and goal elicitation parts of Fig. 2. We have started investigating the decision elicitation part.

References

[Gol99] Golfarelli, M., Rizzi, S.: Designing the Data Warehouse: Key Steps and Crucial Issues. Journal of Computer Science and Information Management 2(3) (1999)

[Hüs00] Hüsemann, B., Lechtenbörger, J., Vossen, G.: Conceptual Data Warehouse Design. In: Proceedings of the International Workshop on Design and Management of Data Warehouses (DMDW 2000) Stockholm, Sweden, pp. 5–6 (2000)

[Mar91] James, G.: How decisions happen in organization. Human-Computer Interaction 6(2), 95–117 (1991)

[Mon86] Montazemi, A.R., Conrath, D.W.: The Use of Cognitive Mapping for Information Requirements Analysis. MIS Quarterly 10(1), 45–56 (1986)

[Ora], http://www.oracle.com/technology/products/database/sql_developer

[Pra04] Prakash, N., Singh, Y., Gosain, A.: Informational Scenarios for Data Warehouse Requirements Specification. In: Atzeni, P., Chu, W., Lu, H., Zhou, S., Ling, T.-W. (eds.) ER 2004. LNCS, vol. 3288, pp. 205–216. Springer, Heidelberg (2004)

[Pra08] Prakash, N., Gosain, A.: An Approach to Engineering the Requirements of Data Warehouses. Requirements Engineering Journal 13(1), 49–72 (2008)

[Pra09] Prakash, D.: Goal Oriented Requirements Engineering for Data Warehousing, M.Tech. thesis, IIIT Bangalore (2009)

[Ste89] Sterman, J.D.: Modeling Managerial Behaviour: Misperceptions of Feedback in a Dynamic Decision Making Experiment. Management Science 35(3), 321–339 (1989)

[Wet91] Wetherbe, J.C.: Executive Information Requirements: Getting it Right. MIS Quarterly 15(1), 51–65 (1991)

Evaluating Goal Achievement in Enterprise Modeling – An Interactive Procedure and Experiences

Jennifer Horkoff[1] and Eric Yu[2]

[1] Department of Computer Science
[2] Faculty of Information,
University of Toronto, Canada
jenhork@cs.utoronto.ca, yu@ischool.utoronto.ca

Abstract. Goal- and agent-oriented models have emerged as a way to capture stakeholder and organizational goals in a complex enterprise. The complexity of such models leads to a need for systematic procedures to enable users to evaluate and compare the alternative actions and solutions expressed in models. Many existing approaches focus on automated procedures, limiting the ability of the user to intervene. Here, we introduce a qualitative, interactive evaluation procedure for goal- and agent-oriented models, allowing the modeler to supplement the evaluation with domain knowledge not captured in the model. We provide a sample methodology to guide model creation and domain exploration which includes the evaluation of alternatives. We illustrate the procedure and methodology with the i* Framework. Case study experience shows that the procedure facilitates analysis, prompts iteration over model development, promotes elicitation, and increases domain understanding. We describe the results of an exploratory experiment designed to test these findings.

1 Introduction

Goal- and agent-oriented modeling frameworks, such as i* [1], have been introduced in order to model and explore socio-technical domains including actors or stakeholders, their goals and responsibilities, dependencies and alternatives. Although this approach has typically been used as a first step in a system development process, as part of "Early" Requirements Engineering, it can be used more generally as a tool in modeling and understanding an enterprise, including its internal operations and relationships to the external environment. Such models can be used to explore alternative courses of action, analyze their impacts on stakeholders, assess whether stakeholder objectives are met, and can help make tradeoffs among competing goals.

Consider a not-for-profit organization that provides phone counseling for youth, but is interested in reaching more youth using the Internet. Online counseling could be viewed by multiple individuals, and may provide a comforting distance which would encourage youth to ask for help. However, in providing counseling online, counselors lose cues involved in personal contact, such as body language or tone. Furthermore, there are concerns with confidentiality, protection from predators, public scrutiny over advice, and liability over misinterpreted guidance. How can such an organization explore and evaluate options for online counseling?

A. Persson and J. Stirna (Eds.): PoEM 2009, LNBIP 39, pp. 145–160, 2009.

Goal- and agent-oriented models which capture such socio-technical situations often form a complex web of relationships, with alternatives in the model contributing positively or negatively to certain goals, which themselves contribute to other goals. It is useful to assess the level of achievement of a goal in the model when a particular alternative is selected by considering the positive or negative evidence a goal has received via relationships with other goals. However, it can be difficult to trace the effect of a particular alternative on the satisfaction of one or more goals in the model when models contain multiple, multi-step paths of relationships represented with links in the model. There is a need for systematic analysis procedures which consider the effects of alternatives throughout the goal network, providing a consistent way to assign goal achievement levels via propagation along the links.

Models developed to consider enterprises at the goal level are often informal and incomplete, focusing on "soft" goals, such as privacy, which are difficult to precisely define. Such models are intended to be used as sketches, interactive recordings of an ongoing discovery process involving stakeholders and analysts. As the stakeholders express their viewpoints, as discussions occur, and as analysts learn more about the domain, such models undergo continuous change. An ideal analysis procedure would facilitate this process, prompting further discussion or elicitation and iteration over models.

A number of analysis procedures for analyzing goal models have been introduced (for example [2], [3], [4], and [5]). Most of these procedures have emphasized automated reasoning over goal models, placing more value in the results of the analysis than in the interactive process of analyzing and exploring the model. However, our experience has shown that the informal and incomplete nature of goal models used for both Enterprise Modeling and Early Requirement Analysis is better served by interactive, qualitative analysis, allowing for the use of domain-specific knowledge to compensate for model incompleteness, and allowing for an interactive process of inquiry and questioning concerning the model domain.

We introduce a qualitative, interactive evaluation procedure for goal- and agent-oriented models, allowing the user to compare alternatives in the domain, asking "what if?"-type questions. Alternatives can include alternative system or process design choices, or alternative courses of actions, capabilities, and commitments. We also introduce a sample methodology using this procedure to guide users through the process of modeling and evaluation. As goal models are often created manually as informal sketches, it is important for analysis procedures and methodologies to be easy to apply. We present the procedure informally, using prose, to facilitate easy understanding and manual application. Although the procedure has now been implemented in the open-source, Eclipse-based OpenOME tool [6], past case studies involved manual application of the procedure. The procedure is presented in terms of the i* Framework; however, the procedure could be applied to other goal- and agent-oriented models, such as those created using the NFR Framework [7] or GRL [3].

The procedure and variations of the sample methodology have been tested via application to case studies, including a long-term project involving a large social service application as summarized in [8], [9], and [10] and an analysis of the intentions behind controversial new technology [11]. Our experience shows that in addition to helping compare alternatives, the analysis facilitates iteration in the modeling process, resulting in an overall improvement in understanding of the model and domain. We have developed and administered an exploratory experiment involving the evaluation procedure in an attempt to test the benefits discovered through case study application.

The procedure introduced in this work expands on a procedure introduced in the NFR Framework [7]. A short description of the procedure in this paper appears in [12]. This paper is organized as follows: Section 2 describes the sample methodology, including a short description of the i* Framework, Section 3 describes the evaluation procedure introduced in this work, Section 4 provides case study examples of the benefits of i* evaluation, Section 5 describes the experiment and its results, Section 6 describes related work, while Section 7 contains discussion, conclusions, and future work.

2   Modeling and Analysis with Goal- and Agent-Oriented Models: A Sample Methodology

Goal- and agent-oriented modeling frameworks, such as i*, are general enough to be used in several contexts, for modeling of the general enterprise (see for example [8]), modeling for early or later-stage system development ([1] or [4]), modeling for knowledge management [9], modeling for process redesign [13], and so on. However, a general methodology can be described, including model analysis, which can be applicable for modeling in multiple contexts. Because of the variety in the context and aims of such types of modeling activities, we advocate this methodology as only a general guide, or series of suggestions. Depending on the context, the role of stakeholders, and the specific required outcome of the modeling process, the methodology can be adapted as needed. The central themes of the methodology are incremental model development with analysis and iteration over models.

Our experience with creating models has indicated that the process of modeling and analysis is as important, perhaps even more important, for understanding and discovery as the resulting models. Ideally, this approach would be applied in cooperation with domain representatives. This allows representatives to have a sense of ownership over the model and the decisions made as a result of the modeling process, as described in [14]. However, it may be difficult to acquire stakeholder buy-in to the modeling process, and in these cases analysts can undertake the modeling process using other sources, including interviews, documents and observations.

As we use i* as an example goal- and agent-oriented framework, a basic knowledge of i* syntax is helpful in understanding the example methodology. The i* Framework facilitates exploration of an enterprise with an emphasis on social aspects by providing a graphical depiction of system actors, intentions, dependencies, responsibilities, and alternatives [1]. The social aspect of i* is represented by *actors*, including *agents* and *roles*, and the associations between them, (is-a, part-of, plays, covers, occupies, instantiates), which can be represented in an Actor Association (AA) model. Actors depend upon each other for the accomplishment of *tasks*, the provision of *resources*, the satisfaction of *goals* and *softgoals*. *Softgoals* are goals without clear-cut criteria for satisfaction. Dependencies between actors are represented in Strategic Dependency (SD) models. Actors can be "opened-up" in Strategic Rationale (SR) models using *actor boundaries* containing the *intentions* of an actor: desired goals and softgoals, tasks to be performed, and resources available. The interrelationships between intentions inside an actor are depicted with *Decomposition* links, showing the elements which are necessary in order to accomplish a task; *Means-Ends* links, showing the alternative tasks which can accomplish a goal; and *Contribution* links, showing the effects of softgoals, goals, and tasks on softgoals. Positive/negative contributions representing evidence which is sufficient enough to satisfy/deny a softgoal are represented by *Make/Break* links, respectively. Contributions with positive/negative evidence that is not sufficient to satisfy/deny a softgoal are represented by *Help/Hurt* links.

Although we present the six steps of our example methodology in a sequence, each step will often lead to changes in the results of previous steps. If the methodology is followed without the direct participation of stakeholders, each stage may result in questions which should be answered by domain experts. This knowledge should be incorporated back into the model at any stage. We will illustrate the method using a simplified example from the first phase of the youth counseling case study described in the introduction, selected results from this phase of the study are described in [8].

1. **Identify scope or purpose of the modeling process.** It is important to identify one or more issues of focus for the modeling process. This determines the scope of the analysis in each of the modeling steps, continually questioning the relevance of including certain actors, dependencies and intentions.
   Example: In the social service example, the purpose of the first phase of the study was to identify and evaluate the effectiveness of various technical alternatives for providing online youth counseling.

2. **Identify model sources.** As stated, ideally the models would be created along with selected domain stakeholders. Alternatively, interviews, enterprise documents, observations or other sources can be used.
   Example: In the example, stakeholders were generally unfamiliar with modeling as a tool for analysis and had difficulty committing significant amounts of time. As a result, models were developed by the analysts using stakeholder interviews and site visits.

3. **Identify relevant actors and associations.** With the model scope in mind, identify relevant enterprise actors and the relationships between them. This could include specific stakeholders or more abstract roles or organizations. Helpful analysis questions include: "Who is involved?" and "How are they related?".
   Example: The actual case study identified 63 relevant actors. For our simplified example we will focus on youth, counselors and the counseling organization.

4. **Identify relevant dependencies.** In the same or a separate model, identify the dependencies between actors. Helpful analysis questions include: "Who needs what?" and "What do they provide in return?".
   Example: The actual case study identified 405 potentially relevant dependencies, a subset of these dependencies are depicted in Fig. 1. To save space we have shown only the SR model, which includes the actors in the AA model and the dependencies in the SD model.

5. **Identify actor intentions.** This stage is divided into three iterative sub-steps:

   a. **Identify actor intentions:** Using the sources, identify what actors want, what tasks they perform, how they achieve things.

b. **Match dependencies to actor intentions:** Using the dependencies found in Stage 4, answer "why?" and "how?" questions for each dependency, linking all dependencies to existing or new intentions within an actor.

c. **Identify relationships between intentions:** Identify how the actor intentions relate to each other, whether it is through a functional AND/OR hierarchy or through positive or negative contributions. New intentions may be discovered. Ideally, no intentions should be isolated.

Example: A subset of the intentional elements identified in the case study is shown in Fig.1. This model captures two alternative ways to provide counseling services: text messaging through a cell phone and an online Cybercafe/ Portal/Chat Room. The effects of each option on the goals of each of example actor are captured via contribution links to softgoals. Even for this simplified example, a complex web of contributions and dependencies are formed.

6. **Evaluate alternatives within in model.** Apply the evaluation procedure introduced in this work, described in more detail in the next section.

The first application of the model typically involves evaluating the most obvious alternative, and often helps to test the "sanity" of the model. Isolated intentions which do not receive an evaluation value can be identified.

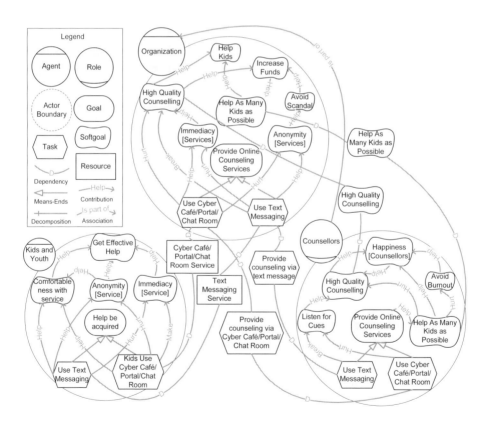

Fig. 1. Simplified Youth Counselling SR Example

Evaluation results which are not sensible can either reveal a problem in the model or an interesting discovery concerning the domain. Changes prompted by the evaluation results should be made in the model.

As the model evolves, more complicated or less obvious questions or alternatives can be analyzed. Further model changes can be made. The process continues until all viable alternatives are analyzed, an alternative has been selected, or a sufficient knowledge of the enterprise has been gained, depending on the initial purpose of the modeling process determined in Step 1.

Example: An example evaluation for the case study is presented in the next section as a means to illustrate the evaluation procedure. In the case study, several online counseling alternatives such as moderated forums, chats, email, and text messaging were analyzed and compared using the evaluation procedure.

3 A Qualitative, Interactive Evaluation Procedure for the i* Framework

Procedure Overview. The proposed procedure starts with an analysis question of the general form "How effective is an alternative with respect to model goals?". The procedure makes use of a set of qualitative evaluation labels, assigned to intentions to express their degree of satisfaction or denial. The process starts by assigning labels representing satisfaction and denial to intentions related to the analysis question. These values are propagated through the model links using defined rules. The interactive nature of the procedure comes when human judgment is used to combine multiple conflicting or partial values to determine the satisfaction or denial of a softgoal. The final satisfaction and denial values for the intentions of each actor are analyzed in light of the original question. An assessment is made as to whether the design choice is satisficed ("good enough"), stimulating further analysis and potential model refinement. More detail concerning the procedure can be found in [15].

Detailed Steps. We describe the steps of the evaluation procedure, followed by an explanation of the required concepts.

1. **Initiation:** The evaluator decides on an alternative and applies the initial evaluation labels to the model. The initial values are added to a label queue.

Iteratively, until the label queue is empty or a cycle is found:

2. **Propagation:** The evaluation labels in the label queue are propagated through all outgoing adjacent model links. Resulting labels propagated through non-contribution links are placed in the label queue. Results propagated through contribution links are placed into a "label bag" for that element.

3. **Softgoal Resolution:** Label bags are resolved by applying automatic cases or manual judgments, producing a result label which is added to the label queue.

4. **Analysis:** The final results are examined to find the impact of alternatives on stakeholder goals. Model issues can be discovered, further alternatives are evaluated.

Note that the procedure assumes that models are well-formed as per the syntax in [1]; however, as propagation is dependent on link type, most models can be evaluated.

Qualitative Evaluation Labels. We adopt the qualitative labels used in NFR evaluation, shown in Table 1. The *(Partially) Satisfied* label represents the presence of evidence which is *(insufficient)* sufficient to satisfy an intention. *Partially denied* and *denied* have the same definition with respect to negative evidence. *Conflict* indicates the presence of positive and negative evidence of roughly the same strength. *Unknown* represents the presence of evidence with an unknown effect. We use the "None" label to indicate a lack of any label. We use partial labels for tasks, resources, and goals, despite their clear-cut nature, to allow for greater expressiveness.

Initial Evaluation Values. In order to start an evaluation of a model, a set of initial values must be placed on the model, reflecting an analysis question and comprising Step 1 of the procedure. For example, in Fig. 1, if we wanted to ask "What is the effect of using a Cybercafe/Portal/Chat Room?", we would place initial values as shown in Fig 2 (circled labels).

Evaluation Propagation Rules. We define rules in order to facilitate a standard propagation of values given a link type and contributing label in Step 2 of the procedure. The nature of a *Dependency* indicates that if the element depended upon (*dependee*) is satisfied then the element depended for (*dependum*) and element depending on (*depender*) will be satisfied.

Decomposition links depict the elements necessary to accomplish a task, indicating the use of an AND relationship, selecting the "minimum" value amongst all of the values. Similarly, *Means-Ends* links depicts the alternative tasks which are able to satisfy a goal, indicating an OR relationship, taking the maximum values of intentions in the relation. To increase flexibility, the OR is interpreted to be inclusive. We expand the order of the values presented in the NFR Framework to allow for partial values, producing: None $< \textbf{✗} < \textbf{✗.} < \textbf{?} < \textbf{≈} < \textbf{✓.} < \textbf{✓}$.

We adopt the *Contribution* link propagation rules from the NFR procedure, as shown in Table 1. These rules intuitively reflect the semantics of contribution links. Note that the "None" label is not propagated or placed in the label queue.

Resolving Multiple Contributions. Softgoals are often recipients of multiple contribution links. We adopt the notion of a "Label Bag" from [7], used to store all incoming labels for a softgoal. Labels in the label bag are resolved into a single label in Step 3, either by identifying cases where the label can be determined without judgment (Table 2), or by human judgment. For example, in Fig. 2, the Immediacy [Service]

Table 1. Propagation Rules Showing Resulting Labels for *Contribution* Links

Source Label		*Contribution* Link Type						
	Name	Make	Help	Some+	Break	Hurt	Some-	Unkn.
✓	Satisfied	✓	✓.	✓.	✗	✗.	✗.	?
✓.	Partially Satisfied	✓.	✓.	✓.	✗.	✗.	✗.	?
≈	Conflict	≈	≈	≈	≈	≈	≈	?
?	Unknown	?	?	?	?	?	?	?
✗.	Partially Denied	✗.	✗.	✗.	✓.	✓.	✓.	?
✗	Denied	✗	✗.	✗.	✓.	✓.	✓.	?

Table 2. Cases where Overall Softgoal Labels can be Automatically Determined

Label Bag Contents	Resulting Label
1. The bag has only one label. Ex: {✗} or {✓•}	the label: ✗ or ✓•
2. The bag has multiple full labels of the same polarity, and no other labels. Ex: {✓, ✓, ✓} or {✗, ✗}	the full label: ✓ or ✗
3. All labels in the bag are of the same polarity, and a full label is present. Ex: {✓•, ✓, ✓•} or {✗, ✗}	the full label: ✓ or ✗
4. The human judgment situation has already occurred for this element and the answer is known	the known answer
5. A previous human judgment situation for this element produced ✓ or ✗, and the new contribution is of the same polarity	the full label: ✓ or ✗

softgoal in Kids and Youth receives a satisfied and a partially satisfied label from incoming contributions links, resolved to a satisfied label using Case 3 in Table 2, reflecting the idea that evidence propagated to softgoals is roughly cumulative.

Human Judgment in Evaluation. Human judgment is used to decide on a label for softgoals in Step 3 for the cases not covered in Table 2. Human judgment may be as simple as promoting partial values to a full value, or may involve combining many sources of conflicting evidence. When making judgments, domain knowledge related to the destination and source intentions should be used. In this way, we compensate for the inherent incompleteness of social models. Areas where human judgment is needed can be considered for further model expansion; however, given the tradeoff between completeness and model complexity, it may not be feasible to altogether avoid human intervention for a particular model.

For example, the resulting label for Happiness [Counselors] in Fig. 2 is determined by human judgment. This softgoal receives partially denied labels from Avoid Burnout and High Quality Counseling, but receives a partially satisfied label from Help as many Kids as Possible, according to the propagation rules in Table 1. Here, using our knowledge of the domain, we decide that Counselors would be mostly unhappy, labeling the softgoal as partially denied. Situations such as this would be good areas for potential discussions with stakeholders involved in the modeling process.

Combinations of Links. Intentions in i* are often the destination of more than one type of link. Following strict i* syntax, this occurs when an element is the recipient of a dependency link and a means-ends/decomposition link or a contribution link. "Hard" links (Decomposition, Means-Ends and Dependency) are combined using an AND of the final results of each link type. If Contribution and Dependency links share the same destination, the result of the Dependency links are treated as a Make contribution, considered with the other contributions in the label bag. An example of this type can be seen in High Quality Counseling in the Organization.

Incomplete Labels. In the procedure, information present in each step is propagated, even if this information in incomplete, i.e., other incoming contributions are missing. As a result, the evaluation labels for an element may change throughout the procedure and the same softgoal may require human judgment multiple times.

Detecting Cycles. Goal models often contain cycles, values which indirectly contribute to themselves and may cause fluctuating values. Our implementation of the procedure places a cap on the number of value fluctuations possible for an intention. Experience has shown that during manual application of the procedure the presence of cycles becomes apparent to the evaluator after a few iterations. We recommend that the evaluator manually selects appropriate converging values, marking the cycle as an area which may need further model refinement.

Example Evaluation. We return to the question posed in Section 2 concerning Fig. 2, "What is the effect of using a Cybercafe/Portal/Chat Room?". Results can be analyzed from the point of view of each actor. For Kids and Youth, the Cybercafe/Portal/Chat Room provides Immediacy as well as a Comfortable Service, but jeopardizes Anonymity, making the overall assessment weakly satisfied for Get Effective Help. From the point of view of Counsellors, the alternative has a positive effect on Help as Many Kids as Possible, but has a negative effect on Burnout and the Quality of Counselling, making the overall assessment to Counsellor Happiness weakly negative. From the point of view of the organization, the service also has a positive effect on Helping as Many Kids and Possible and Immediacy, but has a negative effect on Anonymity, Avoiding Scandal, Increasing Funds, and the Quality of Counselling. There is conflicting evidence for the

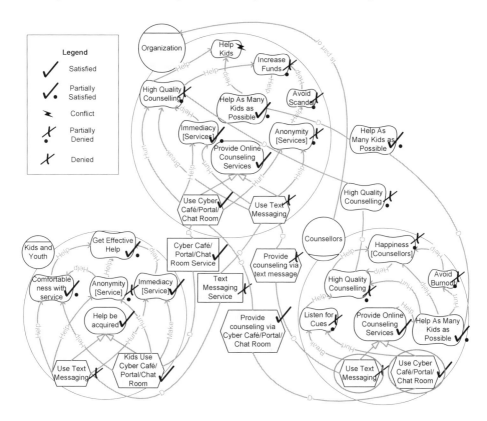

Fig. 2. Simplified Youth Counselling Example showing Final Evaluation Results

ability to Help Kids. Overall, this alternative is judged to be not viable. A further round of evaluation is needed to assess the other alternative in the model, text messaging, and to use the goals in the model to brainstorm further online counselling services which balance concerns more effectively.

4 Experience from Case Studies

We have applied our procedure and methodology to several case studies involving analysis of socio-technical settings, two of which are described here.

In the case study involving a large social service organization, [8], the evaluation procedure was applied in several stages. The first stage of the project is described in Section 2 as an illustrative application of our example methodology. Here the procedure was applied manually to large models (the largest had 353 intentions) in order to analyze and compare the effectiveness of technology options for providing counseling over the internet. The results were presented to the organization using reports and presentation slides containing small excerpts of the model. The analysis was well-received by the organization, bringing to light several issues and provoking interesting discussion. However, due partially to a lack of resources available to handle online counseling traffic, the organization opted to continue to use a modified version of the moderated bulletin board option already in place.

The next stage of the project focused on increasing the efficiency of the existing system. The evaluation procedure was used to analyze various configurations of a moderated bulletin board system, with feedback from the stakeholders used to validate the findings. The final outcome was a requirements specification document provided to the organization. Due to resource limitations and the risks involved in deploying a new system, the organization opted to modify their existing system instead of implementing a new system based on the specification.

A later phase of the project with the same organization focused on applying enterprise modeling to analyze the knowledge management needs of the organization [9]. The evaluation procedure was applied manually to large models in order to evaluate the situational effectiveness of a variety of technologies for storing and distributing knowledge, including wikis and discussions forums. It was discovered, for example, that the features of a wiki were not effective in satisfying the goals of the organization, while a discussion forum, with a set of specific features, showed more promise. We found the procedure to be effective in facilitating a comparison between technologies, with the results reported back to the organization in a series of reports, receiving positive stakeholder feedback. The largest model evaluated in the study contained 544 elements, helping to demonstrate the scalability of the procedure.

We used the opportunity presented by the case study to test the application of model patterns to i* modeling [10]. Here, general models representing technologies were integrated into context-specific models describing the organization. In this case, the patterns and the situational models involved underwent evaluation, using the models to answer various interesting questions, before integration. Our observations in this and other application of the procedure attest to the model iteration provoked by evaluation. For example, before evaluation in the pattern study a context-specific model focusing on communication contained 181 links and 166 elements, while after evaluation the same model had 222 links and 178 elements, a difference of 41 and 12 respectively. In another example, the link count rose from 59 to 96 and the element count rose from 59 to 76. These numbers do not take into account changes such as moving links or changing element names. Models in this study were created by three individuals with evaluation performed by two individuals, helping to demonstrate that this effect is not specific to a particular modeler or evaluator.

Our experience has shown that analysis can also be used as a means of understanding, justifying and explaining complex situations. Examples of this type can be found in a further case study, describe in [11], where evaluation is used to describe the motivations behind stakeholders involved in Trusted Computing (TC). Here, evaluation was used to help demonstrate the differences between proponents and opponents of Trusted Computing Technology, with proponents claiming it help to ensure security for the user, and opponents claiming the technology provided less security and more restrictions by enforcing Digital Right Management. The evaluation procedure helped to show the effects of these different perceptions on the goals of participating actors such as Technology Producers, License/Copyright Owners, Technology Consumers, and Malicious Parties, even when these actors and their goals were not directly connected to the differing effects of TC technology.

Our case study experience demonstrated the ability of the procedure to provoke further elicitation and subsequent model iteration. For example, in the TC case study, although the model appeared to be sufficiently complete, one of the first rounds of analysis of the TC Opponent point of view revealed that Technology Users would not buy TC Technology. Although this may be the case for some Users, obviously the makers of TC Technology envisioned some way in which users would accept their product. These results led the modeler to further investigate the sources, including factors such as product lock-in, more accurately reflecting the domain.

Prompted by our case study experience, we developed and carried out an exploratory experiment designed to test some of the perceived benefits of the procedure, described in the next section.

5   Experimental Results

Observations in case studies have shown that the evaluation procedure described in this work aids in finding non-obvious answers to analysis questions, prompts improvements in the model, leads to further elicitation, and leads to a better understanding of the domain. Our experiment begins to test whether these effects are specific to our procedure or are a product of any detailed examination of a model.

The experimental models were taken from a study applying goal-oriented analysis to the sustainability issues for the ICSE conference [16]. The study produced a series of models focusing on actors in the domain of conference planning. For the experimental investigation, the five participants of that study, including one of the authors, were asked to evaluate two different questions over three models, once without using the procedure and, after training, once using the procedure. The results were compared in terms of analysis findings, questions discovered, model changes, and time taken. The three models contained between 36 and 79 intentions, 50 and 130 links, and 5 and 15 actors. Participants were given two non-trivial analysis questions related to goal satis-faction specific to each of the three models. Participants were asked to answer follow-up questions: Did model changes improve the model quality? Do you have a better understanding of the model and domain? Did this increase more or less, with or without using the procedure? Would you use the procedure again?

We examine several aspects of the results. First the differences in analysis results not using, and then using the procedure, helping to show that the procedure finds non-obvious analysis answers. We observe that the participants made a total of 40 changes to their analysis results after applying the procedure and that changes were made for each question over each model. All participants made changes to their analysis re-sults, with each participant making between 7 and 11 total changes in all question-model combinations. A breakdown of the types of changes is omitted due to space restrictions.

Next, we count the changes made to the models not using and using the procedure. Overall, in evaluating two questions over three models, the 5 participants made a total of 71 changes without using the procedure and then 40 changes using the procedure. Changes were made for each model, and all participants made changes. These results may indicate that the iteration provoked by the procedure may have more to do with forcing the user to carefully manually examine the model than with the procedure itself. However, we note that the participants found 40 additional changes using the procedure to answer the questions for the second time.

In examining the model quality improvement, three out of five participants said that changes made to the models improved the quality of the model. These partici-pants indicated the quality was improved through changes made both with and with-out the procedure. The other two participants did not feel they had made significant changes to the models in either stage, with one stating that "additional knowledge information would be needed to really improve the quality of the models", and the other echoing the sentiment. These results help to emphasize the incomplete and iterative nature of such models, and their ability to prompt further elicitation. Along this line, we observe that participants came up with between 5 and 16 questions each, at total of 26 questions were derived without using the procedure, while an additional 19 were derived while using the procedure, for a total of 45. Although many ques-tions were derived without using the procedure, we observe that application of the procedure provoked a number of further questions, even though the same analysis questions were being evaluated.

All five participants reported a better understanding of the domain after this exer-cise, with all participants claiming that they gained a better understanding using the evaluation procedure than using no procedure. The average time to answer a question without the procedure was 9.5 minutes (standard deviation of 4.6) compared to 11.1 minutes (standard deviation of 6.0) using the procedure. Although the variance is high, we see that working with procedure takes only slightly more time than without. Finally, all five participants said they would use the procedure again if they had to evaluate another i* model.

6 Related Work

Goal concepts are prominent in a number of modeling frameworks, notably in "goal-oriented" requirements engineering (e.g. [17] and [18]) as well as in enterprise modeling e.g. [14], [19]. While all of these frameworks provide for the representation of goals and relationships among goals, only some of the frameworks have associated procedures for determining whether goals are met, for example [2], [3], [4], and [5]. Most of these procedures have taken a more formal, automated, or quantitative approach to goal model analysis. We argue that such procedures are more suitable later in the analysis, when more complete and detailed system information is available, and where models are more stable and appropriate for automated reasoning. The interactive, qualitative approach, such as the one introduced in this work, is more appropriate for early analysis, to gain a high-level understanding of the domain, and to discover and evaluate alternatives with stakeholders. Once the number of alternatives has been narrowed using interactive, qualitative evaluation, more detailed information can be added to the model and various forms of quantitative or automated analysis can be applied in order to further test the feasibility of a particular alternative.

An interactive qualitative evaluation procedure based on the notion of goal "satisficing" was first introduced to evaluate Softgoal Interdependency Graphs as part of the NFR Framework [7]. Previous work has used this procedure evaluate i* models, (see [14] for example), assuming that the NFR procedure could be easily extended for use with i*, without describing the necessary extensions, modifications, or additional benefits. Application of the NFR procedure to i* models in case studies such as [11] has shown that the level of interactivity is too restrictive, assigning a conflict label to all goals with conflicting evidence. We build upon this earlier procedure by introducing aspects which cover agent-oriented concepts, providing steps for application, adjusting the use of human intervention and more thoroughly exploring issues such as initial values and convergence.

Alternative methodologies to direct the creation of i* models have been introduced. The RESCUE method, aimed for system design or redesign, directs the development of several streams of models in parallel including i*, activity, use case, and requirements models [21]. The Process Reengineering i* Method (PRiM) builds on this approach, constructing i* models to understand and redesign business processes and associated information systems [13]. The methodology introduced in Section 2 is more general, applicable to modeling aspects of an enterprise which may or may not be specific to an information system or to actors involved in a particular process.

7 Discussion, Conclusions, and Future Work

In this work, we have identified the need for systematic evaluation of alternatives within models capturing the goals of an enterprise. We have introduced a simple procedure which builds on the NFR procedure, expanding the procedure to deal with agent-specific constructs, and more thoroughly exploring issues such as initial values, propagation rules, and human judgment. A sample methodology describing how to use this procedure in the process of enterprise modeling has been presented. We have explored the benefits the methodology and evaluation procedure, including analysis, model iteration, and elicitation by describing application to two case studies.

Experience has shown that it is difficult to acquire stakeholder buy-in to the modeling process, often due to the considerable time taken by the process or unfamiliarity with modeling as an analysis tool. Existing case studies have involved modeling and evaluation by analysts using interviews, documents, or site observations. Although this process is very useful to help the analysts understand and explore the domain, it is difficult to fully present or validate the resulting models and the results of evaluation. While the analysts who have constructed the model and performed the evaluations are able to understand the model and evaluation results, the models are too large and the evaluation results are too complicated to be easily understood by stakeholders. Thus far, we have only investigated model evaluation in the context of a single modeler. Future work should investigate its role in collaborative or group settings. Although experimental results provide some confidence in the ability of users to learn and apply evaluation, participatory studies would help to confirm the ability of domain users to apply the procedure on their own. Such studies would also help to further assess the mechanism of evaluation, including the appropriateness of propagation rules.

Results of our exploratory experiment indicate that the evaluation procedure prompts changes to evaluation results and may prompt model iteration and elicitation beyond analysis without a systematic procedure. The participants have reported that the procedure provides a better understanding of the model and domain. However, the experiment suffers from several threats to validity, including the small number of participants. Using the lessons learned from this experiment, we hope to conduct further experiments with more participants. Future experiments should try to push the limits of evaluation without a systematic procedure by asking participants to examine the model multiple times. Further studies can explore the perceived benefits of the applying the procedure, including studies to determine whether these benefits are specific to the qualitative, interactive procedure introduced in this work, or apply more generally to other Goal- and Agent-Oriented evaluation procedures.

In order to make our description of the evaluation procedure more concrete, we have applied it to the i* Framework, potentially limiting applicability. However, as most other Goal- and/or Agent-Oriented Frameworks, such as the NFR Framework [7] or GRL [3], are syntactic subsets of i*, our procedure can be easily extended to other, similar frameworks. Future work could include adapting and applying the evaluation procedure described in this work for use with other goal modeling frameworks, such as the goal component in EKD models.

The procedure introduced in this work can be expanded in several ways, for example: capturing the rationale and assumptions behind human judgments, evaluating the satisfaction of actors as in [3], expanding analysis in a top-down direction as explored in [22], allowing for constraints as in [2], facilitating the traceability of evidence, and giving users selection over different qualitative scales.

Acknowledgements. Financial support has been provided by the Natural Sciences and Engineering Research Council of Canada, Bell University Laboratories, and the Ontario Graduate Scholarship Program.

References

1. Yu, E.: Towards Modelling and Reasoning Support for Early-Phase Requirements Engineering. In: 3rd IEEE International Symposium on Requirements Engineering (RE 1997), pp. 226–235. IEEE Press, New York (1997)
2. Giorgini, P., Mylopoulos, J., Sebastiani, R.: Simple and Minimum-Cost Satisfiability for Goal Models. In: Persson, A., Stirna, J. (eds.) CAiSE 2004. LNCS, vol. 3084, pp. 20–35. Springer, Heidelberg (2004)
3. Amyot, D., Ghanavati, S., Horkoff, J., Mussbacher, G., Peyton, L., Yu, E.: Evaluating Goal Models within the Goal-oriented Requirement Language. Int. Journal of Intelligent Systems (IJIS) (to appear)
4. Letier, E., van Lamsweerde, A.: Reasoning about Partial Goal Satisfaction for Requirements and Design Engineering. In: 12th ACM International Symposium on the Foundations of Software Engineering (FSE 2004), pp. 53–62. ACM, New York (2004)
5. Franch, X.: On the Quantitative Analysis of Agent-Oriented Models. In: Dubois, E., Pohl, K. (eds.) CAiSE 2006. LNCS, vol. 4001, pp. 495–509. Springer, Heidelberg (2006)
6. OpenOME, https://se.cs.toronto.edu/trac/ome/wiki
7. Chung, L., Nixon, B.A., Yu, E., Mylopoulos, J.: Non-Functional Requirements in Software Engineering. Kluwer Academic Publishers, Norwell (2000)
8. Easterbrook, S.M., Yu, E., Aranda, J., Fan, Y., Horkoff, J., Leica, M., Qadir, R.A.: Do Viewpoints Lead to Better Conceptual Models? An Exploratory Case Study. In: 13th IEEE International Requirements Engineering Conference (RE 2005), pp. 199–208. IEEE Press, New York (2005)
9. Strohmaier, M., Yu, E., Horkoff, J., Aranda, J., Easterbrook, S.: Analyzing Knowledge Transfer Effectiveness - An Agent-Oriented Approach. In: 40th Hawaii International Conference on Systems Science (HICSS-40), p. 188b. IEEE Press, New York (2007)
10. Strohmaier, M., Horkoff, J., Yu, E., Aranda, J., Easterbrook, S.: Can Patterns improve i* Modeling? Two Exploratory Studies. In: Paech, B., Rolland, C. (eds.) REFSQ 2008. LNCS, vol. 5025, pp. 153–167. Springer, Heidelberg (2008)
11. Horkoff, J., Yu, E., Liu, L.: Analyzing Trust in Technology Strategies. In: International Conference on Privacy, Security and Trust (PST 2006), pp. 21–32 (2006)
12. Horkoff, J., Yu, E.: A Qualitative, Interactive Evaluation Procedure for Goal- and Agent-Oriented Models. In: CAiSE Forum. CEUR Workshop Proceedings (2009)
13. Grau, G., Franch, X., Maiden, N.A.M.: PRiM: an i*-based process reengineering method for information systems specification. Information and Soft. Tech. 50(1-2), 76–100 (2008)
14. Stirna, J., Persson, A.: Ten Years Plus with EKD: Reflections from Using an Enterprise Modeling Method in Practice. In: Pernici, B., Gulla, J.A. (eds.) Proceedings of the 11th International Workshop on Exploring Modeling Methods in Systems Analysis and Design (EMMSAD 2007), pp. 99–108. CEUR-WS.org (2007)
15. Horkoff, J.: An Evaluation Algorithm for the i* Framework. Master's Thesis, Department of Computer Science, University of Toronto (2006)
16. Cabot, J., Easterbrook, S., Horkoff, M.J., Lessard, L., Liaskos, S.: Integrating Sustainability in Decision-Making Processes: A Modelling Strategy. In: ICSE 2009 New Ideas and Emerging Results, NIER 2009 (2009)
17. van Lamsweerde, A.: Goal-Oriented Requirements Engineering: A Guided Tour. In: 5th IEEE International Symposium on Requirements Engineering (RE 2001) (invited paper), pp. 249–263. IEEE Press, New York (2001)

18. Kavakli, E., Loucopoulos, P.: Goal Driven Requirements Engineering: Analysis and Critique of Current Methods. In: Krogstie, J., Halpin, T., Siau, K. (eds.) Information Modeling Methods and Methodologies, pp. 102–124. Idea Group (2004)
19. Rolland, C., Prakash, N.: Bridging the Gap Between Organisational Needs and ERP Functionality. Requirements Engineering 5(3), 180–193 (2000)
20. Liu, L., Yu, E.: Designing Information Systems in Social Context: A Goal and Scenario Modelling Approach. Information Systems 29(2), 187–203 (2004)
21. Maiden, N.A.M., Jones, S.V., Manning, S., Greenwood, J., Renou, L.: Model-Driven Requirements Engineering: Synchronising Models in an Air Traffic Management Case Study. In: Persson, A., Stirna, J. (eds.) CAiSE 2004. LNCS, vol. 3084, pp. 368–383. Springer, Heidelberg (2004)
22. Horkoff, J., Yu, E.: Qualitative, Interactive, Backward Analysis of i* Models. In: 3rd International i* Workshop, pp. 43–46. CEUR-WS.org (2008)

The Impact of Secondary Notation on Process Model Understanding

Matthias Schrepfer[1], Johannes Wolf[1], Jan Mendling[1], and Hajo A. Reijers[2]

[1] Humboldt-Universität zu Berlin
Unter den Linden 6, 10099 Berlin, Germany
jan.mendling@wiwi.hu-berlin.de
[2] Eindhoven University of Technology
PO Box 513, 5600 MB Eindhoven, The Netherlands
h.a.reijers@tue.nl

Abstract. Models of business processes are usually created and presented using some visual notation. In this way, one can express important activities, milestones, and actors of a process using interconnected graphical symbols. While it has been established for other types of models that their graphical layout is a factor in making sense of these, this aspect has not been investigated in the business process modeling area. This paper proposes a set of propositions about the effects of the secondary notation, which entails layout, on process model comprehension. While individual graphical readership and pattern recognition skills are known mediators in interpreting visual cues, these propositions take expertise into account. The goal of this paper is to lay the foundation of follow-up, empirical investigations to challenge these propositions.

Keywords: process modeling, secondary notation, comprehension, modeling expertise.

1   Introduction

Business process models have become an integral part of organizational engineering efforts. They are used both on the business level for describing business operations in a consistent way as well as on the technical level for specifying requirements that have to be supported by enterprise software. As a consequence, business process design is now one of the major reasons for conducting conceptual modeling projects [14]. The process models created in these initiatives capture among others what tasks, events, states, and control flow logic constitute a business process. The different symbols for these elements are part of the graphical notation of process modeling languages. Using a process modeling tool, these symbols are typically placed on a modeling canvas and connected with arcs. The result is a visual model that represents a business process.

Business process models play an important role in facilitating documentation and communication between different stakeholders in a process design project.

A. Persson and J. Stirna (Eds.): PoEM 2009, LNBIP 39, pp. 161–175, 2009.

Therefore, they should be created in a way to best serve this purpose. A major requirement is that they reveal their content in an intuitive and easily understandable manner [15]. Prior research has shown that several factors influence the understanding of a process model; for instance, complex models created by human modelers are more likely to contain errors [26], modeling expertise appears to improve understanding performance [24], and characteristics of the modeling notation have a direct impact on comprehension [19].

While these factors are well covered by current research, the influence of graphical layout on understanding is partly acknowledged (e.g. in [24]) but not yet thoroughly investigated for process models. We address this research gap by revisiting empirical findings on graph aesthetics in this paper. We also discuss in detail how modeling expertise interacts with the quality of the graphical layout of a process model. Our contribution is a set of propositions that builds on a sound theoretical foundation of cognitive research. These propositions are a starting point for investigating the influence of graph layout on process model understanding empirically.

The paper proceeds accordingly. Section 2 motivates the importance of graphical layout by the help of a process model example. Furthermore, we introduce secondary notation as a cognitive dimension relevant to this problem. Section 3 discusses expertise as an important factor that interacts with layout quality. We revisit related work on computer programme comprehension, and discuss its relevance to process model layout. Section 4 presents propositions that build on the theoretical discussion of the previous sections. In Section 5 we discuss different measurement options for an operationalization of the propositions in an experiment. Section 6 closes the paper with a conclusion and an outlook on future research.

2   Graphical Layout and Understanding

This section discusses the relevance of graphical layout for model understanding. We stick to the Business Process Modeling Notation (BPMN) to illustrate our argument. The BPMN specification provides a standardized graphical notation that is meant to be easily understandable by all relevant stakeholders [37]. It offers notation elements for activities, events, and routing conditions (gateways), which are connected by control flow arcs.

Figure 1 presents a sales process modeled in BPMN. The process starts with the submission of a quote. The customer and the company then negotiate the contract. If both parties cannot agree on the contract, they can re-negotiate it. Instead, they can also decline the contract such that it is archived. Once the parties agree on the contract, the responsible department approves it depending on the contract value. If it is below five million dollar, the sales department approves the contract. If the value is larger or equal to that amount, the regional manager must approve the contract. Following the approval, the user deal is concluded. After the contract is archived, the business process ends.

The whole process in Figure 1 is built using different BPMN notation elements that are connected by arcs. The process is initiated with a start *event* which is

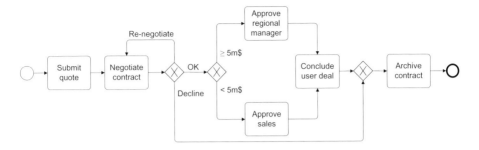

Fig. 1. Sales Process Model in BPMN (Good Layout)

depicted as a circle. There are different events in BPMN which usually affect the process flow. Events occur due to a trigger or they mark a result [37]. Rounded-corner rectangles mark *activities* in the process model, which represent different tasks to be performed within a process. After the activity 'Negotiate Contract' an XOR *gateway* is reached and shown as a diamond shape. It defines a decision point. BPMN offers different gateways including XOR, AND, and OR to control the sequence flow in a business process model. The BPMN process terminates with an end event, drawn as a circle with a bold line.

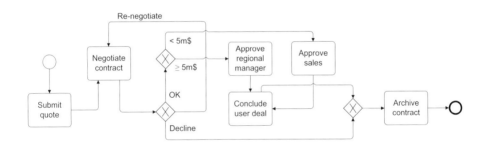

Fig. 2. Sales Process Model in BPMN (Bad Layout)

Although BPMN specifies the set of notation elements to be used in a process model, it does not make any normative statements on how the elements should be positioned. Figure 1 and Figure 2 illustrate this fact by showing the same sales process using two different layouts. Although the processes differ in their visual representation, the process models are identical from a logical point of view. Their semantics are the same, but their effect on the human reader might still be different in terms of understanding. Cognitive research into program compre-hension has coined the terms first notation and secondary notation to describe this phenomenon. The modeling notation as a formal set of symbols is defined as *first notation*. First notation specifies the semantics of all graphical elements of a particular notation such as BPMN. However, the visual characteristics of the model are not limited by first notation. By enriching the process model with information beyond the formal notation (e.g. color, line strength, etc.), the reader may access the information captured in the model with a differing degree of ease [28]. Visual cues, which are not part of a notation, are known as *secondary notation* [28,29]. Among others, the model designer is free in selecting the graphical position of model elements. Accordingly, we can state that the models presented in Figure 1 and Figure 2 differ in terms of secondary notation. Although these visual cues do not change the semantics of a model, they have been identified as an important factor of model comprehension in prior research [27,28].

It is important to note that secondary notation is not constrained in its use. Graphical layout is one particular aspect of secondary notation that is known to influence understanding [30]. It is an appealing feature of graphical layout that it can be traced back to a number of layout parameters. For some domains, e.g. electronics, several hints and rules exist how and when secondary notation should be used [20]. Also model designers often use rules of thumb when changing layout parameters [28]. The priority of these rules may even be adjusted while a model is created. Prior research has shown that the comprehension of graphical layout of a model depends upon a number of parameters [10,28,30,31]. Some of these parameters have been identified as having a strong influence with respect to the understanding of a model [28,30]. In the following, the most relevant layout factors with respect to graphical layout are presented by mentioning their effect on overall understanding and by relating them to the two versions of the sales process.

- **Line Crossings:** The higher the number of crossings within a graphical layout, the lower the readability of that layout [28]. In [30] it is shown that line crossings influence the understanding most of all. The model in Figure 1 does not contain any line crossings while the model in Figure 2 contains three crossings.
- **Edge Bends:** The number of edge bends negatively affects the understanding of a process model [30,31]. The graphical layout of the process model in Figure 1 contains eight edge bends, the model shown in Figure 2 exhibits 12 bends.
- **Symmetry:** Graphical layouts where elements are placed more symmetric are easier readable. However, the effect of symmetry is lower than the one of line crossings [30,31]. The graphical elements, activities 'Approve regional manager' and 'Approve sales', are shown symmetrically in the model presented in Figure 1 while in the other model they are not placed symmetrically.
- **Use of Locality:** Graphical elements which are related to each other shall be placed close to each other making them easier recognizable and leading to a higher understanding of the model [29]. The activity 'Approve sales' in the model depicted in Figure 2 is not positioned close to the preceding XOR-gateway.

The significance of these layout parameters for comprehension builds on cognitive insights regarding the process of reading and understanding a process model. There are two aspects of this process that are influenced by the visual representation. *Graphical readership* describes the ability to read a business process model. This means, first, to identify the graphical elements and visual cues shown in the model, and second, to interpret their individual meaning specified in the modeling notation [13,28]. The process of reading a process model is less a matter of intuition because the reader has to understand the semantics of modeling notation. Order is an important concept of process models, and Figure 2 aims to illustrate that it can be obfuscated by unappropriate layout. The second important aspect is *pattern recognition*. As the term emphasizes, a model usually contains certain patterns that altogether describe a specific behavior within a business process. Several workflow patterns such as the Exclusive Choice have been described in [1]. A model reader must recognize a pattern in the graphical layout in order to access the information described by the pattern. The sales process includes the Exclusive Choice pattern combined with a Simple Merge. Together they define a more complex decision block, which is obfuscated in Figure 2. Furthermore, there is a Structured Loop pattern (see [34]) at the activity 'Negotiate contract'. Again, this pattern is easily visible in Figure 1, but not in Figure 2. In large process models, it is likely to be more difficult to recognize workflow patterns that are obfuscated by bad layout. Both aspects, graphical readership and pattern recognition, are influenced by layout parameters, and they contribute to the understanding of a process model.

3   Modeling Expertise and Understanding

In the previous section we identified the impact of layout on graphical readership and pattern recognition. Clearly, graphical readership and pattern recognition skills vary between readers of a model. Therefore, model comprehension has to be correlated with these individual skills.

Consider again the two versions of BPMN sales model from the previous chapter, and assume it is presented to both a first-year Bachelor's student in Information Systems, and a professor with a research focus on process modeling. Both individuals get the task to read and interpret these process models. Even without a proper analysis of knowledge and skills of both individuals, we would assume that the professor is much faster and more accurate in understanding compared to the first-year student. The advantage of the professor can be traced back to his gained expertise and his extensive knowledge in the field of process modeling. This does not only cover the graphical elements of the notation (graphical readership) which might be new or even unfamiliar to the student. Furthermore, the professor will likely be able to recognize common patterns in the model (pattern recognition). Besides these rather obvious statements, the comparison between the student and the professor is not directly clear when the layout is changed. How will the variation in layout influence the relative performance? Before giving a preliminary answer to this question, we revisit different aspects and constructs related to expertise.

The importance of modeling expertise for process modeling has been confirmed in different works. The survey by Bandara on success factors of process modeling establishes modeler expertise as a critical issue [6]. This success factor describes "the experiences of the person conducting the modeling, in terms of conceptual modeling in general and process modeling in particular." A set of sub-constructs is also identified including *required skills, knowledge* and *experience*. In this way, the factor also covers the criterion *user training* that captures the extent of knowledge given to a users about the modeling tool and modeling procedures. *Language expertise* is mentioned in [5] as a more specific factor. Corresponding scales have been defined by Recker for *familiarity* with a modeling language.

Expertise as a general factor for process modeling comprehension has also been confirmed in experimental designs. Mendling and Strembeck find that theoretical knowledge has a significant influence on process model understanding such that experienced modelers perform better in understanding [25]. Similar observations are made in [24] where understanding tasks were presented to 73 students from three European universities. A significant difference was observed in comprehension performance among the three group, which was traced back to a broader and deeper teaching of Petri nets at one university. This study discusses a potential threat to validity in terms of expertise. Student could be classified as novices, such that the results would not hold for professionals who are experts in the field. For this reason, the results are discussed with 12 professional process modelers for their conclusiveness [24]. In an experiment on modularity, 28 Dutch process consultants are involved who are assumed to be experts [33].

The definition of the concept of expertise turns out to be quite challenging. In demotic definitions the condition of being an expert is used to describe the term expertise. It is often related to extensive skill or knowledge in a particular field [36]. Green et al. describe expertise from a cognitive sciences point of view. "Expertise is not only a characteristic of higher-order cognitive logic but also of perceptual logic, that can be trained to better support cognitive operations through 'perceptual expertise'" [18]. The aspect that expertise is based on trained skills and gained knowledge seems to be of the utmost importance. The field of psychology has analyzed the notion of expert and exceptional performance [16]. There, expert performance is characterized by a "varying balance between training and experience (nurture) on one hand and innate differences in capacities and talents (nature) on the other" whereas "experts knowledge and task-specific reactions must have been acquired through experience". This understanding builds upon the *theory of expertise* formulated by Chase and Simon in 1973 [12]. They postulated that expertise is "the result of acquiring, during many years of experience in their domain, vast amounts of knowledge and the ability to perform pattern-based retrieval". Although expertise is often equated with "the amount and complexity of knowledge gained through extensive experience of activities in a domain", it is stated that this criterion is not sufficient for measuring an individual's performance on a task [16]. Bonner and Pennington noticed that "most experts are highly specialized, and task-specific experience is a better, but still modest, predictor of performance" [8].

An important feature of expertise can be highlighted by the so-called *10-years rule of necessary preparation*. According to this rule, not even the most talented individuals can attain international performance without approximately 10 years of preparation. Ericsson and Lehmann found out that the mere number of years of experience with relevant activities in a domain is typically only weakly related to performance [16]. Individualized training activities designed to improve specific aspects of an individuals performance through repetition and successive refinement seem to play a more important role because they cause physiological and neurological adaption in the body. These training activities where labeled by Ericsson and Lehmann as *deliberate practice*. They found out that a daily amount of four hours of fully concentrated training appears to be a sustainable basis for most humans. In addition, the correlation of talent and expert performance suggests that talent, i.e. innate domain-specific basic capacities, has a small, possibly negligible impact on expert performance. Hence, an individual's performance who solely gained years of expertise is much lower than those of an expert who took part in an substantial amount of training and practice. Experts make extensive use of planning, reasoning, anticipating and controlling in order to face new learning tasks and to increasingly improve their performance.

There are some perspectives on expertise that are prone to wrong conclusions. The levels of expertise are often discussed by referring to the terms *novice* and *expert* in order to indicate a rather weak or strong expertise (see e.g. the notion of 'expert modeler' in [5]). This distinction is problematic because there exists no clear definition of both terms, making it difficult to unambiguously identify people as novices or experts. In this way, the spectrum between low and high expertise is ignored. The terms novice and expert are sometimes also used in a simplifying way by equating novices with students and experts with professionals, which is an classification to be justified. Beyond that, relying on a *self-assessment* has been found unsuitable for identifying novices and experts in different works. In [24] it was shown that self-assessment of students concerning their process modeling knowledge is not correlated to their performance in understanding. Similar observations have been made in [9]. This clarifies the necessity of an objective and systematic assessment of a person's process modeling expertise.

Summing up, current research makes wide use of the terms *novice* and *expert* but evades to define these constructs and tends to use them in a demotic way. This approach may be sufficiently for nominally distinguishing between weak and strong expertise, but can hardly be used for more finely granulated levels of distinction. When talking about process model understanding based on a model's secondary notation, a more detailed distinction between levels of expertise would be useful. Therefore a combination of the presented approaches should be considered using a combination of information given by the individual itself (e.g. duration and frequency of practical experience and training), plus additionally an objective measure of the individual's skills (e.g. the ability of

Table 1. The different Aspects of Expertise

Aspect	Authors
Modeler expertise (skills, knowledge, experience) User training and competence	Bandara [6, p.169]
Modeling language expertise	Aranda [5]
Familiarity with language	Recker [32]
Self-assessment of theoretical knowledge Self-assessment of practical experience Students versus Practitioners	Mendling, Reijers, Cardoso [24]
Theoretical knowledge Time of being involved with process modeling Intensity of being involved with process modeling	Mendling and Strembeck [25]
Years of work experience at process consultancy Years of field experience in process consulting Highest eduction degree Estimated number of modeled processes Estimated average size of modeled processes	Mendling and Reijers [33]
Perceptual expertise	Green et al. [18]
Exceptional performance (training, experience, and talent) Expert performance (amount and complexity of knowledge, and task-specific experience) Experts performance (number of years of experience and deliberate practice)	Ericsson and Lehmann [16] Bonner and Pennington [8]
Experience Knowledge Ability to recognize patterns	Chase and Simon [12]
Non-validity of self-assessment	Mendling, Reijers, Cardoso [24] Burton-Jones and Meso [9]

pattern-recognition and graphical readership). In contrast to earlier research experiments, this approach should highlight the aspect of individual skills and abilities and do not only focus on the amount of both theoretical and practical knowledge and experience. An important step will be to reveal *how* and *to what extent* individuals gained perceptual expertise through intensive training and make use of certain mechanisms, e.g. planning, reasoning, anticipating and controlling, that distinguishes the expert from the novice. Table 1 lists the different aspects of expertise, that piece together the term *expertise*.

4 Propositions

In this section, we bring together observations on layout and expertise as factors of process model understanding. We argue that the effect of secondary notation on model comprehension must also take individual expertise into account, as recognition capabilities can be trained. Indeed, the interaction between a model's

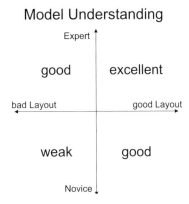

Fig. 3. 2-dimensional 2x2 Matrix displaying Process Model Understanding

layout quality and modeling expertise is partly considered in several studies. One of the most comprehensive studies concerning the layout-expertise interaction was undertaken by Petre [28]. When analyzing readership skills and graphical programming, Petre discovered that novice modelers usually create models that are less comprehensible due to poor use of the secondary notation. The secondary notation allows expert modelers to concentrate on relevant graphical elements, to disregard irrelevant information and recognize patterns. Furthermore, novice users of graphics tend to lack reading and search strategies. These strategies correlate with modeling experience and are the result of extensive learning.

Building on the arguments of the previous sections, we can assume that:

- Given an arbitrary process model, a good graphical layout increases model understanding, whereas a bad graphical layout decreases model understanding.
- Given an arbitrary process model, an expert performs significantly better when it comes to model understanding, compared to an individual classified as a novice.

Based on these two basic propositions, we can reason about the joint impact of graphical layout and expertise on process model understanding. Let us again consider the professor and the student trying to comprehend a process model. We illustrate the problem in a 2-dimensional matrix, including graphical layout and expertise as the two axis (see Figure 3). This matrix contains four areas for each combination of the two factors. According to propositions (1) and (2), the professor would perform significantly better than the student on both good and bad layout. Furthermore, good layout would be understood significantly better by both professor and student. We expect that the student will struggle with the bad layout, whereas he is able to cope with the good one. Instead, the professor is able to perform well even with the bad layout, whereas he performs excellent with the good one.

Taking the consolidated findings from the previous sections into account, we are able to formulate the following propositions:

H1a. For process models with bad layout, experts are likely to perform significantly better than novices for tasks of model comprehension. We expect that experts, although layout cues are obfuscated, can demonstrate their knowledge of reading and understanding information from the models. Experts are presumably capable to recognize hidden workflow patterns and visual cues using their modeling expertise and perceptual training. Contrarily, we expect novices to lack practical expertise on graphical readership and pattern recognition. Therefore, novices face problems of perceiving and interpreting relevant information in process models.

H1b. For process models with layout that use secondary notation for providing visual cues, we expect that experts perform significantly better than novices for comprehension tasks. We assume that experts exhibit their perceptual and practical expertise especially when good layouts are presented. Due to their gained experience experts perform faster and better than novices in understanding these process models. Novices might be slower as they lack efficient reading and search techniques in order to access information in a fast way.

H2a. For novices with a lack of modeling expertise, we hypothesize that good layout of process models significantly enhances model understanding. Bad layout makes it difficult or impossible for novices to extract information while good layout greatly supports the information extraction process. Novices might not recognize workflow patterns in badly layouted models due to missing expertise. Thus, they cannot uncover all information shown in the layout. Therefore, process models with a good layout support the understanding of novices.

H2b. For experts with practical and theoretical experience, we postulate that bad layout of process models significantly decreases the performance of model understanding. We expect experts being able to extract and interpret information from bad layouts with the help of perceptual expertise. However, good layout should increase the performance of experts as it supports graphical readership and pattern recognition. Even though experts know sophisticated search strategies, bad layouts hinders both abilities of graphical readership and pattern recognition. Therefore, we expect a higher understanding of experts for good layout.

H3. We expect that the effect of layout on model understanding will be greater for novices than for experts. Experts will be faster and more accurate in reading relevant information from a process model, even if it is obfuscated by bad layout. Since novices do not know appropriate search strategies, they will be more dependant on an intuitive presentation of the information using a supportive process model layout.

Altogether, we assume that both groups will be affected by the way how the process model is graphically laid out, but this impact will be greater for novices.

5   Experimental Setup

In this section, we discuss the experimental setup. We will focus on potential interactions, and how we aim to track them. Section 5.1 elaborates on the stimulus and the general setup of the experiment. Section 5.2 discusses the dimensions of performance that we aim to measure. Section 5.3 emphasizes potential interaction effects, and how we aim to deal with them.

5.1   Stimulus

In order to investigate the impact of graphical layout on process model understanding, we have to use structurally equivalent models with different layout. There are different challenges in this regard. First, due to learning effects, it is not possible to show the same model to the same person, once with good and once with bad layout. We therefore have to use a block design where participants are randomly assigned to one of two groups such that they either see the good or the bad version of the model. Second, we have to investigate the level of variation in layout parameters in order to find out which changes are significant. The authors of [7] conducted a pre-test to study the strength of impact of their stimulus. Based on the results they used three classes of variation. Analogously, we plan to investigate how huge the variation in layout parameters like bending points and edge crossings should be in the experiment to have a potential impact.

5.2   Comprehension Performance

We aim to measure comprehension performance in different dimensions. Accuracy (number of correct answers), efficiency (comprehension time), and efficacy (accuracy divided by time) are the major performance measures in the context [17]. Since layout is highly perceptual, we also aim to record perceived difficulty. The selection of questions on model comprehension requires specific care. It is common practice to utilize questions, for which an answer can be objectively judged to be correct or wrong [24,25]. This call for objectivity implies ignoring the (informal) content of activity labels, and using abstract letters as activity names instead. The focus will then be on binary relationships between two activities in terms of execution order, exclusiveness, concurrency, and repetition. These relationships play an important role for reading, modifying, and validating the model. Respective statements such as "Executing activity a_i implies that a_j will be executed later" can be easily verified using the reachability graph of the process model. A reachability graph captures all states and transitions represented by the process model and it can be (automatically) generated from it. For some classes of models, several relationship can be calculated more efficiently without the reachability graph. For instance, the concurrency relation can be constructed for those process models that map to free-choice Petri nets in $O(n^3)$ time [22].

There is also a debate on how representative a question is for the overall model understanding. As the number of questions can become quite large for estimating understanding within the boundaries of a given confidence interval [21], we rather plan to identify difficult questions based on a notion of distance in the process model graph. A different option is to choose questions randomly, and later calculate measures of consistency like Cronbach's Alpha for the actually given answers. The rationale here would be that consistent sets of answers were likely to be a good estimate for general model understanding. The disadvantage of the latter option is that confidence in the measurement can only be established post-hoc. We expect a greater variation in understanding by using difficult questions instead of selecting random questions. Still, it can easily be combined with a consistency analysis after gather data.

5.3   Potential Interactions

There are several factors that might have a potential influence on process model understanding. In the previous sections, we have already discussed that we aim to analyze different aspects of process modeling expertise as main covariates. There are other factors discussed in literature including model size and complexity, domain knowledge, modeling purpose, and modeling notation.

The importance of model characteristics is the foundation for work into process model metrics. Metrics have been defined for different structural and behavioral aspects of a process model including *control-flow complexity (CFC)* [11], size, complexity, and coupling [4], modularity [2], or structuredness [26]. Their impact on model understanding and error probability has been studied in different works – see [26] for an overview. In our experiment we aim to neutralize the impact of size and structure on understanding as much as possible. Similar to [24] we plan to choose models of comparable size.

Domain knowledge might also have an impact. If someone is knowledgable in health-care and he answers questions on hospital process models, it is not directly clear whether a good performance can be attributed to model comprehension or domain knowledge. In general, people may find it easier to read a model about the domain they are familiar with than other models. While this has not been established for process models, it is known from software engineering that domain knowledge affects the understanding of particular code [23]. We aim to neutralize the impact of domain knowledge by using abstract letters as activity names.

The understanding of a model may be affected by the specific purpose the modeler had in mind. The best example is that some process models are not intended to be used on a day-to-day basis by people but instead are explicitly created for automatic enactment. In such a case, less care will be given to make them comprehensible to humans. The differences between process models as a result of different modeling purposes are mentioned, for example, in [15]. Empirical research into this factor is missing.

In the presence of many different notations for process models, e.g. UML Activity diagrams, EPCs, BPMN, YAWL, and Petri nets, it cannot be ruled out that some of these are inherently more suitable to convey meaning to people than others. Empirical research that has explored this difference is, for example, reported in [35]. According to these publications, the impact of the notation being used is not very high, maybe because the languages are too similar. Similar observations are made in [32]. Other research that compares notations of a different focus identify a significant impact on understanding [19,3]. We try to neutralize the impact of the notation on an experiment by using the BPMN notation. It is a widely accepted standard and it covers those routing elements that are also found in other languages like EPCs or YAWL. Furthermore, we will focus on those BPMN elements actually used in modeling practice [38].

6   Conclusion

This paper is motivated by the importance of comprehension for the use of business process models. We have discussed expertise and graphical layout as two important factors affecting the ease of process model comprehension. Our contribution is a set of hypotheses that build on a sound theoretical foundation. In particular, we argue that graphical layout influences model comprehension for both experts and novices, but that the effect would be greater for the latter. From these arguments, our plans for future work follow naturally: the proposed hypotheses will be challenged by empirical research that we plan to conduct at our universities in Berlin and Eindhoven.

A clear limitation of our work that needs to be noted is that further interacting factors may be at work that influence process model comprehension. For example, some notations display a wider variety of graphical constructs than others, so that the considered process modeling language may mediate the effect of the secondary notation as we discussed. Considering the early state of research in the area of process model understanding, we see no other option than to try and study the various factors in combinations that are manageable from an experimental perspective. At the same time, it would be a very welcome development if other researchers would engage in these topics, so that progress can be made in distinguishing the most important interactions. Indeed, the presentation of our hypotheses at this stage may be considered as an explicit encouragement and invitation.

References

1. van der Aalst, W.M.P., ter Hofstede, A.H.M., Kiepuszewski, B., Barros, A.P.: Workflow Patterns. Distributed and Parallel Databases 14(1), 5–51 (2003)
2. van der Aalst, W.M.P., Lassen, K.B.: Translating unstructured workflow processes to readable BPEL: Theory and implementation. Information and Software Technology 50(3), 131–159 (2008)
3. Agarwal, R., De, P., Sinha, A.P.: Comprehending object and process models: An empirical study. IEEE Transactions on Software Engineering 25(4), 541–556 (1999)
4. Rolón Aguilar, E., García, F., Ruiz, F., Piattini, M.: An exploratory experiment to validate measures for business process models. In: First International Conference on Research Challenges in Information Science, RCIS (2007)

5. Aranda, J., Ernst, N., Horkoff, J., Easterbrook, S.: A framework for empirical evaluation of model comprehensibility. In: MISE 2007: Proceedings of the International Workshop on Modeling in Software Engineering, Washington, DC, USA, p. 7. IEEE Computer Society, Los Alamitos (2007)
6. Bandara, W., Gable, G.G., Rosemann, M.: Critical success factors of business process modeling (2007)
7. Batra, D., Wishart, N.A.: Comparing a rule-based approach with a pattern-based approach at different levels of complexity of conceptual data modelling tasks. Int. J. Hum.-Comput. Stud. 61(4), 397–419 (2004)
8. Bonner, S.E., Pennington, N.: Cognitive processes and knowledge as determinants of auditor expertise. Journal of Accounting Literature 10(1), 1–50 (1991)
9. Burton-Jones, A., Meso, P.: How good are these uml diagrams? an empirical test of the wand and weber good decomposition model. In: Applegate, L., Galliers, R., DeGross, J.I. (eds.) Proceedings of the Twenty-third International Conference on Information Systems (ICIS), pp. 101–114 (2002)
10. Byron, L., Wattenberg, M.: Stacked graphs – geometry & aesthetics. IEEE Transactions on Visualization and Computer Graphics 14(6), 1245–1252 (2008)
11. Cardoso, J.: Evaluating Workflows and Web Process Complexity. In: Workflow Handbook 2005, pp. 284–290. Future Strategies, Inc. (2005)
12. Chase, W.G., Simon, H.A.: The mind's eye in chess. Visual Information Processing (1973)
13. Chattratichart, J., Kuljis, J.: Some Evidence for Graphical Readership, Paradigm Preference, and the Match-Mismatch Conjecture in Graphical Programs. In: 13th Workshop of the Psychology of Programming Interest Group (2001)
14. Davies, I., Green, P., Rosemann, M., Indulska, M., Gallo, S.: How do practitioners use conceptual modeling in practice? Data & Knowledge Engineering 58(3), 358–380 (2006)
15. Dehnert, J., van der Aalst, W.M.P.: Bridging The Gap Between Business Models And Workflow Specifications. International J. Cooperative Inf. Syst. 13(3), 289–332 (2004)
16. Ericsson, K.A., Lehmann, A.C.: Expert and exceptional performance: Evidence of maximal adaptation to task constraints. Annual Review of Psychology 47(1), 273–305 (1996)
17. Gilmore, D.J., Green, T.R.G.: Comprehension and recall of miniature programs. International Journal of Man-Machine Studies 21(1), 31–48 (1984)
18. Green, T.M., Ribarsky, W., Fisher, B.: Building and applying a human cognition model for visual analytics. Information Visualization 8(1), 1–13 (2009)
19. Hahn, J., Kim, J.: Why are some diagrams easier to work with? effects of diagrammatic representation on the cognitive integration process of systems analysis and design. ACM Transactions on Computer-Human Interaction 6 (1999)
20. Horowitz, P., Hill, W.: The art of electronics, 2nd edn. University Press, Cambridge (1989)
21. Reijers, H.A., Seese, D., Melcher, J., Mendling, J.: On measuring the understandability of process models. In: Proceedings of BPM Workshops 2009 - ER-BPM Workshop. Springer, Heidelberg (to appear)
22. Kovalyov, A., Esparza, J.: A polynomial algorithm to compute the concurrency relation of free-choice signal transition graphs. In: Prof. of the International Workshop on Discrete Event Systems, WODES 1996, Edinburgh, pp. 1–6 (1996)
23. Lakhotia, A.: Understanding someone else's code: Analysis of experiences. Journal of Systems and Software 23(3), 269–275 (1993)

24. Mendling, J., Reijers, H.A., Cardoso, J.: What makes process models understandable? In: Alonso, G., Dadam, P., Rosemann, M. (eds.) BPM 2007. LNCS, vol. 4714, pp. 48–63. Springer, Heidelberg (2007)
25. Mendling, J., Strembeck, M.: Influence factors of understanding business process models. In: Abramowicz, W., Fensel, D. (eds.) BIS 2008. LNBIP, vol. 7, pp. 142–153. Springer, Heidelberg (2008)
26. Mendling, J.: Metrics for Process Models: Empirical Foundations of Verification, Error Prediction, and Guidelines for Correctness. LNBIP, vol. 6. Springer, Heidelberg (2008)
27. Moher, T.G., Mak, D.C., Blumenthal, B., Leventhal, L.M.: Comparing the Comprehensibility of Textual and Graphical Programs: The Case of Petri Nets. In: Cook, C.R., Scholtz, J.C., Spohrer, J.C. (eds.) Empirical Studies of Programmers: Fifth Workshop: Papers Presented at the Fifth Workshop on Empirical Studies of Programmers, December 3-5, pp. 137–161. Ablex Pub. (1993)
28. Petre, M.: Why looking isn't always seeing: readership skills and graphical programming. Commun. ACM 38(6), 33–44 (1995)
29. Petre, M.: Cognitive dimensions 'beyond the notation'. J. Vis. Lang. Comput. 17(4), 292–301 (2006)
30. Purchase, H.C.: Which aesthetic has the greatest effect on human understanding? In: Di Battista, G. (ed.) GD 1997. LNCS, vol. 1353, pp. 248–261. Springer, Heidelberg (1997)
31. Purchase, H.C., McGill, M., Colpoys, L., Carrington, D.: Graph drawing aesthetics and the comprehension of uml class diagrams: an empirical study. In: APVis 2001: Proceedings of the 2001 Asia-Pacific symposium on Information visualisation, Darlinghurst, Australia, pp. 129–137. Australian Computer Society, Inc. (2001)
32. Recker, J., Dreiling, A.: Does it matter which process modelling language we teach or use? an experimental study on understanding process modelling languages without formal education. In: Toleman, M., Cater-Steel, A., Roberts, D. (eds.) 18th Australasian Conference on Information Systems, Toowoomba, Australia, pp. 356–366. The University of Southern Queensland (2007)
33. Reijers, H.A., Mendling, J.: Modularity in process models: Review and effects. In: Dumas, M., Reichert, M., Shan, M.-C. (eds.) BPM 2008. LNCS, vol. 5240, pp. 20–35. Springer, Heidelberg (2008)
34. Russell, N., ter Hofstede, A.H.M., van der Aalst, W.M.P., Mulyar, N.: Workflow Control-Flow Patterns: A Revised View. BPM Center Report BPM-06-22, BPMcenter.org (2006)
35. Sarshar, K., Loos, P.: Comparing the control-flow of EPC and petri net from the end-user perspective. In: van der Aalst, W.M.P., Benatallah, B., Casati, F., Curbera, F. (eds.) BPM 2005. LNCS, vol. 3649, pp. 434–439. Springer, Heidelberg (2005)
36. TheFreeDictionary.com. Expertise (2009)
37. White, S.A.: Introduction to BPMN. BPTrends (July 2004)
38. zur Muehlen, M., Recker, J.: How much language is enough? theoretical and practical use of the business process modeling notation. In: Bellahsène, Z., Léonard, M. (eds.) CAiSE 2008. LNCS, vol. 5074, pp. 465–479. Springer, Heidelberg (2008)

Towards Cross Language Process Model Reuse – A Language Independent Representation of Process Models

Khurram Shahzad, Mturi Elias, and Paul Johannesson

Department of Computer and Systems Science (DSV),
Royal Institute of Technology (KTH) / Stockholm University, Sweden
{mks,mturi,pajo}@dsv.su.se

Abstract. Process model reuse is becoming a key approach to addressing the challenges of modeling business processes from scratch. A repository is, therefore, essential to store and manage process models for future reuse. In this paper, we develop a logical data model that enables a Universal Process Repository to store process models in the form of process elements, independent of any process modelling language. In order to store process models in the process repository we propose an algorithm that automatically extracts data from the repository and converts them to process models on the fly. Finally, we use a case study to present data stored about a process model in the repository and to illustrate the development of process models from the data stored in the repository.

1 Introduction

The reuse of process models can help business users simplify the work of modeling business processes [1], improve efficiency as well as substantially reduce the cost of modeling business processes [2, 3]. A repository is, therefore, necessary to store and manage process models for future reuse. The available process repositories (like IBM process repository [4], IBM BPEL repository [5] and SAP Business Maps [6]) are not publically open for change and growth, which hinders the reuse of process models [7].

We are working on a Universal Process Repository (UPR) that is independent of process modeling languages and is open for changes and extensions by potential users. The UPR aims to provide basic understanding of business processes and it offers a starting point for modeling business processes, by providing fundamental elements of process models.

There are several modeling languages (like YAWL [8], BPMN [9], EPC [10], IDEF0 [11] etc.) which can be used for modeling business processes. These process modeling languages have different elements and control structures [12], therefore, the specification of a business process varies from one language to another. In order to provide support for different modeling languages in the UPR, a common format for storing and sharing process models is needed, where the common format only stores fundamental elements of process models.

The XML Process Definition Language (XPDL) [13] and Business Process Modeling Ontology (BPMO) [14] are used for storing and sharing process models between different modeling languages and tools. However, the XPDL has a complex conceptual

A. Persson and J. Stirna (Eds.): PoEM 2009, LNBIP 39, pp. 176–190, 2009.

model [15] and captures detailed information about business processes. These details are redundant in the context of the scope of the UPR.

BPMO mainly intends to provide semantically rich definition of business processes, and it is focused to align the business and technical view of a process [14]. Therefore, neither XPDL nor BPMO fits the UPR's requirements for storing and sharing process models (i.e. capturing and storing only fundamental elements of process models), and an automated method for storing and retrieving process models is missing. In this paper, we propose a generic data model for storing and sharing process models between different modeling languages that only captures fundamental elements of a process. In addition, an automated method of extracting process model is given.

In section 2 of this paper, we present the research approach used to develop the generic data model for UPR. In section 3, we present the generic metamodel for a business process and the generic process description. In section 4, process description for specific languages is presented and in section 5, we present the generic data model and discuss how it can be used. Finally, we discuss and draw conclusions in section 6.

2 Research Approach

Reusability is the likelihood that artifacts can be used again with slight or no modification. The UPR intends to provide a mass of reusable process models that captures fundamental elements of a business process. For storing the fundamental elements we propose a generic data model for process description DB (a component of UPR), that can store reusable process models independent of any process modeling language. Therefore, it is likely that some language specific details of process models may not be captured.

Processes are modeled in specific languages (like BPMN, YAWL etc.) and in UPR their fundamental elements are stored in a generic format. Therefore, in order to facilitate the conversion from generic metamodel to language specific metamodel and vice versa we use a *mapping specification*. This specification is an association between elements of generic metamodel and language specific metamodels. In the remaining part of this section, we present the approaches used to develop the generic data model for process description DB (a part of the UPR). The *generic data model* consists of a *partial data model* and *mapping specification*, where *partial data model* is used to store data about processes independent of language and a *mapping specification* is used for interpretation of stored data.

Based on the definition of process model and a business process, process description is defined. However, the definition is high-level so the concrete elements of process description are not visible. Therefore, a generic metamodel is generated in order to provide concrete elements of a business processes. The generic metamodel is matched to the definition of process description to form a generic process description that is further used to develop the *partial data model*.

In order to define the *mapping specification* (another part of the generic data model), the elements of generic metamodel are matched to the elements of modeling languages. Based on the matching and the generic process description we define a language specific process description that further contributes to defining the *mapping specification* as shown in figure 1. Each label in figure 1 is of the form *'label (number)'*, where *label* is the name of the step and *number* represents the corresponding section of the paper in which the step is discussed. The boxes with the borders represent the steps, while the ones without borders represent the output of preceding step and input to the next step.

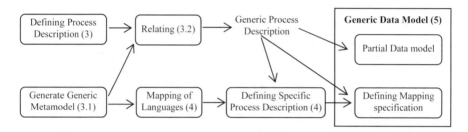

Fig. 1. Research Approach for Designing Generic Data Model for Process Description DB

3 Process Description for Storing Business Processes

In the Universal Process Repository, process definitions exist at two levels, *user level* and *repository level*. The *user level* is a higher level at which a business process is viewed as a process model. At this level a business process is modeled by using graphical constructs of a process modeling language, like BPMN, EPC, YAWL etc. However, the process model is not directly stored in the repository. The *repository level* is a lower level at which a business process is stored as a *process description*. The process description is not directly accessible to users of the repository, but it can be modified by changing its respective process model at the user level because a process description in the repository is derived from a process model. Figure 2 shows the relationship between the two levels.

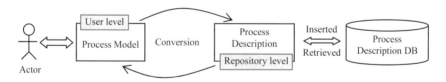

Fig. 2. Relationship between Process Model and Process Description

The benefits of storing process descriptions (non-graphical form) over process models (graphical form) includes, a) efficient retrieval and manipulation of the stored processes, b) easy and flexible way to control process models, because access to parts of a process model can be defined. Definitions of a process model and a business process are as follows [16, 17]:

A process model is defined as

> *"A graphical depiction of a business process detailing the arrangement of task interdependency, controls, and allocated resources."*

A business process is

> *"A collection of related, structured activities or tasks that produce a specific service or product (serve a particular goal) for a particular customer or customers."*

From the two definitions the following can be observed about a business process, a) it consists of activities (may also be called as tasks), b) activities are related with each other and dependences may exist between them, c) activities are related to resources, and d) activities are related to agents. Therefore, from these observations we define the specification of a process description as:

$$PD = \{Elements, \ Control\text{-}flow, \ Process \ Logic\} \ \text{-------------------- (equation 1)}$$

Elements of a process model are the fundamental units of a process model, i.e. activities, resources and agents. *Control-flows* are the possible structures (control structures) between multiple elements in a process model e.g. sequence, AND, OR etc. *Process logic* is a logical association/binding between elements of a process model and it is defined between two elements of a process model e.g. a sequence between two activities, or resource allocation to an activity.

3.1   Generic Metamodel for Business Processes

The process description defined in the preceding section is very abstract so the concrete elements of process description are not visible in equation 1. Therefore, a generic metamodel is required to provide concrete elements of business processes. These concrete elements are used (in section 3.2) for extending the equation 1 to form the generic process description.

Process model represents information about what is done, where and when it is done, who does it, how, why, and who is dependent on its being done. In order to capture these business concepts, Curtis [18] has presented four perspectives of a business process. Here, we use the four perspectives, as defined in Curtis framework, to develop a generic metamodel for a business process shown below in figure 3.

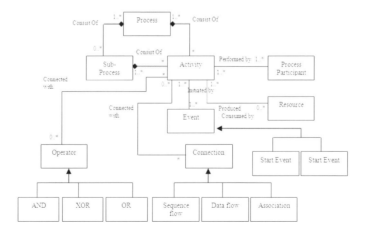

Fig. 3. Generic Metamodel for Business Processes

The four perspectives are functional, behavioral, organization and informational perspective.

Functional Perspective. The functional perspective defines the elements which are being performed. This perspective represents *'what'* elements (activities) of a process model are performed [18].

It is established that a process consists of a set of *activities*, and a process may consist of *sub-processes* [19] which also consist of activities. The execution of a business process is initiated by an event called *start event* and terminated by an event called *end event*. A *sub-process* is a part of a process that can exist independently, whereas an *activity* is a concrete instance of a task that is obtained while executing a particular case of a business process [20].

Behavioral Perspective. This perspective defines the order in which activities are executed and the point(s) where they are be executed. The behavioral perspective represents *'when'* and *'how'* activities of a process model are performed [18]. It gives dependencies between activities and how they are to be executed. These dependencies are called control flow

Control flow is a relationship between two or more activities and it can be of two types [19], *operators* and *connection*. *Operator* is a node that is used to split or join more than two elements and can either be an XOR, OR or AND. *Connection* is an edge that connects two activities, an activity with a participant, an activity with an events, or an activity with a resource. There are three types of connections: sequence flow, data flow and association.

Organizational Perspective. This perspective defines the organizational units where business activities are performed and the involved agent. The organizational perspective represents *'where'* and *'by whom'* business activities are realized.

It is established that an activity can consume, produce, or transfer a resource between *participants* [21]. *Participants* are the entities that can execute a task to take/transfer control of a resource [22] and they could be an organizational unit or agent [19]. Organizational units may have predefined duty-descriptions called roles, that are assigned to agents. Agent can be a person, software, machine or a service.

Informational Perspective. This perspective defines *resources* that are consumed or produced during the execution of a business activity. The resources are the information elements and the documents in which these elements are stored.   Information elements are the messages or data about the activity e.g. messages about output of an activity that can affect execution of the following activity.

3.2 A Generic Process Description

In this section, we relate the elements of generic metamodel and the definition of process description (given in equation 1) to form a generic process description. The process description becomes.

$$PD = \{Elements,\ Control\text{-}flow,\ Process\ Logic\}$$

Where, Elements = {start-event, activity, participant, resource, end-event}

Control flow = {operator, connection}

     ; connection = sequence flow, dataflow, association

Process logic = {*(start-event, activity, connection)* *(activity, activity, connection)*, *(participant, activity, connection)* *(task, operator, connection)* *(operator, activity, connection)* (task, stop event, connection) (resource, activity, connection) (activity, resource, connection) (operator, operator, connection)}

Equation 2

And connection is a combination of the *type* and *label* of the connection.

4 Matching Process Modeling Languages to the Generic Metamodel

In this section we use the concepts of generic metamodel and the concepts of specific languages for matching the concepts. Later, the matching results and equation 2 (Definition of Process Description) are used for producing language specific process descriptions.

For matching concepts, we have selected four languages, Activity Diagram (AD) [23], BPMN [9], EPC [10], YAWL [8]. *Activity Diagram*, because it is a form of UML diagrams that is widely accepted and used in industry. *BPMN*, because it is a standard language, developed by OMG [24]. *YAWL*, because it is one of the most researched process modeling language. *EPC*, because it has been initiated by industry leaders in BPM, and it is supported by several tools like Oryx, ARIS etc.

Table 1. Matching Concepts of Generic Metamodel and Process Modeling Languages

Generic Metamodel	Activity Diagram	BPMN	EPC	YAWL
Subprocess		Subprocess	Sub process	
Activity	Activity	Task	Function	Task
Event				
Start Event	Initial node	Start Event	Pre-activity Event	Input condition on activity
End Event	Final node (process)	End event	Post-activity Event	Output condition on activity
Control Flow				
Operator	Forknode, join, decision, merge	AND/OR/XOR , Complex	XOR, AND, OR connector	AND, XOR, OR split & join
Connection	Control flow, Object flow	Sequence flow, association, message flow	Control flow	No formal name of the construct
Participant		Pool	Org. Unit, Org Role	
Resource				
Informational resource	Object Node	Data objects	Information objects	

Table 1 shows the results of matching concepts between generic metamodel and specific languages. The purpose of activity in generic metamodel is the same as the purpose of *activity* in AD, *function* in EPC and *task* in YAWL/BPMN. Therefore, the activity concept in generic metamodel can be matched to activity, function and task in AD, EPC and BPMN/YAWL. Similarly, the concepts in the generic metamodel are matched to specific languages as shown in table 1.

By using the matching (from table 1) and process description (from equation 2), language specific process description can be produced. This is done by considering equation 2 as a template and filling values from the matching table 1. The language specific process description for BPMN is as follows.

Language Specific Process Description: BPMN

Elements = {start event, tasks, pools, dataobject, end event}
Operators = { AND, OR, XOR}
Connection = {sequence flow-ID, message flow-ID, association-ID} ; ID is unique identifier
Process logic = {(start-event, task, connection) (task, task, connection), (pool, task, connection) (task, operator, connection) (operator, task, connection) (dataobject, task, connection) (task, dataobject, connection) (task, stop event, connection) (operator, operator, connection)}

Similarly, process description for YAWL, Activity Diagram and EPC can also be defined.

5   Generic Data Model for Process Description DB

The generic data model is a logical data model that defines structure and content of a generic process description in the UPR. The generic data model is used for capturing and storing fundamental elements of process models in the repository. The generic data model consists of a *partial data model* and *mapping specification*, where the *partial data model* is used to store data about processes independent of modeling language and *mapping specification* is used for interpretation of the stored data.

The generic data model is generated from a generic process description as defined in equation 2 of section 3.2. The model consists of entities, attributes and relationship between entities as shown below in figure 4. The entities are derived from the elements and control flow and the relationships are derived from the process logic.

Event. In the generic process description there is a start and an end event. In order to capture the information about start and end event an entity (labeled *Event*) is included in the data model. The event consists of three attributes, (a) EventID that describes a unique identification of an event in the table (b) EventName that describes the name of an event (i.e. Illness Occur), and (c) EventType which specifies a type of a particular event and it can be either a start event or end event.

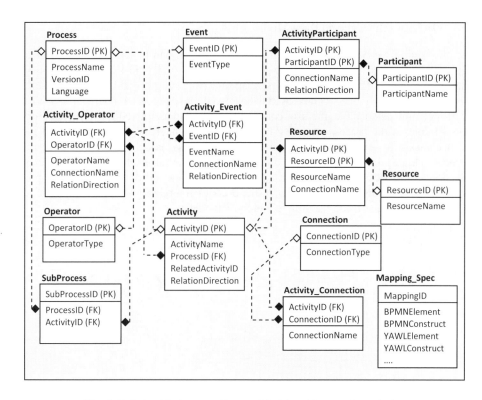

Fig. 4. Relationship between Process Model and Process Description

Activity. In the generic process description we have activity as an element, therefore, in order to capture the information about activities we include an entity labeled as *Activity* in the data model. The activity consists of the following attributes (a) ActivityID that specifies a unique identifier for each record in the table. (b) ActvityName describes the name of an activity (i.e. Prepare Order) and (c) ProcessID as a foreign Key for the entity Process.

Similarly, the participant and resource (as elements) and operator and connection (as controlflows) in the generic process description are represented by the entities participant, resource, operator and connection in the data model. The entities ActivityEvent, ActivityOperator and ActivityConnection are generated from many to many relationships between the three entities (Event, Operator and Connection) and the Activity.

In order to facilitate the use of the data model we introduce a mapping specification as a disjoint entity in the generic data model. The *mapping specification* entity is derived from the generic process description and language specific process description. It consists of elements of a generic process description, their corresponding elements in the specific process description and their associated construct.

5.1 On Using the Generic Data Model

In this section we describe how the generic data model can be used in the Universal Process Repository for storing and extracting process models in the form of process description. Once the mechanism of storing and extracting process models is established, the process models can be used to share and reuse process model.

From a user perspective, the user can interact with a modeling editor to model processes in one of the process modeling languages. At the backend of the editor we have a mechanism for extracting information from a process model and to store it in the Process Description DB. Similarly, a mechanism for the retrieval of data and its conversion to a process model is also used. In the remaining part of this section, we present the mechanism (in the form of pseudo code) for retrieving data from Process Description DB and its conversion to a process model.

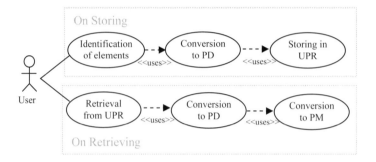

Fig. 5. Relationship between Process Model and Process Description

The algorithm for storing process model is similar to the one used for retrieval, therefore, to avoid redundancy it is not presented in this paper. However, figure 5 shows high-level use cases for storing and retrieving process models.

Pseudo Code of Extraction Algorithm. The algorithm shows the retrieval of a process with the assumptions that the process is identified and will be retrieved in the language in which it was stored. Primarily, it is a three phase algorithm, a) data retrieval from process description DB, b) generation of process description (PD) from the retrieved data, c) conversion from PD to BPMN process model. As soon as the retrieval takes place from DB, the process description is generated. However, for clarity these phases are separated from each other.

Input: identified process description
Output: a process model in BPMN
Create alias for the data model
        { activity → task,
           resource → dataobject
           participant → pool   }

a) Retrieval from Process Description DB:
Use *event* and *process* table
> {   Identify *(start event)*
> Identify *(end event)*   }

Use *task*, *event* and *connection* table
> {   Identify (the *task/s* related to *start event*)
> & *connection* from *start event* to each *task*   }

For each related *task* **do**
> { Identify (*task* related to *task*) & *connection* from *task* to *task*
> Identify (*pool* related to *task*) & *connection* from *pool* to *task*   Identify (*data object* related to *task*) &
> connection from *data-object* to *task*
> Identify (*task* related to *operator*) &
> connection from *task* to *operator*   }
> **While** *task* is not null

For each *operator* **do**
> { Identify (*operator* related to *task*) &
> connection from *operator* to *task*
> Identify (*operator* related to *operator*) &
> connection from *operator* to *operator*   }
> **While** *operator* is not null

b) Conversion to Process Description:
The template of the process description for BPMN is given below and is used to struc-ture the data before it is converted to process model. The template given below is instantiated.

Elements = {start event, tasks, pools, dataobject, end event}
Operators = { AND-ID, OR-ID, XOR-ID} ; where
> ID is used to uniquely identify each operator

Connection = {sequence flow-ID, message flow-ID, association-ID} ; ID is unique identifier

Process logic = {(start-event, task, connection) (task, task, connection), (pool, task, connection) (task, operator, connection) (operator, task, connection) (dataobject, task, connection) (task, dataobject, connection) (operator, operator, connection) (task, stop event, connection)}

c) Conversion to Process Model:
The structured form of data is converted to a graphical form (called process model). Input to this step is each instance of process logic and draw function is used for mod-elling a process on-the-fly. A process model is completed when all instances of the process logic are passed to the Draw function.

> Draw (X, Y, Z)   /*where X is the first element, Y is follow up element and Z
> is the connection between X and Y.
> {
> If (X & Y= *'NotNull'* and *not represented already*)
> { Find (*construct* of X from *mapping specification*)
> &   (*construct* of Y from *mapping specification*)
> &   (*construct* of Z from *mapping specification*)

Place construct X and Y and link them by Z.
And Add Label X, Y, Z
}
Else if (X is *represented already*)
{   Find (*construct* of Y from *mapping specification*)
&   (*construct* of Z from *mapping specification*)
Place construct of Y and link X,Y by Z
And label Y, Z.
}
Else Get next instance and continue.
}

5.2   Generating Process Model from Process Description DB: An Example

In order to exemplify the use of the proposed algorithm and the generic data model, we consider a process model from the Swedish healthcare sector, as shown below in figure 6. For the process model we presented how the data is stored in the process description DB and from which we reproduce the same model. The purpose of this exercise is to exemplify the use of the algorithm and identify the information lost during storing and retrieving process model. This is done by comparing the original and the retrieved process model.

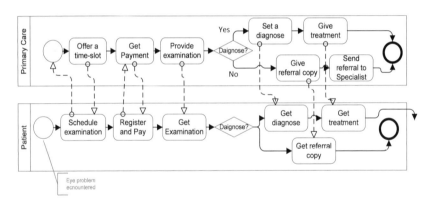

Fig. 6. Example Eyecare Referral Process

The instances of the tables become as follows, where each tuple is separate by ";":
Process = *1, eye care referral process, 1, BPMN;*
Event = *1, start event; 2, end event*
Activity = *1, offer a time-slot, 1, 2; 2, get payment, 1, 3;...*
ActivityEvent = *1, 1, receive a call, null, 1; 1, 2, eye problem encountered, null, 1; 10, 2, null, null, 1;...*
Operator = *1, OR;*
ActivityOperator = *5, 1, diagnose, null, 1; 7, 1, diagnose, yes, 1; ...*
Connection = *1, sequenceflow; 2, dataflow ;*
ActivityConnection = *1, 1, null, 1; 1, 2, null, 0;...*
Participant = *1, primary care; 2 patient;*
ActivityParticipant = *1, 1, null, 1; 2, 2, null, 1;...*

The start event, tasks, pools, dataobjects, operators and connection are given above, so they are not repeated here. Whereas the process logic is as follows.

(start-event, task, connection) = *(receive a call, 1, sequenceflow-null)* // where in sequenceflow-null, sequenceflow is the type of flow null is the label. 1 is the taskID.
(task, task, connection) = *(1, 2, sequenceflow-null); (2, 4, messageflow-null)...*
(pool, task, connection) = *(patient, 2, messageflow-null); (primaycare, 1, messageflow-null)...*
(task, operator, connection) = *(5, OR-diagnose?, sequenceflow-null)*
(operator, task, connection) = *(OR-diagnose?, 7, sequenceflow-yes); (OR-diagnose?, 8, sequenceflow-no)...*
(task, stop event, connection) = *(12, A, sequenceflow-null); (10, B, sequenceflow-null)...*

By using the draw function of the algorithm, a process model can be developed. Figure 7 shows the step by step development of a process model. When the first instance of process logic of the type *(start-event, task, connection)* is passed to the draw function, *start event* its related *task* and *connection* between them (start event and task) is created as shown in step 1 in figure 7. On passing *(task, task, connection)* the second step is executed.

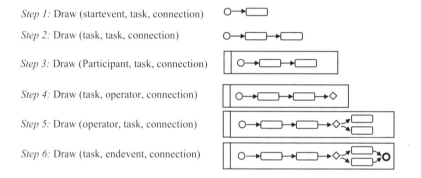

Step 1: Draw (startevent, task, connection)

Step 2: Draw (task, task, connection)

Step 3: Draw (Participant, task, connection)

Step 4: Draw (task, operator, connection)

Step 5: Draw (operator, task, connection)

Step 6: Draw (task, endevent, connection)

Fig. 7. Step by Step Process Model Generation

Figure 8 shows the process model produced by the draw function, when all instances of the process logic (of health care process) are passed to it.

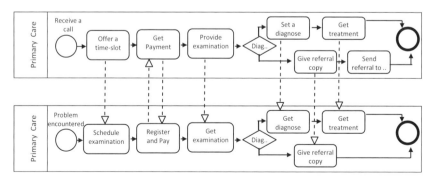

Fig. 8. Example Eyecare Referral Process: On Retrieval

6 Discussion and Conclusions

Modeling of processes is a complex and time consuming task which can be simplified by reuse of process models. A repository is, therefore, necessary to store and manage process model. However, the mass of process models available in repositories cannot be reused because, process models are either domain specific processes or the repositories are not publically open for change and growth [7]. Furthermore, most repositories are proprietary and not extensible. To overcome these limitations, work on a Universal Process Repository is in-progress.

In this paper, a generic data model of process description DB (a component of UPR) is proposed that is capable of storing fundamental information of processes independent of any language. For developing this data model we start from the definition of business process and process model and follow step-by-step procedure to generate the logical data model.

Users of the repository interact with the process editor, and model their processes which are automatically stored in the process description DB in non-graphical form. Similarly, the retrieval process is also automated and transparent to users. Data from Process description DB is retrieved and converted to process models with the help of the algorithm presented in section 5.2. Also, we applied the approach on an eye care referral process to demonstrate the applicability of the proposed approach.

From the study it can be concluded that, a) the generic data model is capable of storing fundamental elements of a process model in a format that is independent of any process modeling language, b) the automated way of storing and retrieving process models can facilitate users in storing and retrieving process models without any additional effort and c) once stored, the process models can be shared and reused. Only the fundamental elements of process models are captured, therefore, only basic understanding of a process can be provided that can be used as a starting point for process modeling. Thus, some advanced features that are specific for each language may not be captured by the logical data model. Examples of these features are token and composite task in YAWL, sending signal to outside and activity partition in AD, and intermediate event in BPMN. This may in some cases result in losses during translation, i.e. the translation will not preserve the semantics of the original model. Such losses may be unacceptable for certain applications but are less problematic for UPR, as we only intend to provide basic understanding and fundamentals of process models.

Transforming process descriptions between different languages and elicitation of guidelines for populating the repository are some of the future research directions.

References

[1] Rodrigues, J.A., Souza, J.M., Zimbrao, G., Xexeo, G., Neves, E., Pinheiro, W.A.: A P2P Approach for Business Process Modelling and Reuse. In: Eder, J., Dustdar, S. (eds.) BPM Workshops 2006. LNCS, vol. 4103, pp. 297–307. Springer, Heidelberg (2006)

[2] Hornung, T., Koschmider, A., Oberweis, A.: A Recommender System for Business Process Models. In: Proceedings of the 17th Annual Workshop on Information Technology and Systems (WITS 2007), Montreal, Canada (2007)

[3] Ma, Z., Leymann, F.: A Lifecycle Model for Using Process Fragment in Business Process Modeling. In: Proceedings of the 9th Workshop on Business Process Modeling, Development and Support (BPMDS 2008), in Conjunction with CAiSE 2008 Conference, France, (2008)

[4] IBM Process Repository,
`http://publib.boulder.ibm.com/infocenter/wchelp/v5r6m1/`
`index.jsp?topic=/com.ibm.commerce.business_process.doc/`
`concepts/processPrice_order.htm` (last accessed on May 20, 2008)

[5] Business Process Execution Language Repository,
`http://www.alphaworks.ibm.com/tech/bpelrepository?open&S_|`
`TACT=105AGX59&S_CMP=GR&ca=dgr-eclpsw03awbpelrepository`
(last accessed on May 20, 2008)

[6] SAP Business Map,
`http://help.sap.com/saphelp_sm40/helpdata/EN/5e/c8145e3a9d9`
`340913099159d80fc87/frameset.htm` (last accessed on May 20, 2008)

[7] Shahzad, K., Andersson, B., Bergholtz, M., Edirisuriya, A., Illayperuma, T., Jayaweera, P., Johannesson, P.: Elicitation of Requirements for a Business process Model Repository. In: Ardagna, D., et al. (eds.) BPM 2008 Workshops. LNBIP, vol. 17, pp. 42–53. Springer, Heidelberg (2008)

[8] Aalst, W.M.P., Hofstede, A.H.M.: YAWL: Yet Another Workflow Language. QUT Technical Report, FIT-TR-2002-06, Queensland University of Technology, Brisbane (2002)

[9] BPMN Specification Release, Object Management Group (OMG),
`http://www.omg.org/spec/BPMN/1.2/` (last accessed on June 30, 2009)

[10] Aalst, W.M.P.: Formalization and Verification of Event-Driven Process Chains. Information and Software Technology 41(10), 639–650 (1999)

[11] IDEF0, FIPS Publication 183, Computer Systems Laboratory, National Institute of Standards and Technology (NIST), `http://www.idef.com/idef0.html`

[12] Lu, R., Sadiq, S.: A Survey of Comparative Business Process Modeling Approaches. In: Abramowicz, W. (ed.) BIS 2007. LNCS, vol. 4439, pp. 82–94. Springer, Heidelberg (2007)

[13] XML Process Definition Language (XPDL), Standard by Workflow Management Coalition (WfMC), `http://xml.coverpages.org/XPDL20010522.pdf`

[14] Cabral, L., Norton, B., Domingue, J.: The Business Process Modeling Ontology. In: Proceedings of the International Workshop on Semantic Business Process Management, collocated with ESWC 2009, Crete, Greece (2009)

[15] Chinosi, M.: Representing Business Processes: Conceptual Model and Design Methodology. PhD Thesis, Department of Computer Science, Università degli studi dell'Insubria, Italy (2009)

[16] `http://www.cecausa.com/business_process_glossary.htm`   Process model definition

[17] Johannesson, P., Andersson, B., Bergholtx, M., Weigand, H.: Enterprise Modelling for Value Based Service Analysis. In: Stirna, J., Persson, A. (eds.) POEM 2008. LNBIP, vol. 15, pp. 153–167. Springer, Heidelberg (2008)

[18] Curtis, B., Kellner, M.I., Over, J.: Process Modeling. Communications of ACM 35(9), 75–90 (1992)

[19] List, B., Korherr, B.: An evaluation of conceptual business process modelling languages. In: Proceedings of ACM Symposium on Applied Computing (SAC 2006), Dijon, pp. 1532–1539 (2006)

[20] Axenath, B., Kindler, E., Rubin, V.: An Open and Formalism Independent Meta-Model for Business Processes. In: Proceedings of the BPRM 2005, in conjunction with 3rd BPM 2005, Nancy, France, pp. 45–59 (2005)

[21] Edirisuriya, A., Johannesson, P.: On the Alignment of Business Models and Process Models. In: Ardagna, D., et al. (eds.) BPM 2008 Workshops. LNBIP, vol. 17, pp. 68–79. Springer, Heidelberg (2008)

[22] Johannesson, P., Andersson, B., Bergholtz, M., Weigand, H.: Enterprise Modelling for Value Based Services Analysis. In: Stirna, J., Persson, A. (eds.) POEM 2008. LNBIP, vol. 15, pp. 153–167. Springer, Heidelberg (2008)

[23] Dumas, M., ter Hofstede, A.H.M.: UML Activity Diagrams as a Workflow Specification Language. In: Gogolla, M., Kobryn, C. (eds.) UML 2001. LNCS, vol. 2185, pp. 76–90. Springer, Heidelberg (2001)

[24] Object Management Group (OMG), http://www.omg.org/

[25] BPMN Specification Release, Object Management Group (OMG), http://www.omg.org/spec/BPMN/1.2/ (last accessed on June 30, 2009)

Service–Driven Information Systems Evolution: Handling Integrity Constraints Consistency

Nicolas Arni-Bloch, Jolita Ralyté, and Michel Léonard

University of Geneva, CUI, 7 route de Drize, CH-1227 Carouge, Switzerland
{Nicolas.Arni-Bloch,Jolita.Ralyte,Michel.Leonard}@unige.ch

Abstract. Changes and extensions of enterprise information systems (IS) often engender their fragmentation and redundancy. In order to overcome these problems, service-driven IS development is considered as a potential solution to support IS evolution when guaranteeing its integrity and consistency. In this work we consider the integration of new information system services (ISS) into a legacy IS and, in particular, how the consistency of integrity constraints (IC) governing the IS and the new ISS has to be handled in order to guarantee their validation. Five IC handling strategies are proposed in the form of method chunks and the impact of their application is measured with four service evolution indicators.

Keywords: Information system service, service integration, integrity constraint.

1 Introduction

Enterprise Information Systems (IS) are generally built on several applications or components that support business activities. Due to several factors such as business innovation, IT evolution, addition of new applications, these components become heterogeneous and specialized. This situation leads to fragmented IS and therefore to the redundancy between different IS components sharing some common parts. To organize the modularity of the IS and to manage these common parts the notion of information system service is proposed [2, 3].

Current service engineering approaches and architectures like SOA [7, 11, 12] concentrate their study on the rebuilding enterprise IS architecture in terms of autonomous services that can be composed afterwards in different ways. The autonomy principal is reached by reengineering the IS where the modularity of each service is carefully (painfully) defined. In this perspective, services are elaborated from scratch with the objective to avoid any overlap between them. However, in reality the lifecycle of the enterprise IS is a continuous incremental and evolutionary process. It is not possible at each iteration to rethink the entire IS in order to guarantee the autonomy and correctness of the existing and new services. Therefore, we need theories and methods for IS service evolution as proposed in [15] as well as formalisms and indicators to evaluate the impact of the extension of the IS with new services. This impact is, among others, influenced by the granularity and abstraction level of a service, which varies from a simple utility that logs errors to a more abstract complete business process [10, 17].

A. Persson and J. Stirna (Eds.): PoEM 2009, LNBIP 39, pp. 191–206, 2009.

Depending on service granularity and abstraction level, its integration into an existing IS is more or less complex. In this work we focus our attention on services with a rather high level of modularity each of them representing a work unit with a precise semantic; we call them information services or Information System Services (ISS). An ISS provides the information space and capabilities to the actors that have the responsibility to use them in order to perform their daily activities restrained by the regulation polices. When the granularity of an ISS is high, the overlap with other IS services becomes hard to avoid. Some service normalization techniques [7] exist to limit the functional redundancy. However, in order to guarantee IS data and process quality it is important to handle the overlap of its services by consolidating their data, capabilities, rules and responsibilities and specifying their cooperation strategy.

While integration of IS data schemas and models was largely discussed in the literature [4, 16, 19], other IS spaces (dynamic, rules and responsibilities) had less attention. In this work, we discuss the consolidation of the IS rule space and handling integrity constraints (IC) consistency when integrating new ISS into a legacy IS. The topic of IC validation has been studied for many years [9, 8] and is closely related to the transaction theories [6, 14]. Our aim here is not to propose a yet another way to ensure the integrity of data or transactional properties but rather to take the orientation of service change management and to study how handling the IC validation can affect the modularity and autonomy of the ISS. ICs are the basis for guaranteeing the information quality and the business rules preservation. They are also an important cause of dependency between different ISS and thus are in tension with the loose coupling and autonomy principles of the conventional SOA approach [7, 11].

In the following we define and illustrate the notion of ISS (section 2) and formalize the overlap which can appear when integrating new ISS into a legacy IS (section 3). Section 4 discusses the generic overlap situations and proposes five method chunks for handling IC consistency. Evaluation of the impact when applying these method chunks is discussed in section 5 and section 6 concludes our paper.

2   Information System Service

An *ISS* is a component of an information system representing a well defined business unit that offers capabilities to realise business activities and owns resources (data, rules, roles) to realize these capabilities. Formally, an ISS is defined as follows:

Definition 1 (Information System Service). An Information System Service is an autonomous coherent and interoperable component of an information system composed of four spaces: static, dynamic, rule and role: $\varsigma=<sSs, sDs, sRs, sOs>$ where:

- $sSs(\varsigma)$: *{Class}*, represents the set of classes of the service ς,
- $sDs(\varsigma)$: *{Action}*, represents the set of actions defined by the service ς,
- $sRs(\varsigma)$: *{Rule}*, represents the set of rules that govern the service ς,
- $sOs(\varsigma)$: *{OrganizationalRole}*, represents the set of organizational roles that have rights and responsibilities on the service ς.

Fig. 1 illustrates an ISS, named *DiplomaManagementService (DMService)*, providing diploma management capabilities for a University. In fact, this service is extracted

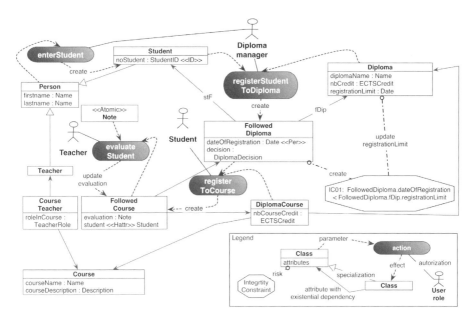

Fig. 1. Partial specification of the DiplomaManagementService (DMService)

from the effective IS of the University of Geneva. For the reason of readability the models used in this paper are simplified. As shown Fig. 1, the four ISS spaces are represented in the same model.

The static space of an ISS embodies its data structure and is represented by a class diagram. Naturally, the main concepts defined in this space are: *class* (e.g. *Student*, *Diploma*), *attribute* (e.g. *diplomaName*), *key* (e.g. *noStudent*) and *method* (not shown in Fig. 1). In order to guarantee the consistency of the data model we limit our model to only two types of relationship, *existential dependency* (e.g. the existence of an object of the class *Followed Diploma* depends on the existence of one object of the class *Student* and one object of the class *Diploma*) and *specialization* (e.g. the class *Student* is a specialisation of the class *Person*).

The dynamic space of an ISS represents the behaviour of service capabilities. For example, the *DMService* (Fig. 1) offers several capabilities: to create the curriculum of each diploma by defining courses and linking them to their teachers, to manage students' registration to different diplomas and to the corresponding courses as well as their examination. The main concepts of this space are *action* and *effect*. An action (e.g. *registerStudentToDiploma*) provokes an effect (e.g. *create* an object of the class *Followed Diploma*) during the execution of its process. The notion of effect is used to characterize the result of the action and allows to evaluate the impact of the action on the rule space.

Definition 2 (Effect). An effect is a tuple < *pr, target* > where *pr* defines the kind of effect from the set of primitives *pr* ∈ {*create, enter, exit, delete, update, list, read, return, call*} and *target* is either a class or a class and a set of attributes or an action.

$sDs_{effects}(\varsigma)$: *{effect}* represents the set of effects that the service ς can generate when executing its actions.

The objective of the rule space is to preserve the correctness and consistency of the ISS during its exploitation. Two types of rules, *conditions* and *integrity constraints*, have to be considered. While conditions regulate the execution of service actions, the role of integrity constraints is to ensure the integrity of service data. In this paper we focus our attention on the integrity constraints. Fig. 1 illustrates one of the *DMService's* integrity constraints named *IC01* which restricts the period of students' registration to a diploma – the date of effective registration has to be inferior to the predefined registration limit date.

Definition 3 (Integrity constraint). An integrity constraint (IC) is a rule that has to be verified in each state of the service or at each modification of it. Given a service ς, and an IC $ic \in sRs(\varsigma)$, the classes and attributes that participate in the validation of the *ic* define its validation context *(context(ic): {class})*. The *ic* also has a *scope(ic): {effect}* which includes all the effects that could transgress this rule. Each effect is called a *risk* of the IC.

In order to be able to validate the IC defined in its rule space *(sRs)*, the ISS has to know all the classes defined in each rule's context. For this purpose we define the *rule completeness* that aims to ensure that the ISS is defined on the static space *(sSs)* that offers all the information needed by its rules.

Rule completeness. Given a service ς, $\forall rule \in sRs(\varsigma) : context(rule) \subset sSs(\varsigma)$ where *context(rule)* is a set of classes needed for the evaluation of the rule, i.e. the context of the rule.

   Finally, the role space of an ISS defines the organizational roles and their rights and responsibilities on the service. A role is an element of an organization that has responsibilities in achieving activities to reach a common objective of the organization. In our example (Fig. 1), the main roles using the *DMService* capabilities are *Student*, *Teacher* and *Diploma manager*. More details about the notion of ISS and its metamodel MISS can be found in [3][1].

3   Defining ISS Overlap and Inconsistency

IS evolution in service-driven perspective means that new ISS are integrated into the legacy IS. Integrating two ISS will certainly create overlap situations in different spaces (shared data, duplicated actions, conflicting rules and responsibilities) that have to be handled in order to ensure each service consistency and also to preserve their modularity and autonomy. Let us consider the *DMService,* discussed in the previous section, as a legacy one which has to be extended with a new service supporting on-line registration of students to the University named *UniversityRegistrationService (URService)*.

---

[1] The role space is added to the original ISS metamodel MISS presented in [3].

Fig. 2 illustrates the new *URService* (simplified for the reason of readability) to be added to the Unversity IS. This service publishes two actions as public methods: *OnlineRegistration* and *RegisterTo-University*. The first action allows to create a *UniversityRegistrationRequest* on the web. It is a complex process (not detailed here) that builds the registration including different required documents according to the integrity constraints defined on the *UniversityRegistrationRequest*. The second action is dedicated to validate the on-line created registration request by the administration, to record the corresponding person as a student and to register him/her to a diploma.

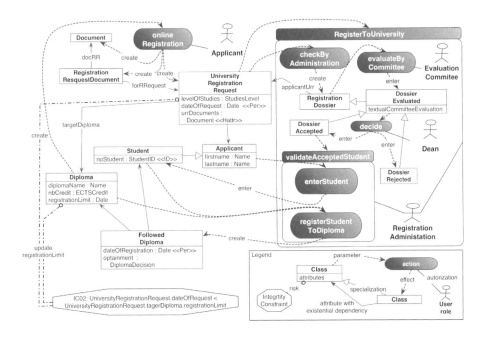

Fig. 2. Partial specification of the new UniversityRegistrationService (URService)

This case illustrates several overlap situations between the two services, the legacy and the new one. In fact, we can see that there is a static overlap between classes *Person*, *Student*, *Diploma* and *FollowedDiploma* as well as a dynamic overlap between actions *registerStudentToDiploma*. If an object, class or action belongs to several services of the same IS, some redundancy of information and inconsistency of rules and responsibilities can be expected and, therefore, has to be managed. In this section we define the notion of overlap which appears in different ISS spaces when integrating an ISS into an IS. Because of the lack of space we limit the number of definitions to those necessary to handle rule space inconsistencies.

We say that a class is in overlap if it is used in the definition of the static space of more than one service. It means that the definition of the given information is used by several services to offer their capabilities.

Definition 4 (Class overlap). Given a class *cl*, we say *cl is in overlap if* $\exists \varsigma, \varsigma'\ \varsigma \neq \varsigma'$ *: cl* $\in$ *sSs(*ς*)* $\wedge$ *cl* $\in$ *sSs(*ς'*)* where *sSs(*ς*)* represents the static space of the service ς, i.e. its set of classes.

The role that a class plays in a service is specified by the effects that this service can cause on the class. For example, some services can only access the objects of the class in overlap but cannot change their state; other services can only create new objects of the class but cannot modify or delete them. In order to refine the notion of overlap, we define the *effect overlap*. An effect is in overlap if it can be generated by more then one service. It means that several services share the same responsibility on the information represented by the class. For example, the effect *<create, an object of the class FollowedDiploma>* can be generated by both services (Fig. 1 and Fig. 2) and therefore it is in overlap.

Definition 5 (Effect overlap). Given an effect *ef*, we say *ef is in overlap if* $\exists \varsigma, \varsigma'\ \varsigma \neq \varsigma'$ *: ef* $\in$ *sDs$_{effects}$(*ς*)* $\wedge$ *ef* $\in$ *sDs$_{effects}$(*ς'*)*. *sDs$_{effects}$(*ς*)* represents the set of effects that the service ς can generate.

A rule is in overlap if some classes of its context are in overlap. It means that some part of the validation context of the rule is shared by several services. In the case of IC, it is essential to consider the effects in overlap that could violate this IC. For that, we define the *IC risk overlap*. For example, the context of the *IC02* (Fig. 2) defined in the rule space of the *URService* contains the class *Diploma* which is also belongs to the static space of the service *DMService*. Therefore, this rule is in overlap.

Definition 6 (Rule overlap). Given a rule *r*, we say *r is in overlap if* $\exists cl: cl \in$ *context(r)* $\wedge$ *cl is in overlap*.

Definition 7 (Integrity constraint risk overlap). Given integrity constraint *ic*, we say *ic is in risk overlap if* $\exists ef: ef \in$ *scope(ic)* $\wedge$ *ef is in overlap*.

An IC in overlap can be either a part of each service for which it is in overlap, or belong to only some of the services and be missing in the others. In the first case, all services guarantee the handling of the IC and the consistency of the IS regulatory policy is assured. In the second case, as the IC is not known by some services and the IS regulatory policy can be transgressed. We should therefore harmonize this policy by identifying the inconsistencies in the IC overlap.

Definition 8 (Integrity constraint overlap inconsistency). An integrity constraint *ic* has an overlap inconsistency with a service ς *if* $\varsigma \in$ *Risk-OSS(ic)* $\wedge$ *ic* $\notin$ *sRs(*ς*)* where the *Risk-OSS(ic)* (named risk overlap service set) is the subset of IS services that include at least one effect from the scope of the *ic: Risk-OSS(ic) = {*ς *:* $\exists ef, ef \in$ *scope(ic)* $\wedge$ *ef* $\in$ *sDs$_{effects}$(*ς*)* $\wedge$ *ef is in overlap}*.

An IC overlap inconsistency appears when the IC is in risk overlap with a service but is not defined in its rule space. From the legacy IS point of view, this inconsistency leads to a service that is not governed by the concerned IC. The service can therefore transgress it without knowing about its existence, the IS rules policies can be compromised and the IS consistency is not guaranteed. From the new ISS point of view, the process of the service can be stopped by an external IC unknown to the service. In this case, the service does not have the necessary information to handle this violation. The actors using the service are unable to perform the work because the service does not provide the required knowledge to resolve the violation of the IC. Several strategies can be defined to resolve this kind of inconsistency. We discuss them in the next section.

4 Handling Integrity Constraints Consistency

Integration of a new ISS into a legacy IS mainly consists in identifying and characterising the overlap in the four information spaces (static, dynamic, rules and roles), handling it (modifying, merging, adding or removing elements in the four spaces) and consolidating the integrated specifications [2][2]. In this paper we focus our attention on the rule space overlap handling and propose five IC consistency handling strategies formalised in the form of method chunks [13]. Selection of the appropriate method chunk depends on the overlap situation and the impact that the application of the chunk results on the concerned service.

4.1 Integrity Constraints Overlap Situations

Because of the static space overlap occurring when integrating a new ISS into a legacy IS some inconsistencies in IC overlap can appear. We identify two generic integrity constraints overlap situations – *total* and *partial* – that generate corresponding inconsistencies and have to be resolved during the ISS integration.

Total IC overlap (see Fig. 3a) appears when the context of an IC (the collection of classes required for this rule validation) defined in one service totally belongs to the static space of the other service. If the IC is in overlap inconsistency with the service (i.e. the IC is not defined in the rule space of the service) we say that this IC is in *total overlap inconsistency* with the service. In this situation, the service owns the required information to handle the IC (i.e. to validate and deal with the potential violation) and the inconsistency can be resolved by simply adding the IC to the service rule space; no evolution of the static space is required.

Definition 9 (Integrity constraint total overlap inconsistency). An integrity constraint *ic* has a total overlap inconsistency with a service ς if *ic is in overlap inconsistency with the service $\varsigma \wedge context(ic) \subseteq sSs(\varsigma)$.*

Partial IC overlap (see Fig. 3b) appears when the context of an IC defined in one service partially belongs to the static space of the other service (not all the classes of the IC context exist in the static space of the service). We say that this IC is in *partial overlap inconsistency* with the service. In this situation, the service does not own enough information to handle the IC and it is not possible to simply add this IC to the service rule space; some evolution of the static space of the service has to be done, or the IC has to be modified.

---

[2] In the paper [2] we have proposed a process model for IS integration into a legacy IS.

a) Total IC overlap   b) Partial IC overlap

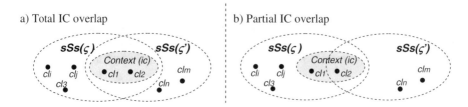

Fig. 3. Generic IC overlap situations

Definition 10 (Integrity constraint partial overlap inconsistency). An integrity constraint *ic* has a partial overlap inconsistency with a service ς if *ic is in overlap inconsistency with the service* $\varsigma \wedge context(ic) \cap sSs(\varsigma)$.

In our case, the *IC01* and *IC02* illustrated in Fig. 1 and Fig. 2 respectively are examples of integrity constraints in overlap inconsistency. The *IC01* defined in the *DMService* is in total overlap inconsistency with the *URService* because its context *{Diploma, FollowedDiploma}* is included in the static space of the *URService*. The *IC02* defined in the *URService* is in partial overlap inconsistency with *DMService* because its context *{Diploma, UniversityRegistrationRequest}* partially belongs to the static space of *DMService*. In both situations, the IC overlap has to be resolved – the missing rule has to be added into the corresponding service rule space and/or different elements of the service have to be modified. In order to validate an IC, the service containing it needs to have access to all the classes of the IC context. It means that the introduction of a new IC can require some evolution of the concerned service static space. In the contrary, if the decision is do not include the IC into the rule space of the service the overlap has to be settled by other means, for example by reducing service responsibility or by transforming the IC into a simple condition. For each situation we define several strategies to handle IC inconsistencies that we present in the form of method chunks[3].

4.2   Method Chunks for Integrity Constraints Consistency Handling

The collection of method chunks presented below is representative but not exhaustive; we aim our approach to be progressive and easily extensible with new method chunks and therefore to follow the situation-driven way of thinking.

Simple IC Addition Strategy. To deal with the total IC overlap inconsistency we propose to add the missing IC into the rule space of the corresponding service. It is clear that the rule completeness has to be validated during such an operation. We call this strategy *simple IC addition strategy* and the method chunk supporting it is illustrated in Table 1. Because all the classes of the IC context are already included in the service static space, the service has enough information to handle this IC. The service has to be updated to take into account this new rule and the actors using this

---

[3] In [13] a method chunk is defined as an autonomous and coherent part of a method supporting the realisation of some specific IS development activity.

service have to be informed about the new rule but the addition of the IC does not require any evolution of the static space of the service. An example of this situation is the *IC01* (see Fig. 1) that is in total overlap inconsistency with the *URService*. This service has actions (e.g. *validateAcceptedStudent*) that cause effects which are risks for the *IC01*. To resolve this inconsistency the *IC01* can be added to the *URService* without any modification of the static space of this service.

Table 1. Method chunk for IC consistency handling following simple IC addition strategy

Chunk name	Simple IC addition
Situation	< Integrity Constraint *ic*, Service ς >
Preconditions	c1) *context(ic)* $\subset$ *sSs(ς)*
	c2) *ic* $\notin$ *sRs(ς)*
Intention	Settle the integrity constrain *ic* overlap with the service ς following simple IC addition strategy
Postconditions	c1) *ic* $\in$ *sRs(ς)*
Guideline	1) Add the integrity constraint *ic* to the service ς.
	2) Verify that all the actions of ς that have effects included in the scope of *ic*, validate the constraint.

Service Static Space Extension Strategy. In the case of partial IC overlap inconsistency, it is not sufficient to add the IC to the service rule space – the missing classes from the IC context have to be added into the service static space in order to respect the completeness of the rule. It means that the static space of the service is extended with new classes. We call this strategy *static space extension* and the method chunk supporting it is illustrated in Table 2. For example, the *IC02* (Fig. 2) is in partial overlap inconsistency with the *DMService*. The *DMService* does not have enough information to handle this rule (*context(IC01)* $\not\subset$ *sSs(DMService)*) but can violate it. The *UniversityRegistrationRequest* class can be added to its static space in order to resolve the inconsistency.

Table 2. Method chunk for IC consistency handling by extending the static space of the service

Chunk name	Service static space extension
Situation	< Integrity Constraint *ic*, Service ς>
Preconditions	c1) *context(ic)* $\not\subset$ *sSs(ς)*
	c2) *ic* $\notin$ *sRs(ς)*
Intention	Settle the integrity constrain *ic* overlap with the service ς by extending the static space *sSs* of the ς with classes from the *ic* context
Postconditions	c1) *ic* $\in$ *sRs(ς)*
	c2) *context(ic)* $\subset$ *eSs(ς)*
Guideline	For each classe *cl* $\in$ *context(ic)*:
	if *cl* $\notin$ *sSs(ς)*:
	add *cl* to the static space of the ISS (add to sSs(ς))
	add ic to the service by applying the method chunk "Simple rule addition".

Service Responsibility Reduction Strategy. Another way to deal with the IC overlap (total or partial) is by reducing the responsibility of the service. In the contrary to the previous cases, the IC is not added into the rule space of the service but the responsibility of the service is modified in order to handle the IC overlap inconsistency. To reach this objective, it is necessary to remove from the service all the actions that have effects which could violate the IC. By doing that, the responsibility of the service is decreased as well its capability. We name this strategy *responsibility reduction* and the method chunk is presented in Table 3. In our example, applying this method chunk on the *IC02* and the *DMService* would require to remove from the *DMService* the responsibility of updating the objects of the class *Diploma*, more exactly to update its attribute *registrationLimit*.

Table 3. Method chunk for IC consistency handling by reducing service responsibility

Chunk name	Service responsibility reduction
Situation	< Integrity Constraint *ic*, Service ς>
Preconditions	c1) *context(ic)* $\cap$ $sSs(\varsigma)$$\neq\varnothing$
	c2) *ic* $\notin$ $sRs(\varsigma)$
Intention	Settle the integrity constrain *ic* overlap with the service ς by reducing the responsibility of the ς
Postconditions	c1) $scope(ic) \not\subset sDs_{effect}$
Guideline	For each action $act \in sDs(\varsigma)$:
	if $\exists ef_i \in effects\ (act), ef_i \in scope\ (ic)$: remove *act* from $sDs(\varsigma)$.

Control Extension Strategy. This method chunk (see Table 4) aims to guarantee the non-violation of an IC in partial or total overlap without adding this IC to the service and by preserving the responsibility of the service. This objective is reached by the introduction of an overlap protocol defined with new IC having a more restrained scope. This allows to maintain the IC without increasing the information coupling and without decreasing the responsibility of the service. Meanwhile, the service will be more constrained by the new rules. The strategy is named *service control extension*. In the case of the *IC02*, we can add a state to the *Diploma* class, as for example *DiplomaInElaboration* and *DiplomaInProduction*. The *DMService* can modify the attribute *registrationLimit* while a diploma is in the *elaboration state*, but cannot modify it when a diploma is in the *production state*. In the *URService* side, the registration is allowed only to diplomas that are in production and therefore the *IC02* cannot be violated by the *DMService*.

Table 4. Method chunk for IC consistency handling with service control extension strategy

Chunk name	Service Control Extension
Situation	< Integrity Constraint *ic*, Service ς>
Preconditions	c1) *context(ic)* $\cap$ $sSs(\varsigma)$$\neq\varnothing$
	c2) *ic* $\notin$ $sRs(\varsigma$
Intention	Settle the integrity constrain *ic* overlap with the service ς by adding a control element to the service ς
Postconditions	c1) *ic* cannot be violated by any action of ς
Guideline	Add new rules and eventually new elements (attribute, classes) that guarantee that *ic* cannot be violated by any action of the ς.
	Eventually modify the *ic*.

IC Transformation into a Condition Strategy. This method chunk (see Table 5) transforms an IC into a condition and offers therefore the possibility to choose the actions that have to handle this condition. By transforming the IC into a condition, the validation of the rule is not anymore mandatory and the service with which it was in overlap does not need to validate the rule. In the case of the *IC02*, transforming this constraint into a condition will allow to validate *IC02* only by the actions of the *URService*. Registration to diploma through the *URService* will follow the *IC02* condition while the *DMService* will not. This strategy decreases the global level of consistency of the IS by transforming the IC into a simple condition.

Table 5. Method chunk for IC consistency handling by IC transformation strategy

Chunk name	IC transformation into a condition
Situation	< Integrity Constraint ic, Service ς>
Preconditions	c1) $context(ic) \cap sSs(\varsigma) \neq \varnothing$
	c2) $ic \notin sRs(\varsigma)$
Intention	Settle the integrity constrain *ic* overlap with the service ς by transforming the *ic* into a condition
Postconditions	c1) *ic* is a condition
Guideline	Transform *ic* into a condition.

5   Evaluating Integrity Constraints Consistency Handling Impact

The method chunks presented in the previous section demonstrate that the impact of the service integrity constraints consistency handling depends on the selected strategy and can be more or less cumbersome to deal with. We propose here a set of indicators in order to support the evaluation of this impact and the selection of the most appropriate method chunk in each situation.

5.1   Service Evolution Indicators

For this study we select four properties of a service, named *needs (N)*, *capabilities (CAP)*, *overlap (O)* and *consistency (CO)*, and we aim to assess the impact of each IC consistency handling strategy on these properties (i.e. indicate how they evolve).

The evaluation of the evolution of service *needs* consists in detecting if a given method chunk increases or reduces the information necessary for the execution of service capabilities. The evaluation of service *capabilities* property means to identify if a method chunk will cause a loose or an increase of the capabilities offered by the service. Similarly, we evaluate if it will increase or decrease the static space *overlap* of a given service. Finally, the *consistency* property allows the evaluation of the rule system of the service – to measure if the applied strategy will relax or harden the integrity constraints, i.e. more integrity constraints will be defined or some existing integrity constraints will not be validated anymore by the service.

In order to evaluate the impact of the method chunks on the discussed properties we define property evolution indicators. This impact is deterministic when it can be established before the enactment of the method chunk, otherwise it is unknown (?).

Definition 11 (Indicator $\mathcal{I}^{\theta}$). Given a service ς, an indicator $\mathcal{I}^{\theta}$ measures the evolution of its property $\theta \in \{N, CAP, O, CO\}$ between service variants v_i^{ς} and v_i^{ς}. This evolution can be *an increase ($\nearrow$), a decrease ($\searrow$)* or *stay constant ($\rightarrow$)*.

The evaluation of the evolution of service needs after application of a method chunk is based on the number of classes in its static space (sSs), which can stay constant or have more or less classes.

Definition 12 (Needs indicator $\mathcal{I}^{N}$). Given a service ς and its variants v_i^{ς} and v_i^{ς}, we measure the impact on service needs with $\Delta sSs = |sSs(v_i^{\varsigma})| - |sSs(v_i^{\varsigma})|$. The semantic of the needs indicator $\mathcal{I}^{N}(v_i^{\varsigma}, v_i^{\varsigma})$ is defined as: $\mathcal{I}^{N} = \rightarrow \Leftrightarrow \Delta sSs = 0; \mathcal{I}^{N} = \nearrow \Leftrightarrow \Delta sSs > 0; \mathcal{I}^{N} = \searrow \Leftrightarrow \Delta sSs < 0.$

For example, the addition of the *IC02* into the rule space of the *DMService* following the *Service static space extension strategy* will result an extension of the static space of the *DMService* with the class *UniversityRegistrationRequest*. It means that more information will be required to realise the capabilities of this service: the *DMService* will have to access the *UniversityRegistrationRequest* class in order to validate the *IC02* (to ensure rule completeness). Moreover, it is not only a question of rule validation, but also a question of information space modification for the actors using this service. After the addition of this new IC, if an actor will need to modify the attribute *Diploma.registrationLimit* he/she will have to know the *IC02* as well as the new class *UniversityRegistrationRequest*.

The evaluation of service capabilities evolution is based on the actions that it can execute. With the static space constant, the decrease of $\mathcal{I}^{CAP}$ means that the service offers fewer capabilities with the same amount of information.

Definition 13 (Capabilities indicator $\mathcal{I}^{CAP}$). Given a service ς and its variants v_i^{ς} and v_i^{ς}, we measure the impact on service capabilities with $\Delta sDs = |sDs(v_i^{\varsigma})| - |sDs(v_i^{\varsigma})|$. The semantic of the capabilities indicator $\mathcal{I}^{CAP}(v_i^{\varsigma}, v_i^{\varsigma})$ is defined as: $\mathcal{I}^{CAP} = \rightarrow \Leftrightarrow \Delta sDs = 0; \mathcal{I}^{CAP} = \nearrow \Leftrightarrow \Delta sDs > 0; \mathcal{I}^{CAP} = \searrow \Leftrightarrow \Delta sDs < 0.$

If the capabilities indicator decreases the unity of work represented by the service loses some responsibility on the information space. Such a change can result in the incapacity of realising some work with this service, or the work will be harder to do. For example, another possibility for handling the *IC02* overlap with *DMService* is by applying the *Service responsibility reduction* method chunk. In this case, we remove from the *DMService* the possibility to update the registration limit of a diploma (effect *<update, Diploma.registrationLimit>*) and therefore all the actions that can produce this effect. By doing this, we reduce the responsibility space of this service and the actors managing the diplomas will not be able to update this attribute anymore.

The evaluation of the service overlap property is based on the number of classes in the static space that are shared with others services. With a constant number of classes, the increase of service overlap means that some parts of the service that were only used by the service are now shared with other services. In fact, as the overlap is between at least two services, the shared static space will evolve in more then one service.

Definition 14 (Overlap indicator $\mathcal{I}^O$). Let's $sSs_{shared}(\varsigma)$ represents the subset of the classes of $sSs(\varsigma)$ that are in overlap with other services. $sSs_{shared}(\varsigma)=\{cl \in sSs(\varsigma): cl\ is\ in\ class\ overlap\}$ (cf. definition 4). Given a service ς and its variants v_i^ς and v_t^ς, we measure the impact on service overlap with $\Delta sSs_{shared}=/sSs_{shared}(v_t^\varsigma)/-/sSs_{shared}(v_i^\varsigma)/$. The semantic of the overlap indicator $\mathcal{I}^O(v_i^\varsigma,v_t^\varsigma)$ is defined as $\mathcal{I}^O=\rightarrow \Leftrightarrow \Delta sSs_{shared}=0$; $\mathcal{I}^O=\nearrow \Leftrightarrow \Delta sSs_{shared}>0$; $\mathcal{I}^O=\searrow \Leftrightarrow \Delta sSs_{shared}<0$.

For example, adding the *IC02* to the *DMService* by applying the *service static space extension strategy* implies to add the *UniversityRegistrationRequest* class (from the *URService*) to the *DMService*. The consequences for the *URService* and the *DMService* will be an increase of their overlap.

Finally, the last indicator evaluates the preservation of service consistency. It measures if the service will be more or less constrained after applying a method chunk. Due to the difficulty to reason with integrity constraints in its full generality [18], the evaluation of the level of consistency cannot be reduced to the calculation of the number of service rules.

Definition 15 (Consistency indicator $\mathcal{I}^{CO}$). Given a service ς and its variants v_i^ς and v_t^ς, the consistency indicator $\mathcal{I}^{CO}(v_i^\varsigma,v_t^\varsigma)$ decreases ($\mathcal{I}^{CO}=\searrow$) when some IC are removed or relaxed from the $sRs(\varsigma)$, it increases ($\mathcal{I}^{CO}=\nearrow$) when IC are added or hardened, and finally it is stable ($\mathcal{I}^{CO}=\rightarrow$) when IC stay unchanged.

For example, the *IC transformation into a condition* method chunk transforms the *IC02* into a condition in order to validate it only in the *URService*. This transformation can be seen as an elimination of the IC, or as a relaxing of the IC into a condition. Anyway, the service rule space will be less constrained and therefore the consistency of *URService* will decrease.

5.2 Applying the Indicators

Table 6 overviews the impact of the application of the five IC consistency handling method chunks measured with the four service evolution indicators.

Table 6. Overview of the IC consistency handling impact

Method chunk \ Indicator	Needs $\mathcal{I}^N$	Capabilities $\mathcal{I}^{CAP}$	Overlap $\mathcal{I}^O$	Consistency $\mathcal{I}^{CO}$
Simple IC addition	$\rightarrow$	$\rightarrow$	$\rightarrow$	$\nearrow$
Static space extension	$\nearrow$	$\rightarrow$	$\nearrow$	$\nearrow$
Responsibility reduction	$\rightarrow$ or $\searrow$	$\searrow$	$\rightarrow$	$\rightarrow$
Control extension	$\rightarrow$ or $\nearrow^4$	$\rightarrow$	$\rightarrow$	$\nearrow$
IC transformation	$\rightarrow$	$\rightarrow$	$\rightarrow$	$\searrow$

---

[4] The static modularity can increase if the overlap protocol requires new classes.

We can see in this table that the method chunks supporting *simple IC addition* and *IC transformation* strategy have impact only on service consistency; however, while the first increases it the last decreases which can be rather negative especially when the service is a legacy one. Service capabilities evolve only when the *responsibility reduction* method chunk is applied. Reducing service capabilities of a legacy service can be problematic because it concerns an already established work unit. The overlap increases only because of the *static space extension* which means that the autonomy of the involved services is reduced. The application of the *static space extension* method chunk also increases service needs. Adding new classes into the static space of a legacy service is not always appropriate. For example, addition of the *IC02* to the *DMService* following this strategy requires to add the *UniversityRegistrationRequest* class to the *DMService* which is a legacy service. Adding this class (which manages university registration requests) to the service (which manages diplomas) does not make sense from the semantic and responsibility perspective of this service. Finally, if the IC is in overlap with several services, *control extension* strategy can be quite hard to apply as all the involved services will have to implement the overlap protocol.

To summarize, we claim that the objective of these indicators is not to state that one strategy is better than another but rather to indicate the type of impact that should be expected and to help decide which type of impact could be accepted and managed. In general, the impact on a legacy service is always more problematic than the impact on a new one because some conformance invariants, as defined in [1], can forbid some evolution and cause modifications of existing data and processes.

6   Conclusion

Handling information service integration in order to extend an existing IS can be quite cumbersome especially when dealing with service rule space overlap. However, this task is necessary in order to ensure IS policies and integrity on the one hand and to preserve each service modularity and consistency on the other hand. Based on our previous work where we define the notion of ISS [3] and propose a process model for ISS integration into a legacy IS [2], we focus here our attention on the consistency handling of the ISS and IS rule spaces. For this purpose, we define the notion of service rule space overlap and identify generic integrity constraints overlap situations and inconsistencies to be resolved.

The inconsistency of the integrity constraints, which are the most important rules to handle, can be considered in several ways each of them having a different impact on service properties. In this work we propose five IC consistency handling strategies captured in the form of method chunks and we illustrate their application. In order to support the selection of the most appropriate method chunk in a given situation, we analyze the impact that each of them has on four service properties: the *needs* for executing service capabilities, the *capabilities* provided by the service, the static space *overlap* with other services and the *consistency* of the service. As a consequence, we define four service evolution indicators, one for each property. Each indicator shows how the corresponding property can evolve when applying the method chunk and therefore helps to evaluate the impact of its application. It is clear that important changes have to be avoided on the legacy services.

Currently, we focus our effort on identifying and evaluating other method chunks having less impact on service properties, investigating the potential of the service evolution indictors and developing a tool supporting our approach.

The formalization presented in this paper is based on the notion of information service as defined in MISS [3]. However, the proposal can be generalized to other services metamodels such as: WSDL [20], WSPER [5] or Service specification reference model [1]. These metamodels already define the notions of action (named operation or method) and information model (object-oriented or some kind of type system). To apply our approach on these metamodels, we need to extend them with the notion of rule and to annotate the operation or method with the notion of effect. With this pivot concept we are able to identify the actions that can invalidate the IC. We are therefore looking for the possibility to extract service specification knowledge from existing enterprise service registry and to enhance it with the rule knowledge.

References

1. Andrikopoulos, V., Benbernou, S., Papazoglou, M.P.: Managing the evolution of service specifications. In: Bellahsène, Z., Léonard, M. (eds.) CAiSE 2008. LNCS, vol. 5074, pp. 359–374. Springer, Heidelberg (2008)
2. Arni-Bloch, N., Ralyté, J.: Service-Oriented Information Systems Engineering: A Situation-Driven Approach for Service Integration. In: Bellahsène, Z., Léonard, M. (eds.) CAiSE 2008. LNCS, vol. 5074, pp. 140–143. Springer, Heidelberg (2008)
3. Arni-Bloch, N., Ralyté, J.: MISS: A Metamodel of Information System Service. In: Proc. of the 17th Int. Conf. on Information System Development (ISD 2008), Paphos, Cyprus (2008)
4. Batini, C., Lenzerini, M., Navathe, S.B.: A comparative analysis of methodologies for database schema integration. ACM Comput. Surv. 18(4), 323–364 (1986)
5. Dubray, J.-J.: Wsper an abstract soa framework. Technical report (2007),
   http://www.wsper.org
6. Elmagardmid, A.K. (ed.): Database Transaction Models for Advanced Applications. Morgan Kaufmann Publishers Inc., San Francisco (1990)
7. Erl, T.: SOA Principles of Service Design. Prentice Hall PTR, Englewood Cliffs (2007)
8. Fahrner, C., Marx, T., Philippi, S.: Dice: Declarative integrity constraint embedding into the object database standard odmg-93. Data Knowl. Eng. 23(2), 119–145 (1997)
9. Grefen, P.W.P.J., Apers, P.M.G.: Integrity control in relational database systems - an overview. Data Knowl. Eng. 10, 187–223 (1993)
10. Haesen, R., Snoeck, M., Lemahieu, W., Poelmans, S.: On the definition of service granularity and its architectural impact. In: Bellahsène, Z., Léonard, M. (eds.) CAiSE 2008. LNCS, vol. 5074, pp. 375–389. Springer, Heidelberg (2008)
11. Krafzig, D., Banke, K., Slama, D.: Enterprise SOA: Service-Oriented Architecture Best Practices. Prentice Hall PTR, Englewood Cliffs (2004)
12. MacKenzie, M., et al.: Reference model for service oriented architecture 1.0. Technical report, Oasis (2006)
13. Mirbel, I., Ralyté, J.: Situational Method Engineering: Combining Assembly-Based and Roadmap-Driven Approaches. Requirements Engineering 11(1), 58–78 (2006)
14. Papazoglou, M.P.: Web services and business transactions. World Wide Web 6(1), 49–91 (2003)

15. Papazoglou, M.P.: The challenges of service evolution. In: Bellahsène, Z., Léonard, M. (eds.) CAiSE 2008. LNCS, vol. 5074, pp. 1–15. Springer, Heidelberg (2008)
16. Park, J., Ram, S.: Information systems interoperability: What lies beneath? ACM Trans. of Information Systems 22(4), 595–632 (2004)
17. Quartel, D.A.C., et al.: Cosmo: A conceptual framework for service modelling and refinement. Information Systems Frontiers 9(2-3), 225–244 (2007)
18. Queralt, A., Teniente, E.: Decidable reasoning in UML schemas with constraints. In: Bellahsène, Z., Léonard, M. (eds.) CAiSE 2008. LNCS, vol. 5074, pp. 281–295. Springer, Heidelberg (2008)
19. Quix, C., Kensche, D., Li, X.: Generic schema merging. In: Krogstie, J., Opdahl, A.L., Sindre, G. (eds.) CAiSE 2007 and WES 2007. LNCS, vol. 4495, pp. 127–141. Springer, Heidelberg (2007)
20. W3C. Web services description language (wsdl) version 2.0 part 1: Core language. Technical report, W3C (2007)

Socio-instrumental Service Modelling:
An Inquiry on e-Services for Tax Declarations

Göran Goldkuhl

Department of Management and Engineering,
Linköping University, SE-581 83 Linköping, Sweden
{goran.goldkuhl@liu.se}

Abstract. A socio-instrumental service modelling approach is presented through a tax declaration case study. Three different service alternatives have been investigated (two paper form alternatives and one e-service). These service alternatives have been studied through service interaction modelling, contextual service definitions and service pattern analysis. Service effects have been identified at both service parties; the service provider (the Tax Agency) and the service clients (companies). These service effects were dependent on affordances of services and service pre-conditions. These affordances can be of both social and technical-instrumental character. This study has contributed with service modelling methods and a new socio-instrumental conceptualisation of services. Important new notions are: reciprocal service effect, interdependence of services and service pre-conditions, unintended service affordances, reciprocal facilitation through service interaction. These concepts lead to the new concept of co-service.

Keywords: Service, e-service, service modelling, co-service, e-government, socio-instrumental pragmatism, evaluation, practical inquiry.

1 Introduction

Information systems (IS) are no longer restricted to be internal organisational phenomena. They are in a growing extent used externally in interaction with stakeholders outside the organisation. Many such systems include services to other actors. We tend to consider such systems as e-services. The development of e-service applications raises new demands on information systems development (ISD). Initial steps of ISD with a focus on enterprise modelling (EM) need in such cases to involve service modelling (SM). Service modelling can thus be seen as one crucial part of a broader enterprise modelling when developing e-service applications. This means that relations to other parts of EM need to be investigated when clarifying SM. Steps have been taken in this direction concerning SM in relation to modelling of goals and value object exchange [1, 2] and to workflow and use-case modelling [2, 3]. Within service marketing there is a related interest into what is called service maps [4, 5]. These can be seen as a kind of service process models. These are all important contributions to SM, but there is a need for further investigations, especially concerning modelling the interactivity of services. This follows the idea that services to large extent are co-produced by customers (clients) and suppliers (providers) [4, 6, 7, 8].

A. Persson and J. Stirna (Eds.): PoEM 2009, LNBIP 39, pp. 207–221, 2009.
© IFIP International Federation for Information Processing 2009

One great obstacle in conceptualising service modelling is that the service notion is equivocal. Reading the service marketing literature, service can mean resources, activities, processes, results, utilities, benefits, values and experiences [6, 7]. This conceptual vagueness of services spills over to the e-service notion. There seems not to be a consensual and clear definition of an e-service.

This paper addresses challenges of service modelling. Besides issues of method and model uses, this includes foundational conceptual matters of (e-)services and e-service relations to business processes. The paper develops a distinct perspective on service modelling: A socio-instrumental approach to service modelling. This approach has evolved in a multi-grounded fashion through a diagnostic case study. Multi-grounded means that it has been theory-informed as well as emerging through practical use in a real-life modelling situation [26]. This is more fully described in section 2 below. The chosen case study deals with tax declarations; an e-government service. This means that the paper contributes with knowledge concerning egov services (public e-services). The paper can be said to have multiple purposes and contributions. It contributes with

- A socio-instrumental conceptualisation of services, e-services and egov services
- A service modelling approach
- An egov case study

Most important of the paper is the service conceptualisation and the over-all service modelling approach. Specific notations are presented, but the main focus is not on different notational elements. It is beyond the scope to make any comparison with other EM notations.

2   Research Approach

The research approach can be characterised as a *practical inquiry* [9] following the spirits of pragmatism and its notion of pragmatic inquiry [10, 11]. As such, this practical inquiry comprises action research, design research and evaluation research. These three aspects will be further described below. Practical inquiry means a study in one or several local practices with a dual purpose of contributing both to these local practices and to general knowledge. In this respect it coincides with purposes of action research [12]. One difference is that general knowledge of practical inquiry is aimed both for general practices and for the scientific community. The demands on action research are not defined [12] as contributing to general practice outside changed local practices.

The author of this paper has participated in an inquiry at the Swedish Tax Agency (STA). An e-service for companies' tax declarations was launched some years ago. It has not been a success since there are only 30% of the companies that use this e-service. The rest of the companies use the traditional way with a paper form for tax declarations. STA has a clear ambition to increase the amount of e-declarations. A joint project was started by STA and some researchers in order to investigate causes for this missing success and to redesign the e-service to be more attractive in order to increase its usage.

The research reported in this paper is delimited to the initial diagnosis phase. This means that it is based on an evaluative endeavour. The evaluation consisted of modelling of the e-service as well as the paper form service. There was a clear diagnostic purpose to better understand why the companies did not use the e-service. STA had earlier conducted a broad survey among companies concerning tax declarations. This diagnostic study was based on the earlier survey and the purpose was to disclose yet hidden patterns of use and non-use in order to build an informed basis for subsequent redesign. The conducted evaluation contributed to this local practice (STA) with new knowledge as a kind of evaluation research [13]. The evaluation has been used as an exploratory empirical study in the research process. It is exploratory in the sense that the evaluation was used to try out and continually refine the socio-pragmatic service modelling approach described in this paper. This means that the evaluation (both process and product) form the empirical basis for abstraction and theorizing.

The collaboration between Swedish Tax Agency and the researchers can be characterized as action research (AR). It aims at local practice changes besides contribution to scientific knowledge. This part of the research cannot be said to constitute a full action research cycle according to [12]. It is limited to a diagnosis intervention [9]. For a full AR cycle it requires also action planning (=design intervention) and action taking (=implementation) [12, 9]. An evaluation/diagnosis intervention, as conducted in this case, is thus a partial action research [9].

A great part of the evaluation of the services at STA has consisted of service modelling. This means creation of model-artefacts based on languages/notations. Integrated with this modelling there has been an evolution and adaptation of concepts and notations. The creation of model-artefacts and model-languages can be interpreted as a kind of design research (DR). Results of design research are defined as constructs, methods and models [15, 16]. This practical inquiry has led to new knowledge concerning service conceptualisations (i.e. constructs in DR), new and adapted methods/modelling languages (i.e. methods in DR) and the creation of situational models of declaration services (models in DR). The models are parts of evaluative statements concerning the declaration services. The models as such have been continuously (meta-)evaluated concerning their practical usefulness and conceptual cohesion. The evolving socio-pragmatic perspective on services can be seen as an embryonic design theory [17, 18, 26].

3   Some Fundamentals of Socio-instrumental Pragmatism

The basic perspective used for developing this service modelling approach has been socio-instrumental pragmatism (SIP) [9, 19, 20]. This is an eclectic approach adapted for IS studies. SIP is an *integration* and *synthesis* of several action-oriented theories from reference disciplines to IS. SIP has been inspired by speech act theory, pragmatic philosophy, symbolic interactionism, social action theories, affordance theory and activity theory among others. Confer [19, 20] for more details on theoretical background. One key idea behind SIP is that this framework should be possible to use for many different research areas in IS aiming for *seamless theorizing* [19]. This means that it should be possible to use for conceptualization of (e-)services among other areas.

The basic concepts of SIP are *actor/agent*, *action* and *object*. Other important concepts are *action disposition* (by actors/agents) and *relation* (between actors). SIP concepts are visualized in figure 1. This figure describes socio-instrumental action; one actor (the focused actor) conducts an intervention (interventive action) leading to a result object intended for another actor (the addressee). The addressee receives this object which is another type of action. Actions respective objects can be material or communicative. The focused actor can deliver a material object to the addressee or he can express (say or write) something directed to the addressee. Both material and communicative actions give rise to (changed) social relations between the actors [19].

There are different kinds of objects that have different functions in the actions. In order to produce a *result object*, the actor may use some base object and some instrument object. A *base object* is something that is transformed (to a result object) through the interventive action. *Instruments* are utilized in interventive actions in order to enable and/or facilitate the creation of result objects.

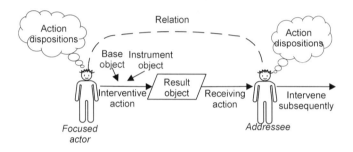

Fig. 1. Socio-instrumental action (based on [19])

SIP acknowledges both the social and instrumental character of interaction between actors. There are communicative objects that inform addressees and regulate the relations between the actors. There may also be technical/material objects which need to be handled by the actors. Materiality constrains and facilitates actions [21, 19]. Actions are performed by human actors; but some actions may be performed by technical artefacts (agents) like IT-systems. Such actions need to be well-defined and they should always be performed on behalf of some human actor.

Another important notion in socio-instrumental pragmatism is *affordance*. This notion emanates from affordance theory [22]; which is an ecological theory of perception. According to this theory, humans (as well as other species) perceive the surrounding world in terms of what action possibilities it affords to us. An affordance is an action possibility for the actor provided/offered to him. It is something that humans can do with, through and in relation to the environment. Instruments and bases are affordances for the actor to act and create a result object. The original affordance concept was mainly focused on material conditions. But there are also socio-communicative affordances which through symbols influence the actor and give rise to action possibilities. Affordances are not only positive. One can also talk about negative affordances, i.e. elements that obstruct or inhibit action. There may be material affordances that are positive (enable or facilitate action) or negative (obstruct or inhibit action). There may also be communicative affordances that are positive (e.g. guidance, advices) or negative (as constraining regulations). Information that is misleading or confusing can also be seen as negative affordances.

4   Socio-instrumental Service Modelling: A Taxation Case Study

This section describes of parts the case study at the Swedish Tax Agency introduced in section 2 above. It describes three types of models:

- Service interaction models
- Contextual service definitions
- Service pattern models

The modelling has been driven by the author/researcher in continual interaction with a STA officer who is responsible for development of the e-declaration service. Empirical bases for the service modelling has, besides dialogues with STA staff, been results from an earlier survey among companies concerning use and non-use of the e-service, taxation regulations, other STA documents and the e-declaration service. The different service models have been continually inspected and validated by the STA officer.

4.1   Service Interaction Modelling

Service is often described as a co-production between a service provider and a client [6, 7, 8]. Even if this concept of co-production may be questionable, it is obvious that there is often an interaction going on between the provider and the client. This makes it important to describe this interaction in order to clarify the service's role for the client as well as for the provider [4, 5]. I would hypothesize that it is often more important to make service interaction models rather than business process models (workflow models) in service analysis and design [9]. Anyhow, in this study both service interaction models and business process models have been created. The process models are not presented or analysed in this paper since they have not influenced the socio-instrumental analysis to any significant degree.

Service interaction modelling consists of describing the basic interaction structure between the service provider and the service client concerning provision and use of the services. The main interest in the inquiry was towards the e-service (eTax Declaration). It was however important to compare it with the alternative service, declaration via a traditional paper form. This comparison was needed in order to better understand why so many companies still chose to use the paper form declaration.

Service interaction modelling started with a describing tax declaration in a generic way independent of how to make and submit the tax declaration. Based on this generic service interaction model, different services cases were identified. There were two main types of service cases (e-service vs. paper form). But there existed also some sub-cases of these two services cases. In this paper I will describe three service variants[1]; two paper form variants and one generalized e-service type. The division

---

[1] The notion of service variant is inspired by the notion of business process variant [23]. It has been found important in process modeling to distinguish between different process variants in order to make a clarifying analysis.

into different service variants was important since it makes a comparison possible and this can lead to conclusions concerning advantages and disadvantages. It is a way of identifying "analysis units". Each such unit (i.e. service variant) will be possible to describe in sufficient detail.

In figure 2 a service interaction model (called "InterActor Diagram") is presented for the ordinary paper form variant. It describes the two main interactors; the Swedish Tax Agency (service provider) and the company (as service client). It depicts also the government as an actor, since it produces tax regulations that govern the tax declaration process. Service interaction modelling relies on an exchange perspective rooted in SIP [23, 9] and the language action perspective [29]. What are the exchanges made in processes of agreement and accomplishment? What exchange actions are performed and thus what objects are exchanged? The regulative character of tax declaration makes this case rather distinctive.

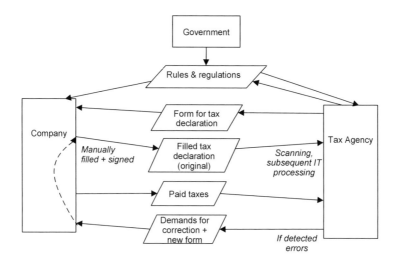

Fig. 2. Paper form declaration (use of original form) – InterActor Diagram

STA delivers paper declaration forms every month to companies. The company fills out the tax declaration form and submits it to the Tax Agency. The paper form is scanned and later IT processed where errors might be detected which might lead to demands for corrections.

The e-service variant is described in figure 3. In this case there is no paper form. The company fills out an e-form within the e-service. The declaration will be signed through an electronic Id. The authorized signatory needs to make request for an eId permit before the e-service is used the first time. The Tax Agency will receive the declaration electronically which will facilitate further IT processing. The e-service application will conduct number checks which will lead to fewer errors in received tax declarations.

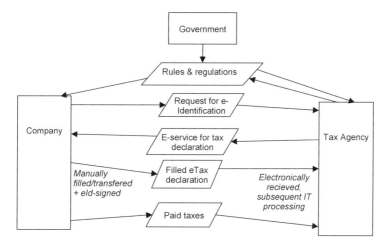

Fig. 3. eTax declaration – InterActor Diagram

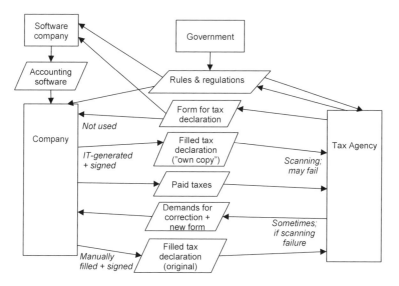

Fig. 4. Paper form declaration (use of "own copy") – InterActor Diagram

There are companies which use the paper form variant together with their account-ing software. The acquired software has capabilities to print out a tax declaration form with filled numbers. There is however one problem with this service case alternative. The Tax Agency's scanning equipment is so sensitive that it cannot (always) process forms that are printed from the companies' software systems. STA personnel might need to manually register the declaration or sometimes it can be resent to the com-pany with demands for a new declaration to be filled out.

4.2 Contextual Service Definition

An e-service should be a *service*. Why else should we call it an e-*service*? As stated in section 1 above, there are however not so clear conceptions of what a service is. Service can for example designate activity, use, experience and effect [6, 7]. In order to analyse and compare services it is pivotal to have a clear service conception. I agree that it is important to understand different service aspects like service actions, service use and service effects. But it is necessary to have a clear conception of what a service is for service evaluation and redesign. It is not acceptable to have equivocal meanings. For a more detailed critique of this vagueness in the service notion cf. [27].

For most services - what is *done* is the most important. Clients do not only request actions. They request something to be done. Clients request that actions will be accomplished leading to results that are useful for the client. This means that it is not the doing; instead what is done that is the essential of a service [27]. 'Service' is not just a noun-making of the verb 'serve'. Service is what is provided to the client through serving. I call the service to the client a *service fact*. This means what is done and thus possible for the client to experience or use. This means that a service comprises also affordances following the reasoning above in section 3. Through the use of a service the client may be able to perform actions otherwise not doable. A service has affordances for further action.

Table 1. Contextual service definition for two tax declaration services

Service type / Service category	Paper form service	Electronic service
Service provider	Swedish Tax Agency	Swedish Tax Agency
Service pre-conditions	Tax regulations	Tax regulations, Internet
Service provision actions	Deliver paper form	Establish e-service application (eTax Declaration)
Service techno-agent	--	eTax Declaration (e-service application)
Service to client (Service fact)	Delivered paper form	E-service
Service client	Company	Company
Service use & effects	Company can fill out, sign and submit declaration by mail	Company can fill out and get declaration checked, sign and submit it electronically

In table 1 contextual service definitions are given for the two declaration services. Contextual means that not only the service itself is defined. Several other (contextual) aspects are also described, as the service provider, service pre-conditions, service provision actions conducted by the provider, the client and the service use and possible effects. The contextual service definition also includes "service techno-agent" which means a technical performer of actions (like an e-service application or some other type of IT artefact). Having two services in one table makes them easier to compare.

4.3 Service Pattern Analysis

Services should be valuable to clients [7, 8]. The use of a service should give rise to effects that are conceived as valuable to the client. The service provider should deliver a service that is valuable to the client. This is essential following the general service discourse. There is a provider that should direct a valuable service to the client. Even if there, in service theory, is acknowledged that the client take part in the production of value [8], the whole focus is on value to the client. Total emphasis is on how the client should be satisfied through the service. There is no or little attention to how the service provision affects the provider in positive or negative terms.

When studying this service case (tax declaration) it is obvious that the different service designs will render different effects to both STA as service provider and the company as service client. It is not sufficient to analyse only service effects at the company. Different effects have arisen at both parties. The inquiry perspective has been on *reciprocal service effects*. This means service effects at both parties.

Service effects might not only be positive. In this case it was important to study *positive and negative effects* at both parties. It was however not sufficient to just identify these different effects. To evaluate the services it was necessary to make a *causal analysis* why these different effects were rendered. To make this causal analysis of reciprocal service effects, the socio-instrumental framework (introduced in section 3 above) was used. Services are considered as *affordances*. They offer action possibilities to a service user. Service affordances can be both *positive* and *negative*. A positive affordance will enable and/or facilitate actions. A negative affordance will obstruct or inhibit actions. The focus in the causal search was not only on the service itself. Different accompanying *service pre-conditions* were analysed, like regulations, accounting software and scanning equipment. This means an interest on both *social* matters (e.g. regulations) and *technical-instrumental* matters (e.g. scanning equipment) and how these different pre-conditions influenced the different parties in their actions. This follows the essence of socio-instrumental pragmatism.

This cause and effect analysis of services was labelled a *socio-pragmatic service pattern analysis*. The three services cases were investigated concerning reciprocal service effects and their socio-instrumental causes. Each service case was described in a service pattern diagram (figure 5-7).

A service pattern diagram is thus a kind of cause-effect diagram (see table 2). It describes socio-pragmatic patterns, which means that actions, different pre-conditions for actions and results and effects of actions are described. Action pre-conditions can be both internal (e.g. intentions, dispositions) and external objects (of both communicative and material character). The main type of relation is "lead-to", i.e. a cause-and-effect relation. The socio-pragmatic character means that it is not always a strict deterministic relation. Deliberation, intentionality and social interactivity are at stake. The diagrams do not only describe causal relations. They can also describe relations of inhibition character. The diagrams are divided in two parts; each part for each actor in order to clarify conditions, actions and effects clearly related to each actor. This makes also the interactivity character of the services to come through. Service pattern diagrams are re-developments of cause-effect problem diagrams [28].

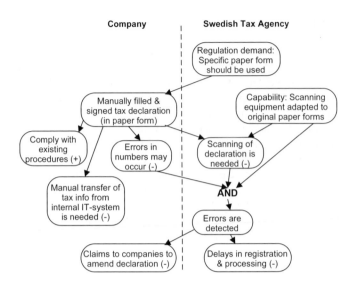

Fig. 5. Paper form declaration (use of original form) - Service pattern diagram

Table 2. Legend Service pattern diagrams

⬭	→	⊸●
Action, action pre-condition, action effect	"Lead-to" relation	"Inhibit" relation

Figure 5 describes the paper form service case; where the company uses the original paper form. As can be seen from this diagram there are negative effects for the Tax Agency, like the need to scan the declaration and thus delays in processing. Why do companies still use this service option? This was a key question in the service inquiry. One answer can be found from the diagram: Habit! The companies are accustomed to this kind of procedure. They tend to follow their routines if they do not see that they can gain a lot from shifting to new services.

More answers can be found from diagram 6 which describes the case where the company uses their accounting software system to generate a tax declaration in paper form ("own copy" alternative). This alternative will give certain advantages to the companies. They do not have to fill out the forms manually. Numbers are checked by the software. This alternative may however have negative consequences for STA. As said above (section 4.1), the STA scanning equipment is so sensitive that it sometimes cannot process forms that are printed from the companies' software systems.

This alternative is dependent on the capabilities of existing software. The accounting systems need to have capabilities (i.e. certain affordances) to print forms according to the standards of the Tax Agency. The software companies have used the STA paper forms to adapt their software (figure 4 above). According to regulations, this alternative is not acceptable. There is a regulation that states that original form should be used. However many companies do not comply with this regulation since their internal efficiency demands give preference to the use of the accounting software for printing the form. This case can be said to be an unintentional service case. It is unintentional from the perspective of the Tax Agency. On the other hand companies use this option intentionally to deliver tax declarations more easily.

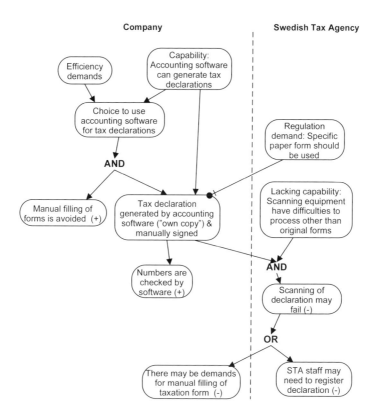

Fig. 6. Paper form declaration (use of "own copy") - Service pattern diagram

Even more answers can be found from the e-service diagram (figure 7). For the companies there might be seen easier to generate a tax declaration from their own software than manually fill out the e-form of the e-service. They need also to acquire an e-Identification to use the e-service. The companies do not have much to win to use the e-service alternative instead of using their own software for generation of tax declarations. The gains of the e-service alternative are to be found at the Tax Agency. They will get the tax declaration in electronic form which will enable a smooth continual processing. Scanning of tax declarations is avoided in this case. The e-service application will check numbers which will lead to fewer errors in declarations.

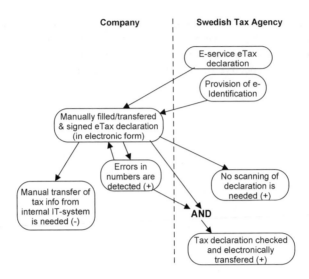

Fig. 7. eTax declaration (e-service) - Service pattern diagram

5 A Socio-instrumental Understanding of Services and Co-services

The socio-instrumental service modelling of tax declaration services described above gave rise to several positive inquiry effects. New circumstances were discovered and revealed concerning use and non-use of the e-service. The different models gave a clarifying picture of why so many companies still do not use the e-service. This was acknowledged through interaction with Tax Agency personnel. The models have also been used as a basis for further inquiries concerning these services.

What conclusions of general character can be drawn from this case study? The study has developed and adopted a socio-instrumental approach to service modelling and inquiry. This approach has been applicable and useful in this egov service case. I would like to claim that the conclusions, clarified below, should be valid for governmental services in general. Concepts have been abstracted in order to be applicable for such service analysis. Some of these concepts, perhaps all, might also be applicable and useful in other service settings. This needs however to be shown through further empirical inquires.

The purpose of this paper is not to compare the socio-instrumental approach and its modelling languages with other EM methods. A few comments will just be interposed. The notations used here (figures 2-7; table 1) are simple and flexible. Sophisticated notational distinctions as e.g. in i* [1, 30] and e³value [1] have been avoided. The underlying perspective (socio-instrumental pragmatism with emphasis on service interactions and service patterns) gives rich expressiveness in models. The basic conceptualisations are used together the notations in a rather free way.

This study has contributed with several important notions. One key notion is *reciprocal service effect*. This means that effects of service use can arise for both parties in the service interaction; i.e. both service provider and service client. These effects can be of both positive and negative character. The different service alternatives and their uses gave rise to different effects for the two parties. Some effects were positive and some effects were negative.

Another key notion in this socio-instrumental service conceptualisation is the *interdependence of services and service pre-conditions*. In order to understand service effects it is necessary to study services as well as service pre-conditions of social and instrumental character at each party. To understand why certain service effects arise (e.g. scanning failure) it was necessary to investigate service pre-conditions at each party (e.g. capabilities of accounting software and scanning equipment). It was not only necessary to understand the capabilities and deficiencies of technical instruments (as mentioned above) but also demands and deliberations of social characters (e.g. tax regulations and companies' efficiency demands).

Another important notion in this emerging service conceptualisation is *unintended service affordances*. Services may have unintended affordances which can be used to give rise to negative affordances and effects. The Tax Agency's paper form led to *unintended positive affordances for the companies*. The distributed paper form enabled software companies to develop accounting software with capabilities to print tax declarations. And this enabled companies to use such software to print tax declarations directly from their accounting systems and thus avoiding manual filling out of forms. Such software-generated declaration forms had the *unintended negative affordances for the Tax Agency* of not being able to scan them through the scanning equipment.

Following these different conceptualisations another important notion appears: *Reciprocal facilitation through service interaction*. This means that the two parties facilitate for each other. It is not only a one-sided service delivery from the service provider to the service client. What the client does and how this is performed will also have effects for the provider. The service is not only for the client. The service is both for client and provider. A new concept emerges from this discussion: *Co-service*.

A co-service is something arranged that should have positive affordances and positive effects for both parties in a service interaction. The co-service perspective emphasises reciprocal facilitation.

This means that it should not be confused with the "co-production of service value" perspective [8]. That perspective involves the customer/client in the service/value production. The service seems however still to be seen as something aimed for and restricted to the client. The co-service perspective emphasises that value for both parties are important and should be acknowledged. The socio-instrumental co-service perspective also acknowledges that co-service interaction (and its design) are processes of "take and give". There are trade-offs and pay-offs between the two parties. Co-service interaction may sometimes comprise reciprocal inhibition. Co-services mean that valuable and non-valuable effects are created by and for both parties.

Is co-service is a special kind of service or is it a special perspective on all kinds of services? It is yet too early to answer this question unequivocally. It is definitely a perspective on services that emphasise the dual roles of some services. I would not yet dare to claim that is a perspective applicable for all types of services. Some services (like governmental e-services) would be easier to consider as co-services than others. Many governmental e-services have a two-way communication character [9, 24, 25], i.e. the client (citizen) and the provider (governmental agency) are both communicators and information recipients. The two parties should facilitate for each other. Public e-services should be seen as co-services.

6 Conclusions

This paper has presented a socio-instrumental approach to service modelling. This approach has emerged through an inquiry on tax declaration services which was presented in section 4 above. The approach to service modelling consists of conceptualisations and modelling methods. The modelling process consisted of three steps: 1) service interaction modelling, 2) contextual service definition and 3) service pattern analysis. Service interaction modelling follows the principle of provider-client interactivity and participation of the client in the service process [4, 6, 7, 8]. Contextual service definition tries to capture several different aspects of services [6, 7, 27]. Service pattern analysis investigates services and service pre-conditions as socio-instrumental affordances [22, 19, 20] and identifies positive and negative effects at both parties through uses of these service affordances.

Through the empirical inquiry and the evolution of modelling methods a socio-instrumental conceptualisation of services have emerged. Several important notions have been put forth (section 5 above) for example the notion of co-services. This means that valuable and non-valuable effects are created for both service parties through service interaction. Further research will demonstrate the domain of applicability of this service conceptualisation. It has here been used in a governmental service setting. Whether different proposed concepts are applicable beyond this context will be shown through future studies. One important contribution of this study is that it once more (cf. [9, 27] for other examples) has shown the applicability and usefulness of socio-instrumental pragmatism as a generative theory for creating new relevant models and methods within IS as well as concrete situational results of value.

Acknowledgments. This research has been financially supported by the Swedish Governmental Agency for Innovation Systems (VINNOVA).

References

1. Gordijn, J., Yu, E., van der Raadt, B.: E-service design using i* and e3value modelling. IEEE Software, 26–33 (May/June 2006)
2. Henkel, M., Perjons, E., Zdravkovic, J.: A value-based foundation for service modelling. In: The European Conference on Web Services (ECOWS 2006), Zurich (2006)
3. Anzböck, R., Dustdar, S.: Modeling Medical E-services. In: Desel, J., Pernici, B., Weske, M. (eds.) BPM 2004. LNCS, vol. 3080, pp. 49–65. Springer, Heidelberg (2004)
4. Kingman-Brundage, J.: Service mapping: Back to basics. In: Glynn, W.J., Barnes, J.G. (eds.) Understanding service management. John Wiley, Chichester (1995)
5. Getz, D., O'Neill, M., Carlsen, J.: Service quality evaluation at events through service mapping. Journal of Travel Research 39, 380–390 (2001)
6. Grönroos, C.: Service marketing and management. Managing the moments of truths in service marketing. Lexington Books, Lexington (1990)
7. Edvardsson, B., Gustafsson, A., Johnson, M.D., Sandén, B.: New service development and innovation in the new economy. Studentlitteratur, Lund (2000)

8. Ramirez, R.: Value co-production: intellectual origins and implications for practice and re-
    search. Strategic Management Journal 20, 49–65 (1999)
9. Goldkuhl, G.: What does it mean to serve the citizen in e-services? - Towards a practical
    theory founded in socio-instrumental pragmatism. International Journal of Public Informa-
    tion Systems 2007(3), 135–159 (2007)
10. Dewey, J.: Logic: The theory of inquiry. Henry Holt, New York (1938)
11. Cronen, V.: Practical theory, practical art, and the pragmatic-systemic account of inquiry.
    Communication Theory 11(1), 14–35 (2001)
12. Susman, G.I., Evered, R.D.: An assessment of the scientific merits of action research. Ad-
    ministrative Science Quarterly 23(4), 582–603 (1978)
13. Van der Knaap, P.: Theory-based evaluation and learning: Possibilities and challenges.
    Evaluation 10(1), 16–34 (2004)
14. March, S.T., Smith, G.F.: Design and natural science research in information technology.
    Decision Support Systems 15(4), 251–266 (1995)
15. Hevner, A.R., March, S.T., Park, J., Ram, S.: Design science in information systems re-
    search. MIS Quarterly 28(1), 75–105 (2004)
16. Walls, J.G., Widmeyer, G.R., El Sawy, O.A.: Building an information systems design the-
    ory for vigilant EIS. Information Systems Research 3(1), 36–59 (1992)
17. Gregor, S., Jones, D.: The anatomy of a design theory. JAIS 8(5), 312–335 (2007)
18. Goldkuhl, G.: Socio-Instrumental Pragmatism: A theoretical synthesis for pragmatic con-
    ceptualisation in information systems. In: Proceedings of the 3rd Intl. Conf. on Action in
    Language, Organisations and Information Systems, University of Limerick (2005)
19. Goldkuhl, G., Ågerfalk, P.J.: IT Artefacts as Socio-Pragmatic Instruments: Reconciling the
    Pragmatic, Social, Semiotic and Technical. International Journal of Technology and Hu-
    man Interaction 1(3), 29–43 (2005)
20. Wertsch, J.V.: Mind as action. Oxford University Press, New York (1998)
21. Gibson, J.J.: The ecological approach to visual perception. Houghton Mifflin, Boston
    (1979)
22. Lind, M., Goldkuhl, G.: Designing business process variants – using the BAT framework
    as a pragmatic lens. In: Bussler, C.J., Haller, A. (eds.) BPM 2005. LNCS, vol. 3812, pp.
    408–420. Springer, Heidelberg (2006)
23. Ancarini, A.: Towards quality e-service in the public sector: The evolution of web sites in
    the local public service sector. Managing Service Quality 15(1), 6–23 (2005)
24. Wimmer, M.A.: Integrated Service Modelling for Online One-stop Government. Elec-
    tronic Markets 12(3), 149–156 (2002)
25. Goldkuhl, G.: Design theories in information systems – a need for multi-grounding. Jour-
    nal of Information Technology Theory and Application (JITTA) 6(2), 59–72 (2004)
26. Goldkuhl, G., Röstlinger, A.: Beyond goods and services - an elaborate product classifica-
    tion on pragmatic grounds. In: Proc. of Quality in Services (QUIS 7), Karlstad (2000)
27. Goldkuhl, G., Röstlinger, A.: Joint elicitation of problems: An important aspect of change
    analysis. In: Avison, D., et al. (eds.) Human, organizational and social dimensions of In-
    formation systems development. North-Holland, Amsterdam (1993)
28. Winograd, T., Flores, F.: Understanding computers and cognition: A new foundation for
    design. Ablex, Norwood (1986)
29. Yu, E.: Towards Modelling and Reasoning Support for Early-Phase Requirements Engi-
    neering. In: Proc. 3rd IEEE Int'l Symp. Requirements Eng. (RE 1997), pp. 226–235. IEEE
    CS Press, Los Alamitos (1997)

A Game Prototype for
Basic Process Model Elicitation

Stijn Hoppenbrouwers and Bart Schotten

Radboud University Nijmegen
Institute for Computing and Information Sciences
Heijendaalseweg 135
6525 AJ Nijmegen, the Netherlands
stijnh@cs.ru.nl, b.schotten@student.ru.nl

Abstract. We present a first prototype of a simple "modelling wizard". We also explain the ideas and rationales behind it: a first exploration of a new type of modelling tool which uses game-like interaction to guide and support the modeller in the process of modelling. After being played, the prototype game renders the basic information for a formal process representation (for example in BPMN), based on structured input given by a domain expert as she plays the game. Rather than offering substantial support for real modellers at this point, the game merely aims to demonstrate what we believe to be a new direction in thinking about methods and support for enterprise modelling. We also report on our experiences and evaluation of the prototype.

Keywords: Method engineering, process modelling, serious games, interactive modelling.

1 Introduction

This paper aims to contribute to the field of methods for business/enterprise modelling. Our work is related to methodological work in information systems analysis and design, and to the sub-field of method engineering [1]. Recently, we have proposed a somewhat alternative approach to the study and development of methods for *operational* modelling [2], meaning that we take the *practice* of modelling as our object of study, emphasizing the detailed actions and interactions that constitute the process of modelling. This contrasts mainstream method engineering, which mostly focuses on the definition of meta-models and high-level phasing of the modelling process, typically in terms of the required creation of various interrelated deliverables, without considering how every single element in such deliverables gets into place.

Our interaction-oriented approach to modelling research aims to be complementary to the mainstream approach in that it addresses issues hardly addressed in the mainstream, like aspects of modelling concerning human-human interaction, human-machine interaction, motivation, strategy and tactics, collaboration, decision making, negotiation, problem solving, and so on. We believe that understanding such aspects is crucial in better understanding requirements and enabling support for operational modelling processes, mainly with respect to the following points:

A. Persson and J. Stirna (Eds.): PoEM 2009, LNBIP 39, pp. 222–236, 2009.

1. Improve its quality [3,4]
2. Improve its focus in view of its utility [5,6]
3. Improve its efficiency
4. Make "lightweight formal modelling" more accessible to non-expert modellers (i.e. enable modelling without the necessary presence of facilitators or expert analysts; this is sometimes called "disintermediation"[7])
5. Improve the possibility to perform (formal) modelling in a truly collaborative setting

The initial results presented here emphasize the fourth point, but also involve the first, second, and third point. We do not address the fifth point. Also, we do not (yet) attempt to provide any solid proof that our approach increases quality, focus, and efficiency of (some aspect of) enterprise modelling. However, we do claim to provide at least a reasonable proof of concept and a demonstration of the possibility and potential of creating a game-like, modelling process-oriented type of modelling tool that goes beyond mere editors.

The sort of model that results from applying the approach presented is a basic process model of the kind usually represented in schema languages like UML Activity Diagrams [8], BPML [9], or YAWL [10], featuring basic concepts like activities, flows, and AND/OR-splits. However, we deliberately refrain from tying ourselves down too much to some specific language for process modelling, because:

- We want to avoid discussion here about detailed differences between languages and their merits, for reasons of focus;
- We observe that in practice, initial phases of process modelling do not normally call for detailed decisions concerning language/representation (whereas later stages often do);
- We aim to primarily elicit *information on the basis of which a schematic model can be generated* rather than needlessly confronting the participant with an actual schema, in particular in the earlier stages of the modelling process (which are our main focus). This does not exclude the use of schematic representations, but the utility thereof is different: they serve to extract information; they do not necessarily constitute the actual final model.

We have chosen to focus on process modelling here because we believe it is the most central type of modelling in most enterprise modelling efforts. Even so, the approach presented already includes some aspects typically related to basic data modelling or ontological modelling. In fact, we work towards the future operational integration of elicitation of (at least) (Business) Process Modelling, Ontological or Data Modelling, and (Business) Rule Modelling, and believe such models can indeed be fruitfully created in parallel, i.e. one model aspect can provide helpful (if not vital) information for the creation and validation of another. This principle will be pivotal in our wider (longer term) approach.

As mentioned, we propose to embody modelling methods in games. As discussed in [2,11], this minimally requires the following elements to be present:

- A clear description of the task to be completed by the player(s), including a victory or end condition for the game;
- A clear description of the game components to be manipulated by the player(s)
- A clear description of the rules to be followed in carrying out the task (i.e. playing the game);
- A clear description of the allowed types of action and interaction within the game;
- A clear description of procedures to be followed by the game system (for example, keeping or calculating a score)

Goals set within the formal context of a game correspond to task descriptions or assignments (what we will call "game-internal goals"). Such goals should not be confused with any goals the playing of the game is supposed to fulfil: its utility goals ("game-external goals"). For example, though our external goal for the game presented is to create a basic process model, the player is not explicitly assigned the task to do this (the terms used instead are "task description", by means of "describing task steps and their ingredients and products").

Game-external goals are explicitly linked (in design) to any desired properties of the resulting model, or even mind-states of modellers and –in collaborative games–social effects (shared understanding, agreement, commitment). Relevant goal categories have been discussed at some length in [12,13], and include utility goals, deliverable goals, validation and agreement goals, syntax goals, interpretation goals, argumentation goals, and efficiency goals.

Designing the goals, rules, score system etc. in line with game-external goals and standing conventions (explicit or implicit) is by no means trivial. In fact it is the main long-term goal of our line of research to discover and develop apt sets of interaction rules for achieving specific external goals in view of different capabilities and expertise of players involved, and of different demands posed by the modelling domain and context. The current game reflects only a very first (yet concrete) exploration of the basic principles.

2   Utilitarian Idea behind the Game

It may be helpful for the reader to view the game as a preliminary design for a "process modelling wizard". We are fully aware that some experienced modellers, or even "not-so-experienced modellers", find the current game restrictive and somewhat tedious. However, this would not necessarily render the game presented useless: its purpose is merely to make a start in creating games embodying playful modelling procedures, opening up process modelling for layman modellers, and to illustrate the more general point that shaping modelling methods as game designs is possible, interesting, and *potentially* useful.

The game in an operational sense works towards a particular type of *result*. We will elaborate on this now. As discussed, creation of an actual process schema is neither the game-internal nor the game-external goal of the game as such: rather, that goal is to *deliver information* that can be directly used to *derive* a process model. In order to obtain some particular sort of structured information (a "pre-model"), in some cases additional information is needed which is not necessarily to be reflected in the final model. We emphasize that this does not mean such information is irrelevant to the modelling *process* (in particular, the thinking process). In fact, we believe that quality-driven, stepwise elicitation of the sort we try to realize in the game *requires* elicitation and conceptualization of knowledge that supports *thinking about aspects underlying the process* in the domain rather than merely the abstract representation of that process in some focused but therefore also restricted modelling language.

For example, in our game we enforce the definition of objects and attributes, making the player provide what can be taken as a structured argumentation for the use of standard AND-joins (also see [12]). For example, as illustrated in the middle column of Fig. 1, a business process model in the standard language BPMN [9] typically shows an ordering of activities, e.g. activities D and E must be completed before activity F can be started. However, the reason why this is the case is that D and E respectively produce entities n and o that are needed in F (resulting in what is technically called an "AND-join"). This is illustrated by the text in the leftmost and rightmost columns of Fig. 1, in which these entities and dependencies are made explicit. However, such dependencies and entities are not made explicit in a regular BPMN diagram, even if they are crucial for creating a useful, "good" one. As a consequence, the entities and dependencies involved are usually left implicit and exist only as concepts in the head of the modeller –in fact, they are probably more concrete to the modeller than the abstract process flow derived from them. Even if the objects in the process are made explicit, perhaps in another model, they are not explicitly used as a basis for deriving AND-joins.

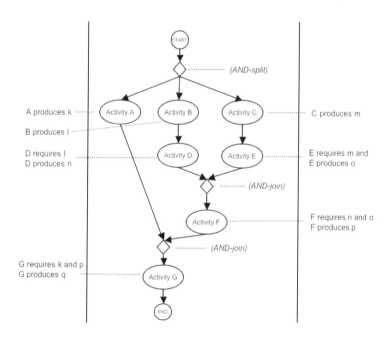

Fig. 1. Reasoning about Basic AND-joins

Put succinctly, the immediate utility goal (i.e. game-external modelling goal) in our game is to put the above argumentation central and strive to *indirectly elicit basic BPMN-like structures with AND-joins*. Note that OR/XOR-joins are excluded for now.

3 The Game

We will first provide an illustrated overview of a simple but typical course of game-play. Following [2] and [11], we will then give a brief decomposed overview of the game design along the lines of Game Design Theory. Please note that we feel the gameplay as described below does insufficient justice to the actual game experience. The static pictures look very much like those one might expect from a regular graphi-cal editor. We emphasize the difference lies in the act of modelling as such; for this, a real demo or, even better, actual experience in playing the game would be required. Also note that the example presented is meant to explain the main game mechanics reflecting the rationale pattern presented in the previous section. It is a toy example that was also used in the tests for the initial, exploratory game round, but is simpler than most assignments used for testing the game.

The external (utilitarian) purpose of the game is to get the player to describe a ba-sic task accurately, in terms of its *steps* (which is the term the game uses for 'activi-ties'). The game looks somewhat like a normal modelling tool, but provides more guidance for stepwise thinking and (most importantly) does not require abstract think-ing about AND splits and joins: it merely inquires about what is needed for a step (i.e. *ingredients*), what items come out of it (i.e. *products*), and (optionally) what change is inflicted on some item in the course of the step (a *link*). The game-like properties of the procedure (please be aware of the fact that it is, after all, a methodical procedure dressed up as a game) are the following:

1) The game can only be finished if the player fulfils a minimal set of demands, because only then the required information can be derived;
2) The player gets immediate feedback on what she is doing, using graphics and sound; also, a score is calculated and made visible;
3) How long the player plays is reflected in the score, while the time is visibly tick-ing away, thus introducing mild time pressure;
4) The player is (hopefully) motivated or entertained by the setup and gameplay, besides being guided.

The player has the option of being shown extra (rather minimal) guiding and explana-tory remarks, meant to help novice players understand the game and not miss some finer points. In the example pictures, we have excluded these (i.e. switched them off), except in the first illustration (Fig. 2). In addition to the optional guidelines, hints are also shown on the bottom of the screen when the player moves his mouse over any object (standard). This is not visible in the figures.

At the beginning of the game the interface provides the player with only one but-ton, allowing the player to create a new step. Other than that the player must give the task a name. When a new step is created it appears as a rectangle that the player can drag around; the next thing to do is to give the step a name (Fig. 2). A guideline for this is to describe the step in no more than four words.

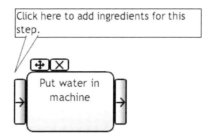

Fig. 2. Creating a step

Not visible in the illustration is the brief appearance of a green, animated number "10" drifting away from the activity symbol, indicating that 10 points have been scored by this action. There is also an accompanying sound.

Next, the player then has to add "items needed" (*ingredients*) and "items created" (*products*) to the step. Each ingredient that is added to a step also shows up in a list in the top left of the screen (Fig. 3). Items from this list can then be dragged to a new step, to be reused. This minimizes repetitive typing and provides a clear overview of items introduced so far. It also encourages re-use of exact terms.

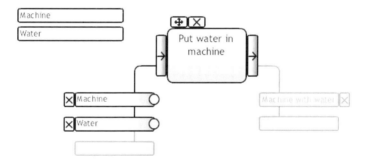

Fig. 3. Adding needed and created items

Next, clicking on a small bubble next to an ingredient and then clicking on a bubble next to a product of the same step can connect ingredients and products; again there is a (rather funny and appropriate) sound effect. This creates a link (Fig. 4). A link can be used to provide extra information about what happens to an ingredient during that step.

However, when an ingredient gets linked, the link should describe what happens to the ingredient. As a conceptual aid, the player may describe the change by filling in the pattern "this ingredient is being ...". The grammatical trick is that the player provides a verb that can also be used as an adjective, and therefore as an attribute of the item (describing a relevant state of it): a *precondition* (though this term is not used in communication with the player). This is useful because if the item is also used in another step, the game will recognize that the item has attributes, and provides the player with the simple option to select one or more existing attributes as relevant to the step (illustrated as part of Fig. 5, "filter::put in machine").

Another option for describing a link (and its underlying precondition) is to combine two ingredients in a pattern known from data modelling: ingredient A [with ingredient B] & ingredient B [in ingredient A]. An extra option the player has here is to graphically connect the links, which automatically render this precondition description pattern (not illustrated).

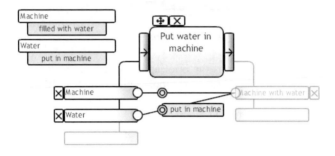

Fig. 4. Adding a state change attribute

When the player has described multiple steps this way, the game derives the connections between the steps. Each step has a set of ingredients with possible preconditions and a set of products as well as ingredients with added preconditions. When an ingredient of one step matches with a product of another step, the two are connected (Fig. 5), and a triumphant sound is played (taDAA!).

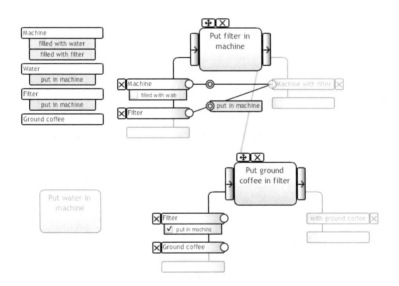

Fig. 5. A connection is found

Optionally, the game can automatically visualize the derived suggested order of connected steps by moving ('floating') them to a relevant position when they are not being used by the player. However, note that this does not amount to the visualization of flow as in an actual flow chart. A flow chart is derived from the above diagram later (outside the game as such).

The player can only finish the game when all the steps she created are connected to at least one other step, but can carry on until the model is complete; this is up to the player to decide (Fig. 6).

We will now briefly describe the main game components (objects to be manipulated in the game), game mechanics (actions allowed to take place on the components), and game rules (goal descriptions, constraints, score system). The rules are not described in great detail, as most of them have been demonstrated already.

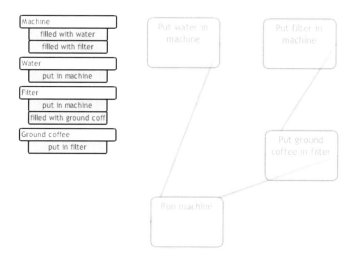

Fig. 6. Finished

3.1 Game Components

The game components are: Task Name field, Step Symbol with Step Description, Ingredient boxes and Precondition Ticks, Product Boxes, Link Circles and Boxes, Item/precondition List Boxes.

3.2 Game Mechanics

First, there are game mechanics for filling in various textual fields: Step Name, Step Description, Ingredients, Products, Link Descriptions. There are also non-textual mechanics: Creating Steps, adding and deleting Ingredients/Products, dragging Item List Boxes to Ingredient or Product Boxes, ticking Preconditions, linking Ingredients with Products.

Layout functions are left out here since they are auxiliary to actual gameplay. They belong to the game interface, which we further disregard here (but see the illustrations for a visual impression).

3.3 Game Rules: Goals, Assignments; End Condition

The (internal) goal of the game is to score points by creating a stepwise description of some (self-)assigned task, within possibilities and rules as embedded in and constrained by the interface. Obligatory: two interconnected steps (minimal end condition), implying at least one product matching one ingredient, so the game cannot be ended without some ingredients and products being entered. Importantly, the actual end condition is that the player herself "calls it quits" when the model is finished. The game as such does therefore not provide means to decide when the game is finished, only when it is not. Note that this is not unheard of in the Gaming world: many modern role playing video games can in principle be played ad infinitum.

3.4 Game Rules: Score System

The scores are calculated as follows:

- 100 points for each step.
- 100 points for each connection between two steps.
- 10 points for each ingredient, product or link.

Note that deleting a step leads to a reduction of the score with 100 points. The final score is the sum of the score so far minus half a point for every second played. However, the amount of points deducted based on the elapsed time can never be more than half of the amount of points scored.

3.5 After the Game: Deriving a BMPN Diagram

Besides the game as such, we also implemented a simple algorithm for deriving a BPMN-like structure from the information gathered. Instead of generating an actual diagram (Fig. 7), we decided that for this prototype an XML-based format, XPDL [14], would suffice.

```
#Start by finding the sets of input and output items for each step:

for each ingredient
    for each precondition
    if precondition is selected
      add "precondition_ingredient" to input set
    if no preconditions are selected
    add "ingredient" to input set

for each product
  if product is relevant
    add "product" to output set
for each link
```

Fig. 7. Algorithm to find dependencies between steps

```
    if link is not empty
       add "link_ingredient" to output set

# Whether a product is "relevant" (not overwritten by
# a link and not present as an ingredient) is known
# beforehand. A link always has a reference to its
# corresponding ingredient and product.

# Next, find the connections between the steps

for each step x
   for each input item
      for each step y
         if step x is not step y
            for each output item
               if input item equals output item
                  step x depends on step y
```

Fig. 7. (*Continued*)

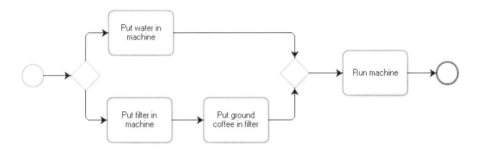

Fig. 8. Generated BPMN Diagram (implemented only as XPDL)

4   Development and Evaluation

The development process was performed within the design science paradigm [15], in a standard yet admittedly somewhat ad-hoc development cycle involving design, implementation, testing and improving the design. Testing was not always done extensively in the initial development stages, but as the game evolved from little more than a list of rules to a digital, more graphical game, more systematic evaluation took place.

We initially tried to stay away from automating the game, focusing instead on a pen and paper approach ("board game"). This gave us the chance to think through the basic setup and rules, without getting lost in details of implementation. However, the down sides of board gaming also became apparent soon. Playing and therefore testing the game proved to be a tedious experience for both the facilitator and the player, mostly because of active relations and dependencies between items, which had to be updated manually.

The first digital version of the game soon appeared, based on a standard spread-sheet implementation, which at least took the task of calculating the score out of the hands of the facilitator, and also made the entering of information by the player much easier. This allowed us to perform the first (successful) tests with "outsiders" (i.e. players other than ourselves), proving that the game system was viable in principle, and that players could at least get through the game.

It became increasingly clear at this point that the expectations for and experience of playing an actual computer game rely not just on its rules, but also on flowing interaction, animation and sound. The choice was made to rebuild the game from scratch in Actionscript 3.0 [16], which, after a few iterations, led to the current prototype.

The game was tested on five players with little to no prior process modelling experience, as well as on five players with significant such experience. Each test player played the game three times. The first two times, simple, standard tasks were described: first, "making coffee" and second, "repairing a flat bicycle tyre". These are tasks everyone in the test population was familiar with, the second generally being a little more complicated than the first. The third game was played with a task of the player's own choice.

The players were given as little introduction as possible, forcing them to rely on the explanation provided by the game. Admittedly, some subtle hints were sometimes given during the game if a player was really stuck. The players were asked to 'think aloud' as much as possible and to voice their possible frustrations or confusion. The attending game developer wrote down observations and interesting comments.

Afterwards the players were given a questionnaire, consisting of 25 statements (with five possible responses, ranging from "strongly disagree" to "strongly agree") and three open questions. The purpose of the questionnaire was to get an idea of the players' general experience. The statements hardly go into aspects unique to this particular game. Examples are: "I was satisfied with the result when I was done" and "I felt the score was a fair representation of how well I was doing". The statements are based on known properties of successful games, described in game design literature [11,17,18] and on general usability heuristics [19].

We aimed for our observations and player comments, as well as the results of the questionnaire, to inform us about the differences between players with and without process modelling experience, with respect to success in and perception of the game. We also looked for differences in player perception when playing the game for the second or third time. In general, we were obviously also interested in whether or not the game was properly designed, and in particular in needs or wishes for further improvement. Note that our game was a very first attempt of creating a game-for-modelling, so finding out what does *not* work was expected to be a prominent part of our effort.

5 Lessons Learned

Our observations suggest that there is indeed a noticeable difference between players with and without modelling experience. Despite our intentions to make the game playable for players with little or no expertise in modelling, most of those players found it hard to get started. It took them a while to understand what was meant by "task", "step", "ingredient" and "product". It was somewhat of a surprise to us that people by nature do not seem to make a sharp distinction even between actions and objects: sometimes they confuse the name of a step with its products, or describe sub-steps instead of ingredients.

Generally the game has a hard time forcing people towards the 'correct' way of thinking, if they are not inclined that way already. For example, while the game is supposed to be played by listing steps, some people naturally start describing a task by listing ingredients. They even search for workarounds to do this, like making one step a super-step encompassing the whole task, or describing a first step 'fetch all ingredients'.

Most experienced players fare better, quickly grasping the concept of the game, although sometimes after some initial confusion. In contrast with the less experienced players, they list ingredients only in their head, and then quickly switch to describing steps. Not surprisingly, experienced players are also more conscious of issues pertaining to abstraction.

When it comes to learning to play the game, the one thing we can clearly identify is the moment that players really 'get the hang of it'. Experienced players generally start working quickly and efficiently near the end of the first game or at the beginning of the second, while less experienced players are still struggling during the second game, and only pick up pace during the third. On the up side, given that playing the game does not take all that much time and effort, this could still be considered reasonably rapid learning.

A further interesting observation is that advanced functions of the game are generally not used. Players simply look for the easiest way to succeed in the game. Only one player so far has used preconditions in his description.

The results of the questionnaire suggest that experienced players found it more important to play well, while the inexperienced players were more satisfied with their results. All players felt there was a trick to easily getting a high score, but still mostly thought that the score was a fair representation of how well they did. This implies that the "trick" (whatever it was) was not actually used.

There was very little variation in how easy players thought it was to get started (most answers were neutral), but surprisingly the experienced players were on average less satisfied with the amount of context-sensitive help.

The first open question of the questionnaire ("What was, according to you, the most important goal in the game?") turned out particularly interesting because it really touches on the conflict between game-internal and game-external goals that we have been dealing with. The question is vague on purpose and results in a variety of answers, such as: "scoring points" (pure game-internal), "finding out what the links between steps are" (basic game-external), and "judging how well people can model" (extreme external: concerning reflection on the modelling process).

5.1 What Went Well

It is encouraging that players generally do not take very long to learn how to play the game and how to produce a reasonable task description. It seems that the main strength of the game is that it provides players with tangible feedback based on what they are doing, giving them at least a general sense of direction in the modeling process. This is an improvement over having to explain goals of modelling in abstract terms to people with little process modelling experience.

Aside from a few specific problems, the players seem to be satisfied with the current interface. By keeping things simple it manages to provide a good overview of the whole task description within one screen, and the feedback it provides by using graphics and sound seems to work well.

5.2 What Went Not So Well

We cannot honestly say that the current score system properly represents the various quality aspects of modelling. Players recognized that they did not really have to provide sensible input to get a good score. There is certainly much room for improvement here, although quantifying quality will never be easy.

It is somewhat disappointing that even though the scope of the game was already limited, most players did not use the advanced functionality such as preconditions. Players may be better encouraged to do this if provided with examples of more complicated descriptions, but we avoided the use of examples so far. Instead we used a wizard-like system to get players started, which is easy to understand, but is limited when things get more complicated.

A more specific problem we encountered concerns the use of links between ingredients and products within a step. If preconditions are not used, the purpose of these links is unclear to players and they consistently tend to forget about them. In fact, there are no clear rules concerning when links are required, so the confusion is entirely understandable. This is something that still requires attention.

6 Conclusions and Further Research

We set out to demonstrate and discuss a very first prototype of a "game for modelling", which is in fact a first implementation of the idea of a "modelling wizard". We explained the rationales behind the idea of creating modelling games/wizards, and proceeded to describe the basic utilitarian purposes (goals) behind our prototype game: deriving some basic information from a game with the purpose of then generating a basic BPMN diagram, focusing only on the derivation of AND-splits and joins.

We then described the game as such, and the process of developing and evaluating it. We finished with the outcome of our evaluation, observations, and lessons learned. In particular we concluded that though the game worked reasonably well, it is certainly not "intuitively playable" at this point. Arguably, this means we failed to achieve our main goal. However, this being a first attempt, we are by no means discouraged, and believe we have demonstrated what a game-for-modelling might look like and –in some respects– what it should perhaps not look like. In the mean time, we consider our first proof of concept a modest success: the game exists, is playable, renders sufficiently usable results, and is considered moderately satisfying by the players. It now serves as a platform from which further explorations can depart.

Whether modelling can ever be remotely as much fun as a dedicated entertainment game remains to be seen, but we can certainly learn a lot in this respect from how games are designed. A good game is more than just a goal to work towards. It lets you know what interactions are at your disposal, it lets you explore what effect your actions have on the game world, and it gives you a sense of how well you are doing.

Similarly, a good modelling process requires more than just a language and a model to work towards.

Future research will, of course, focus on further development of the game. We consider various directions for doing so. Improvement of this actual prototype is a possibility, but we are also interested in developing a more strongly text-oriented version. We also consider expansion of the concepts to be elicited by the game, possibly by combining a number of sub-games (covering different modeling rationales). A PhD project has recently started at our department which aims at the creation of a larger, much more developed game, better rooted in theory and practice involving game design theory and game psychology, cognition (in particular pertaining to abstraction and conceptualization), but also AI (reasoning about information gathered, after the game but also during the game).

Evaluation of games played is a key aspect of the development cycle, and requires extra attention in any effort that claims to engage in "design science". Another ongoing PhD project [20] focuses on advanced evaluation of interactive modelling sessions (including both collaborative and solo modelling), and methodological results will be used to evaluate games played.

References

1. Ralyté, J., Brinkkemper, S., Henderson-Sellers, B.: Situational Method Engineering. In: Fundamentals and Experiences. IFIP, vol. 244, pp. 313–327. Springer, Boston (2007)
2. Hoppenbrouwers, S., van Bommel, P., Järvinen, A.: Method Engineering as Game Design: an Emerging HCI Perspective on Methods and CASE Tools. In: Exploring Modelling Methods for Systems Analysis and Design (EMMSAD 2008), held in conjunction with CAiSE (2008)
3. Krogstie, J., Sindre, G., Jorgensen, H.: Process models representing knowledge for action: a revised quality framework. European Journal of Information Systems 15, 91–102 (2006)
4. Vanderfeesten, I., Cardoso, J., Mendling, J., Reijers, H.A., van der Aalst, W.: Quality metrics for business process models. In: Fischer, L. (ed.) BPM and Workflow Handbook. Future Strategies and Workflow Management Coalition (2007)
5. Lagerstrom, R., Saat, J., Franke, U., Aier, S., Eckstedt, M.: Enterprise Meta Modelling Methods: Combining a Stakeholder-Oriented and a Causality-Based Approach. In: Halpin, T., Krogstie, J., Nurcan, S., Proper, E., Schmidt, R., Soffer, P., Ukor, R. (eds.) Enterprise, Business-Process and Information Systems Modelling. LNBIP, vol. 29, Springer, Heidelberg (2009)
6. Proper, H.A., Verrijn-Stuart, A.A., Hoppenbrouwers, S.J.B.A.: Towards Utility-based Selection of Architecture-Modelling Concepts. In: Hartmann, S., Stumptner, M. (eds.) Proceedings of the Second Asia-Pacific Conference on Conceptual Modelling (APCCM 2005), Newcastle, New South Wales, Australia, January 2005. Conferences in Research and Practice in Information Technology Series, vol. 42, pp. 25–36. Australian Computer Society, Sydney (2005)
7. Faget, J., Marin, M., Mégard, P., Owens, V., Tarin, L.: Business Processes and Business Rules: Business Agility Becomes Real. In: Workflow Handbook 2003, pp. 77–92. Future Strategies Inc. (2003)
8. Booch, G., Rumbaugh, J., Jacobson, I.: The Unified Modelling Language User Guide. Addison Wesley, Boston (1998)
9. Object Modelling Group: Business Process Modelling Notation (BPMN) version 1.0, OMG Final Adopted Specification (2006)

10. van der Aalst, W.M.P., ter Hofstede, A.H.M.: YAWL: Yet Another Workflow Language. Information Systems 30(4), 245–275 (2005)
11. Järvinen, A.: Games without Frontiers, Theories and Methods for Game Studies and Design. PhD Thesis, University of Tampere, Finland (2008)
12. Hoppenbrouwers, S.J.B.A.: Community-based ICT Development as a Multi-Player Game. In: What is an Organization? Materiality, Agency and Discourse. University of Montreal (2008)
13. van Bommel, P., Hoppenbrouwers, S.J.B.A., Proper, H.A., Roelofs, J.: Concepts and Strategies for Quality of Modelling. In: Innovations in Information Systems Modelling: Methods and Best Practices. IGI, New York (2008)
14. Workflow Management Coalition: XPDL 2.1 Complete Specification (Updated October 10, 2008)
15. Hevner, A.R., Ram, S., March, S.T., Park, J.: Design Science in Information Systems Research. MIS Quarterly 28(1), 75–105 (2004)
16. Adobe Labs, ActionScript 3.0 specification, http://labs.adobe.com/technologies/actionscript3/
17. Salen, K., Zimmerman, E.: Rules of Play, Game Design Fundamentals. MIT Press, Cambridge (2004)
18. Desurvire, H., Caplan, M., Toth, J.A.: Using heuristics to evaluate the playability of games. In: CHI 2004, Vienna, Austria, extended abstracts on Human factors in computing systems, pp. 1509–1512. ACM, New York (2004)
19. Nielsen, J.: How to Conduct a heuristic Evaluation. Online paper, http://staff.unak.is/not/nicolaw/courses/hci/HCILab7papers.pdf
20. Ssebuggwawo, D., Hoppenbrouwers, S.J.B.A., Proper, H.A.: Analyzing a Collaborative Modelling Game. In: Yu, E., Eder, J., Rolland, C. (eds.) Proceedings of the CAiSE 2009 Forum at the 21st International Conference on Advanced Information Systems Engineering, Amsterdam, The Netherlands, June 8-12 (2009) Published online (May 28, 2009), http://CEUR-WS.org/Vol-453/

Enterprise Models as Data

Marite Kirikova, Ligita Businska, and Anita Finke

Riga Technical University
{marite.kirikova,ligita.businska}@cs.rtu.lv, anita.finke@rtu.lv

Abstract. In many cases enterprise models are considered as a part of enterprise knowledge. This paper examines the status of enterprise model as an artifact that is a part of organizational information system. In this view, the enterprise models are a part of information flow in the organization, and in their static state can be regarded as data rather than knowledge. This view helps to understand why the usability of enterprise models is still quite low in spite of the availability of powerful and sophisticated enterprise modeling tools and environments that allow to construct, analyze, maintain, configure, and integrate different types of models and even generate code and configure software subsystems on the bases of models amalgamated in the tools.

Keywords: data, information, knowledge, information system, enterprise model.

1 Introduction

Usually enterprise models (EM) are considered as a part of organizational knowledge [1]. Not denying this perspective of EM, in this paper, we analyze in more detail the nature of this artifact and we look at it from the point of organizational information system (IS) in a somewhat non-traditional way, namely, using the extended IS approach where the IS is considered not merely as a data flow that supports organizational operation and management, but also as a flow of data that supports organizational changes including the changes in IS itself. The EM is considered as an essential part of IS with multiple possible ways of use and development.

The research question addressed here is as follows: what is the role of EM in the organizational IS and when can EM be considered as knowledge, when as data, and when as information?

In order to answer the above mentioned question Section 2 starts with the analysis of notion of information. Section 3 examines three potential roles of EM in organizational IS. Section 4 presents a simplified organizational IS model that considers EM as data. Section 5 analyzes problems that arise in the use of EM as information in organizational processes. Section 6 consists of brief conclusions and points to further research directions.

2 On the Notion of Information

Information may be regarded as nonmaterial entity which allows describing real (material) and mental (nonmaterial) entities with any degree of precision [2, 3, 4, 5]. This

A. Persson and J. Stirna (Eds.): PoEM 2009, LNBIP 39, pp. 237–244, 2009.

view about information differs to some extent from the well known interpretation of Shanoon's use of the term that suggests information as a successful selection of symbols or words from a given vocabulary [6] that pays less attention to the meaning of the information. According to [2] information has the following features:

- Information does not exist outside of interaction between objects
- Objects do not lose information during interaction
- Information is delivered with the purpose of satisfying some goals of the receiver
- Informational interaction may happen only if a particular fit exists between the provider and receiver of information.

This means that information is a phenomenon that exists at the momentum of interpretation of data by a particular knowledge system. The interpretation may be done by natural knowledge system (human knowledge) or, if we use software as a part of IS, the interpretation may be done by artificial knowledge system, i.e., human knowledge coded in a particular software system [7]. Thus, it is essential that EMs that are produced by a particular group of people are meaningfully perceivable by human and artificial knowledge operating in the enterprise. On the other hand, it is essential to distinguish between two different types of information availability. First, information may be available without the purpose of information provision. Second, information may be provided purposely by "pushing" it to the intended receiver or making it available for some known or unknown "poolers" [8]. Sticking to the point that information is (1) interpreted data [8] and (2) exists only at the momentum of interaction between at least two natural or artificial objects, we can conclude that there are two phenomena that are essential for existence of information, namely data which is interpreted and knowledge that interprets the data. Furthermore, taking into consideration the dynamic nature of knowledge (knowledge changes in each moment of data interpretation) [1, 8, 9], we can conclude that the only static tangible phenomenon, changes of which can be relatively easily traced, is data. In the next section we analyze three different roles of EM in organization, namely, data, information, and knowledge.

3   Three Roles of EM

In order to view EM in three different roles (data, information, and knowledge) it is necessary to examine the nature of EM and the process of its creation. Usually the EM is created on the basis of already existing tacit and explicit knowledge [1, 10]. In general, in order to locate knowledge sources it is important to distinguish between master's knowledge and observer's knowledge concerning the object of interest (Figure 1). Both, master and observer have tacit knowledge and can provide explicit knowledge.

However, there can be quite considerable difference not only regarding the tacit but also explicit knowledge provided by the master of the object in comparison to the knowledge provided by the observer of the object. Thus, the agent (in case of EM creation – the enterprise modeling group) that seeks knowledge about a particular object has the following main sources of knowledge (Figure 1):

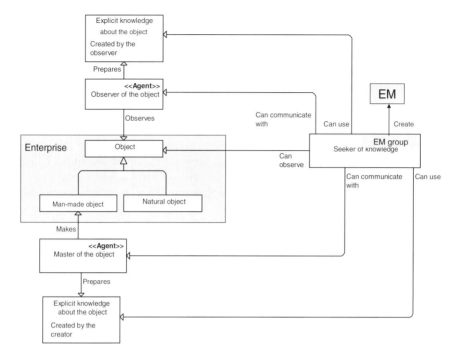

Fig. 1. Knowledge sources of EM

- The object of interest that represents knowledge, i.e., an enterprise consisting of natural and man-made objects.
- The agents that have made man-made objects (masters of the object), e.g., employees and managers of the enterprise
- The agents that have observed (or investigated) the object (observers of the object), such as business analysts, systems analysts, consultants and to some extent IS staff in general.
- Explicit knowledge that has been prepared by the masters of the object (externalized master's knowledge)
- Explicit knowledge that has been prepared by the observers of the object (externalized observer's knowledge)
- Seeker of knowledge, e.g., EM development group whose purpose is to create an EM

Actually, EMs developed at different times may be represented as man-made objects, explicit knowledge about the object and as a result of work of EM group. In Figure 1 active possessors of knowledge are divided in three classes, namely - master of the object, observer of the object, and seeker of knowledge. In EM development one and the same person and one and the same group of persons may belong to several classes of knowledge possessors. The master of the object is an agent who has made the object, the observer of the object is an agent who has investigated the object by methods available at its disposal. The knowledge seeker is an agent whose goal is to obtain knowledge about the object. Human agents can obtain knowledge even without a conscious aim of knowledge acquisition [9]. In Figure 1 the situation of purposeful knowledge acquisition is reflected. There is a difference in quality, richness and completeness between the knowledge of the master of the object and the knowledge of the observer of the object. Actually, as experience shows, the observer must learn to make himself or herself an object to obtain knowledge that is adequate with the master's knowledge (see the example about the development of bread making machine in [11]).

Figure 1 reflects knowledge sources from the point of view of the knowledge seeker at a particular point of time t_i. However, two other agents can be also considered as seekers of knowledge. Actually, the observer of the object would not be used as a source of knowledge if it had not been a seeker of knowledge at some point of time $t_j = t_i - \Delta t$, $\Delta t \geq 0$. None of the agents depicted in Figure 1 can possess complete knowledge about natural objects; therefore, the master of the object becomes a seeker of knowledge when it observes a natural object or the object that includes natural objects. On the other hand, the seeker of knowledge likewise can take the roles of the observer and the master [12].

In view of the abovementioned complexity of knowledge development during enterprise modeling, EM at its particular development sate at a particular point of time t_j may be regarded as data (hard or soft depending on the means of representation) looking from the point of independent observer: it may be regarded as an amalgamation of pieces of knowledge of individuals participating in enterprise modeling activities; and it may be considered as information at moments when EM is processed by the brain of its human users or by particular software tools. Thus, in order to become useful information in IS development, EM and natural or/and artificial knowledge supposed to use it are to fit one another (see section 2). In case of non-fit EM may become useless. A simplified model of the role of EM in enterprise IS is provided in the next section. It will allow to look closer at the issues of fit between EM and the knowledge that can interpret it.

4   A Simplified Model of Use of EM

There are several reasons why EMs are used in organizations [13]. In this paper we consider two purposes of EM use, first, managing an enterprise and, second, developing and maintaining the enterprise IS (Fig. 2). The situation is quite straightforward and to some extent controllable at the first go of EM creation. In this situation those involved in EM development become its users for organizational management and IS development purposes. A new situation arises when new versions of EM are developed. Due to the dynamic nature of knowledge, all human knowledge that has been involved in EM development has changed and software has changed due to its maintenance. Consequently, the fit between the previous EM and actual knowledge that processes it may not be present. When a new EM is developed, the fit between the previous version of EM and the new one could be established using sophisticated modeling tools and human effort. However, the question is whether this fit makes any sense in terms of both enterprise management and IS development. It would make sense if at any moment of time the "vertical" fit between natural and artificial knowledge involved in enterprise management and data processing had been maintained.

However, in practice it would mean continuous extra effort and continuous information overload to all human knowledge possessors in the enterprise. Theoretically it is achievable that every single change relevant to IS development and maintenance is reflected in the EM [7]. However up to this time nobody has actually examined how much effort and time it would require. In practice, in many cases, new EM are built from scratch again and again when new IS are to be developed or organizational problems resolved [14].

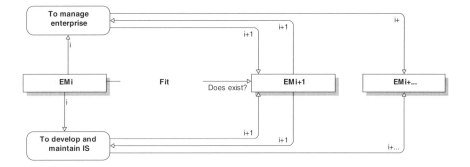

Fig. 2. Use of EM

According to Steven Alter [15] "an IS is a work system whose processes and activities are devoted to processing information, that is, capturing, transmitting, storing, retrieving, manipulating, and displaying information. A work system is a system in which human participants and/or machines perform work (processes and activities) using information, technology and other resources to produce specific products and/or services for specific internal or external customers". According to this definition an EM is a product of enterprise IS. Thus, the main question to be answered is who (what) are the customers of EMs and what specific value EMs can bring to their customers at specific time points of enterprise life cycle. Here we focus only on one essential requirement for EM to be valuable, namely, the EM should enable information circulation in organization, i.e., it should be interpretable by human and artificial knowledge of the enterprise. In the next section we consider some problems that currently hinder enterprise IS from obtaining value from enterprise modeling efforts.

5   Difficulties in Obtaining Information from EM

One of the essential aspects of EMs is that their construction is a time and effort demanding process. This, to some extent, is in contradiction with the need for frequent changes perceived in current historical situation of global economic development. For enterprise to be changeable, its IS also has to be changeable, and, in turn, the EM as a part of IS has to follow these changes. It means that data provided by EM has to change rapidly and the ability to interpret this data by humans or software also has to change rapidly. According to [16], changeability involves four essential features namely, agility, adaptability, robustness, and flexibility.

Agility usually is related to speed. The more rapidly the system will operate, the quicker the users will react to changes; that will lead to the user satisfaction. Still, the agility of the system is not reflected only in the speed of operations. It is reflected also in the time needed to complete any of the intended operations. If the system is designed in a way that allows the user to perform a certain action as simply as possible, the amount of time spent is small; therefore we can define that action as one that is relatively easy to carry out. Thus to achieve the agility needed for changeability the development and use of EM should be perceived as a simple activity by the "customers" of the EM [17]. This differs from the current practice of enterprise modeling.

Nowadays systems are designed to adapt to the users and the intensity of operations. We should note that all users are not the same and everyone has professional and personal peculiarities when it comes to the use of systems. Adaptability can be referred to moments when the system is adapted or adapts to work in a certain way at definite moments and with definite users. IS that includes EM has to successfully trace the moments when it can save some of the resources (e.g., time of EM developers or users), or vice versa – use all the available resources. Adaptability of EM has not been researched properly and may imply the use of artificial intelligence techniques in EM building and maintenance.

The environment that surrounds us is stochastic (changing). There is a continuous introduction of new technologies, new needs and changing market conditions, etc. It is important for the system to be robust, i.e., to be stable and to be able to last apart from a certain range of changes. How to achieve robustness of enterprise models is still an open question. Probably it is necessary to distinguish between stable and frequently changeable parts of EMs.

Changing the system each time a new product appears is unfavorable. In systems with high level of flexibility options should be introduced that allow the user without any specific preliminary knowledge to quickly add additional parameters that previously have not been listed in the system. Some improvements here are related to active knowledge modeling [1]. Nevertheless flexibility in current developments does not always go hand in hand with simplicity if we consider the use of EM as a whole not just role-oriented parameterization of particular parts of the EM.

Changeability includes all the previously mentioned factors. In view of the problems in EM in connection with these factors we can conclude that there is still a long way to go before we achieve genuine development and use of EM in practice.

6 Conclusions

This paper examined the role of EM in enterprise IS focusing on its use as mere data rather than knowledge. This approach helped to reveal and partially structure basic problems of EM development and use, such as lack of agility, non-investigated adaptability, vague requirements for robustness, and fragmentary flexibility. These problems highlight the following directions in EM usability research: (1) How to balance simplicity and complexity in EM development and use; (2) What are the possibilities of the use of artificial intelligence in EM development and maintenance; (3) How to achieve robustness of EM without losing flexibility.

Those research directions show that while EMs usually are considered in the context of organizational knowledge management, it is still necessary to be aware of the fact that without the possibility to be interpreted EMs are nothing more than data; and in many cases may become just useless data to be discarded from organizational memory despite of availability of powerful and sophisticated enterprise modeling tools and environments that allow to construct, analyze, maintain, configure, and integrate different types of models and even generate code and configure software subsystems on the basis of models amalgamated in the tools.

Acknowledgment

The research work reflected in this paper is partly sponsored by Latvian Council of Science, Grant No. 09.1245.

References

1. Lillehagen, F., Kroghstie, J.: Active Knowledge Modeling of Enterprises. Springer, Heidelberg (2008)
2. Jankowski St.: A concept of general theory of information (Станислав Янковски Концепции общей теории информации), http://n-t.ru/tp/ng/oti.htm
3. Moon, T.: Information Theory, Electrical and Computer Engineering, Utah State University, http://ocw.usu.edu/Electrical_and_Computer_Engineering/Information_Theory
4. Carter, T.: An introduction to information theory and entropy (2007), http://astarte.csustan.edu/~tom/SFI-CSSS/info-theory/info-lec.pdf
5. Corning, P.A.: Control Information Theory: The 'Missing Link' in the Science of Cybernetics. System Reseach and Behavioral Science, Syst. Res., 297–311 (2007)
6. Shannon, C.E.: A Mathematical Theory of Communication. Reprinted with corrections from The Bell System Technical Journal 27, 379–423, 623–656 (1948)
7. Kirkova, M., Grundspenkis, J.: Using knowledge distribution in Requirements Engineering. In: Leondes, C.T. (ed.) Knowledge-Based Systems, Four-Volume Set: Techniques and Applications. Academic Press International, London (2000)
8. Tiwana, A.: The knowledge management toolkit: Orchestrating IT, Strategy, and Knowledge Platforms, 2nd edn. Prentice-Hall, Englewood Cliffs (2002)
9. Anderson, J.R.: Cognitive Psychology and its Implications, 4th edn. W.H. Freeman and Company, New York (1995)
10. Bubenko Jr., J.A., Persson, A., Stirna, J.: User Guide of the Knowledge Management Approach Using Enterprise Knowledge Patterns, deliverable D3, IST Programme project Hypermedia and Pattern Based Knowledge Management for Smart Organisations, project no. IST-2000-28401, Dept. of Computer and Systems Sciences, Royal Institute of Technology, Stockholm, Sweden (2001), http://www.dsv.su.se/~js/ekd_user_guide.html
11. Nonaka, I., Takeuchi, H.: The Knowledge Creating Company: How Japanese Companies Create the Dynamics of Innovation. Oxford University Press, New York (1995)
12. Kirikova, M., Grundspenkis, J.: Types of knowledge and knowledge sources. In: Scientific Proceedings of Riga Technical University, Series Computer Science: Applied Computer Systems, RTU, Riga, pp. 109–119 (2002)

13. Persson, A., Stirna, J.: An explorative study into the influence of business goals on the practical use of Enterprise Modelling methods and tools. In: Harindranath, G., et al. (eds.) New Perspectives on Information Systems Development: Theory, Methods and Practice, pp. 215–288. Kluwer Academic, New York (2002)
14. Ambler, S.: Introduction To Agile Modeling, white paper. Ronin International (2002)
15. Alter, S.: Defining information systems as work systems: implications for the IS field. European Journal of Information Systems 17, 448–469 (2008)
16. Fricke, E., Shulcz, A.P.: Design for changeability (DfC): Principles to enable changes in systems throughout their entire lifecycle. Systems Engineering 8, 342–359 (2005)
17. Maeda, J.: The laws of simplicity. The MIT Press, Cambridge (2006)

The IT-Socket:
Model-Based Realisation of the Business and IT Alignment Framework

Robert Woitsch, Wilfrid Utz, and Vedran Hrgovcic

BOC Asset Management, Bäckerstraße 5, 1010 Wien, Austria
{Robert.Woitsch,Wilfrid.Utz,Vedran.Hrgovcic}@boc-eu.com

Abstract. As a result of recent changes in the IT, where the role of IT has shifted from an enabler to an industrial sector in its own right, the necessity to provide framework which would allow seamless alignment of the business and IT rose. The goal was to allow the stakeholders from the business as well as IT perspective to model the requirements for the IT service provisioning using the modeling languages they are familiar with and to apply semantic technologies as a mediator that will allow translation between them. IT-Socket, the model based approach for business and IT alignment, developed in the European Research project – plugIT, aims to realize the vision of businesses "plugging-in" to IT by introducing graphical modeling languages as mediators between the domain experts and IT. The research challenges identified include the ability to perform integration and translation between graphical modeling languages by building the reference ontology, enabling automatic generation of machine interpretable domain ontologies from graphical models and allowing automatic translation between domain ontologies. The results of the application of the IT-Socket for business and IT alignment are presented within three use cases: (1) "Certification" of IT infrastructure, (2) "Virtual Organization" by evolving the current service orientation to a higher and more business driven abstraction and (3) "Governance" of IT infrastructure.

Keywords: Next Generation Modelling Framework, Knowledge Management, Semantics, IT-Socket, Virtual Organisation, IT-Governance, Certification.

1 Introduction

Information technology (IT) has changed during the history in many ways (e.g. Mainframe to Client-Server, SOA, etc) and those changes have influenced the way how we see and use the IT in our everyday work. Currently the IT is influenced by many different factors, the external factors such as rapid changes in the market environment, legal requirements, different regulations as well as the internal factors such as Software as a Service, SOA, etc, which impose the necessity to align the business and IT in order to survive in highly competitive markets. The change in the IT that we are witnessing today is a ground-breaking change from an enabler –supporting business - to an industry on its own – doing business. [13], [11].

A. Persson and J. Stirna (Eds.): PoEM 2009, LNBIP 39, pp. 245–257, 2009.
© IFIP International Federation for Information Processing 2009

The change resulted in IT moving away from back-office support toward becoming a core business process (e.g. in branches Airline Transport, Finance, Automotive Industry or Health Care, IT is a strategic factor in business) [6].

Model based approaches are seen as a viable solution to support this change and to allow seamless transition between the enabler to provider, by allowing the alignment based on externalized requirements from both the business and IT perspective.

IT has to support different business coming from various domains and having diverse requirements. The EU research project plugIT - FP7-3ICT-231430 [36] aims to develop a model-based IT-Socket that would allow business to plug-in into the IT. The domain specific scenarios which will evaluate the IT-Socket within the project include (as detailed in [50] and [33]):

- The "Certification Use Case" demonstrates how the alignment between the business area and the IT domain during the certification process for regulations such as SOX, EuroSOX, ITIL®, CoBIT®, ISO20000 or BASEL II can be established.
- The "Virtual Organization Use Case" demonstrates how virtual organizations can be supported using business driven requirements and semantically described SLA's for intelligent interpretation.
- The "Governance Use Case" demonstrates how intelligent agents are used to identify the IT infrastructure of data centres. Graphical models are regarded as mediators between system administration and an intelligent discovery environment.

The structure of the paper is as follows: after this introductory section a brief overview on the idea and background of the IT-Socket is presented – focusing on the related work and the analysis of the IT-Socket. Following section is dedicated to the model based realization approach of the IT-Socket. Last section summaries the work presented and provides overview on planned future work.

2   Idea and Definition of the IT-Socket

The standardisation and industrialisation of everyday work which affected more and more business sectors in last decades did not make halt before the IT. The trend being currently observed, when analysing the industrialisation phenomenon in the IT, can be easily compared with the industrialisation of the electricity where electric power is provided and consumed via power sockets [15], [25].

Building on this observation the plugIT [36] defined a challenge to realise an IT-Socket similar to the aforementioned electric power socket, providing a standardized and industrialised access to consumers of the IT services.

The first step in order to realize the IT-Socket in plugIT was the research on related approaches (as depicted in section 2.1) that range from formal, to unstructured and up to intuitive mechanisms in order to define the modelling framework that will be used for modelling and configuring domain specific IT-Socket.

It is assumed that expert knowledge from both parts – business and IT perspective – can be externalized, formalised and used to support the business and IT alignment by applying semantic technologies for integration, translation and transformation of the externalized knowledge.

2.1 Related Work

The importance of the business and IT alignment has been recognized as a significant part of the enterprise life cycle by various actors coming from different areas of business and IT world.

Due to this diversification of research we witness different approaches on business and IT alignment which focus mainly on technical transformation, like described in [39] and [9], or on the other hand involving also the business aspects as elaborated in [41] and [4].

The business perspective – the set of initiatives, vendors and guidelines has been described in [43] – as one of the parts of the alignment has been underestimated in the SOA based approaches. A survey of 175 research papers about SOA from 2000 to 2008 outlines this statement [46].

The goal of solving the issue and integrating the aforementioned business perspective is done through provision of the detailed description of the alignment between business requirement specification and IT and it is fulfilled by externalization of participants' knowledge within the alignment process. The model-based approach applied in the plugIT provides a way to conceptually link the business requirements and IT [47], [21].

By applying the model-based approach the alignment is described by models representing the initial step of formalization. The key challenge is the integration of different modeling languages that are used to describe the business and IT perspective.

The alignment of the business and IT can be achieved by following different approaches and thus yielding different results. Some of the approaches in this area that have been evaluated by plugIT include:

- The Formal approach – is following the strategy of applying mathematical models in order to identify best-suited IT products for a specific business scenario. An example of the formal approach for the alignment include IT-Portfolio Management from Zimmermann [49] and the identification of services based on business process model analysis from Esswein et al, [12].
- The Heuristic approach – applies the similar approach as the previously mentioned Formal approach, but it reduces the formalisms details level. Prominent examples include the questionnaires provided by Technology Evaluation Centre [42] in order to support the end user to formulate the business request, the model driven business application system development [22] or the SOAM framework [34].
- The Informal approach – is probably the most common approach found today. It involves usage of Request for Information (RFI), Request for Quotation (RFQ), Request for Tender (RFT) and Request for Proposal (RFP) in order to align the business requirements and provided IT services. An overview on this approach can be found in [28] and [38].
- The Intuitive Alignment approach – is a human-driven approach for alignment, which relies on initiative human competence to align business requirements and existing IT products. The advantage is that it includes experts in the alignment process and possible disadvantage could be that it relies solely on the expertise of the involved persons.

The alignment followed by the IT-Socket approach does not follow any specific alignment approaches nor tries to create a standard business and IT alignment approach but introduces a holistic model-based framework that can be used in different ways to ensure business and IT alignment.

2.2 The Analysis of the IT-Socket

In order to address the definition and analysis of the IT-Socket the first task was to analyse both business and IT perspective and to identify the relevant parts playing major role in the business and IT alignment. The starting point to identify these requirements were the business processes for the business perspective and IT products – the commercially exploitable bundle of IT services – for the IT perspective. The process of analysing the IT-Socket was based on three aspects:

- Interviewing experts in order to externalize the required knowledge in interviews and number of modelling sessions. These initial tasks were carried out with the plugIT use case partners - iTG[1] , HLRS[2] and CINECA[3]
- Complement experiments at universities in order to validate the results of the interviews and modelling sessions against the visionary challenge of the IT-Socket
- Extensive survey in the literature [3], [7], [10], [14], [23], [29], [31], [40] and [48]

The result of the analysis, as shown in Fig 1, was the definition of three aspects for both the business and IT perspective: the competence aspects – providing the human knowledge, technical aspects - consisting of software, hardware and IT infrastructure and organisational aspects - taking over responsibility for parts of the IT-Infrastructure. They are divided on the perspective basis and include:

- Competence requirement to correctly specify the IT products.
- Technical requirements of the IT products.
- Organisational requirements to correctly specify the IT products,

for the business perspective and

- Competence provision of an IT service.
- Technical provision of an IT service.
- Organisational provision of an IT service.

for the IT perspective.

The IT services are defined in following pillars [50]:

- IT services in form of competence provision like helpdesks, training or consulting,
- IT services in form of technical provision like applications, middleware or housing as well as

---

[1] ITG, Innovation Technology Group SA, http://www.itg.pl
[2] HLRS, High Performance Computing Center Stuttgart, http://www.hlrs.de
[3] CINECA, Consorzio Interuniversitario, http://www.cineca.it

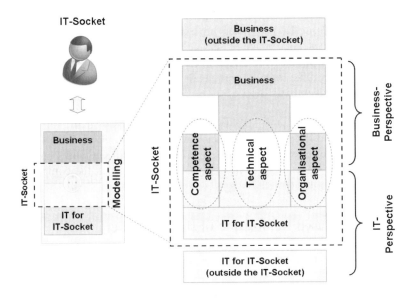

Fig. 1. Identified aspects of the IT-Socket, [35]

- IT services in form of organizational provision like maintenance processes, user administration or infrastructure monitoring.

Another important factor in the analysis of the IT-Socket that has to be taken into account is the so-called abstraction layer of the IT-Services. This simplified means that IT services like data storage or server housing are considered to have lower abstraction than services providing for example ERP functionalities.

Abstraction layer signals the distance of the IT service to the specific activity of the business process that is consuming the IT-Service [50]. More detailed definition of these abstraction layers is currently not possible as different application domains may have different abstraction levels – see [44], [18], and different implementation at the client site (plugIT Use Cases).

This results in the issue that the IT-Socket has to support service provision considering different abstraction layers and different classification of the abstraction itself.

The answer to this question is the introduction of the model based framework which is easily adaptable by the service provider in order to comply with the imposed requirements of the end user (on any abstraction layer), thus being generic in such way to support the requirements (in any specific instantiation of the IT-Socket) and still be capable of handling the available IT services.

The alignment between the requests and the provisioning, required to allow the usage of the presented framework, is assured through formalizing the request performed by the end user so that following conditions are satisfied [50]:

- the correct abstraction layer for the specified IT service can be easily identified,
- the required IT service parameters are explicitly described to allow the identification of the most appropriate IT service for the specific business use case and
- the appropriate product framework in terms of legal aspects, responsibility, additional services like training, service, or helpdesk as well as the financial conditions can be identified.

ACS [1], CISR [8], ISACA [16], ITGI [17] and OCG [32] provide different alignment approaches, whereas [45] provides an overview on 17 different methods to reach the desired goals. The selection of one of the approaches within the model based framework presented here depends on complexity of the IT product, the competence, the organizational culture and the like.

3   The Model-Based Realization of the IT-Socket

As outlined in the related work section of the paper, the model based realization of the alignment framework has to deal with different alignment approaches. The model based approach builds on the foundation that the relevant knowledge, both for the business and IT part, can be externalized in both semi-formal and formal way using graphical models. The ability to translate between the different languages (one of the research challenges defined in section 3.2) allows both stakeholders, the business and IT managers to use the languages they are familiar (e.g. BPMN, UML, etc) with in order to describe the requirements for a specific use case.

3.1   The Six Elements of the IT-Socket

Fig. 2 depicts the two perspectives: business – the "plug" containing two elements and IT – the "IT-Socket" and corresponding six elements of the IT-Socket. The first two elements forming the "plug" include:

- Business – this is expressed using models in order to graphically describe such aspects as knowledge, business processes, business rules, etc. The model based modelling framework of the IT-Sockets takes into account all business aspects that are relevant for the IT-Socket and specific use case (e.g. business processes requiring alignment with the underlying IT) and those that are not directly relevant for the IT-Socket (e.g. business strategies that do not directly influence the business and IT alignment),
- Business Requirements – this is applied in the definition of the T services used. Based on the selected approach the requirement specification may be expressed in mathematical formulas, fulfilled questionnaires and the like – as described in section 2.1

The second part depicted in the Fig 2 is the IT-socket consisting out of six elements, where first four describe the IT perspective and last two are describing the business perspective of the IT-Socket. Starting from bottom up following elements are available:

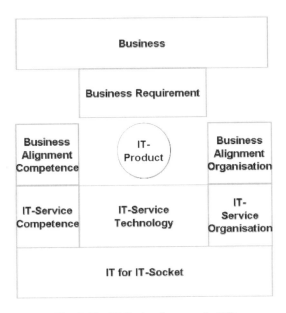

Fig. 2. The IT-Socket framework, [35]

- IT for the IT Socket – this element includes basic items required to provide IT services to end users. This includes software, hardware and corresponding infrastructure. This element, depending on the level of detail in which IT governance is applied in the alignment process, may be considered as not relevant for the IT-Socket.
- IT Service Technology – this element represent all services (e.g. software based services) that are offered to the end users having different abstraction layers as defined in section 2.2
- IT Service Competence – this element represents and describes all services in terms of competence provision. These services include such functionalities like helpdesk, training, etc., which may not be seen as technical services but are nevertheless included as they assure the deployment of technical services.
- IT Service Organisation – organisational IT services handle such aspects for which the provider of the IT service is also responsible, e.g. backup, maintenance, test, etc.
- Business Alignment Competence – the goal within this element is to explicitly define the skills required to execute the select approach and perform the business and IT alignment.
- Business Alignment Organisation – defines the processes that are performed during the alignment.

All described elements may use different languages and each of the applied modelling languages can have different formal expressions. This manifests in having collections of different models designed using different languages and having different levels of formality.

3.2   The Semantic within the IT-Socket

The alignment scenario presented in the paper requires IT-Socket to be able to handle different modelling languages describing different perspectives, aspects and formalisation levels. This involves the necessity to utilize the semantic technologies in order to act as a mediator between the (1) modelling languages and (2) business and IT models. The major task is to guarantee that imposed service requirements by the end user which are designed in the language that end user is familiar with are understood by IT service providers which may use different modelling languages with different formal expressiveness.

Models describing one of the aforementioned elements of the IT-Socket (section 3.1) may, based on the alignment procedures requiring different formalisation levels, be formal, semi-formal or unstructured. So in one use case stakeholders may be confronted on one hand with text documents and on other hand with mathematical definitions. In order to be able to mediate between these different definitions, semantic technology is used to translate between the used modelling languages, namely it is used to provide an integrated and coherent view of data stored in multiple, heterogeneous information sources. The integration of the available information is an important research field and have been prominently represented in recent research activities.

Different forms of integration can be distinguished [50]:

- Schema integration: Design a global unified schema
- Data Integration: Take into account both schema and actual data
- Semantic integration: Take into account ontologies, schemata and data which can be structured, unstructured or semi-structured

Three dimensions of the semantic integration techniques are applied in the IT-Socket [50]:

- Mapping discovery: Given two ontologies/schemas, how do we find similarities between them, determine which concepts and properties represent similar notions, and the like.
- Declarative formal representations of mappings: Given two ontologies, how do we represent the mappings between them to enable reasoning with mappings?
- Reasoning with mappings: Once the mappings are defined, what do we do with them, what types of reasoning are involved?

Based on aforementioned semantic integration techniques we try to address following five research challenges (as depicted in Fig. 3. and detailed in [50]):

- RC1 – The first research challenge focuses on the development of the modelling language ontologies (marked as MLO in Fig.3). The MLO is created by transforming the expressions of the graphical modelling languages into a well formed ontology used to represent the modelling principles of the modelling language in question. Besides the meaning that is extracted from the graphical elements, a textual description has to be exposed too in order to allow interoperability. This approach is applicable to any modelling language; example would be to specify the elements of UML or BPMN as ontology – see [19].

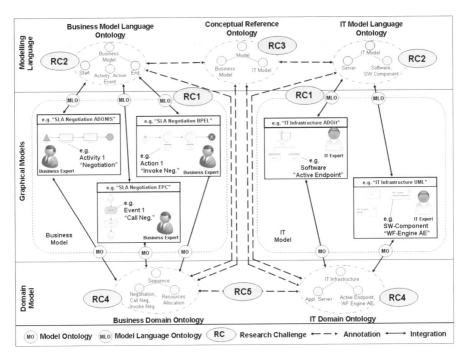

Fig. 3. An overview on the research challenges indentified in the project in order to realize the IT-Socket, [50]

- RC2 – The second research challenge is dedicated to the integration and translation of the modelling languages used by different stakeholders that will use the IT-Socket. In order to allow the integration and translation it is necessary to take into account syntactic and semantic layers (as elaborated in [24] and [30]). The syntactic layer is provided as a result of the RC1. The representative ontology is used in order to make possible the mapping between the source modelling languages (stakeholder describing the scenario) and target modelling languages (stakeholder as service provider). Such an approach is elaborated in [5], [26], [27] and [37]

- RC3 – The third indentified research challenge is focused on developing the reference ontologies for the modelling languages used in the plugIT with the goal to analyse the ability to use such ontology to explicitly transform between different modelling languages. This will be handled on the meta-level. The meta meta level (comp. [20]) for modelling languages – as used in ADONIS, MOF, etc, – describes the generic elements of the modelling languages (comp. [24], [30]). The meta level used in the RC3 is in the example of modelling languages the description of the aforementioned elements as derivations of the meta meta element, e.g. activity, process start, etc. The ontology developed in the RC3, the Conceptual Reference Ontology (marked with CRO in Fig. 3) is based on the meta meta level but requires parts of the meta level in order to be used for mapping.

- RC4 – The fourth research challenge is tackling the issue of automatic generation of the machine readable domain specific ontologies out of the graphical
  models. Such an ontology (the modelling ontology – marked with MO) is generated out of graphic model where each model was annotated with the previously available MLO. By doing this the machine-interpretability is assured and
  on the other hand these mechanisms ensure   continuous evolution of the domain ontology and enable cooperative modelling by different domain experts
  using different tools.
- RC5 – The fifth research challenge is dedicated to the translation between domain specific ontologies using the MLO and CRO ontologies as a bridge to
  map the ontology concepts. This provides the functionality to the stakeholder to
  use their own language (e.g. business manager using BPMN and IT Manager
  using UML) to define and model the requirements for a specific case and to
  present them to the counterpart in their own language as mapping and translation will be handled by the IT-Socket.

4   Conclusion

The work presented here introduced a business and IT alignment approach applying
the model-based IT-Socket. Currently this approach is being implemented by the
consortium of the EU research project plugIT. As the project is currently in its early
phase only the initial results such as definition of the research challenges as well as
the analysis of the IT-Socket are presented.

Further work is separated in two parts, first one focusing on stronger involvement
of semantic technologies – through application of semantic and meta modelling
matching patterns [24] – conceptual integration, development of the Next Generation
Modelling Framework and application of the abstract workflows in order to support
the execution of the IT-Socket aligned processes – the technical integration of the
framework and on the other hand the evaluation of the IT-Socket in the three end user
use cases.

Following the Open Model paradigm[4], The Next Generation Modelling Framework
will be available as a public service to attract the community to use the web-
modelling platform to design and the execution environment to deploy the IT-Socket.

Acknowledgments. The authors would like to thank the members of Elsag Datamat,
Consorzio Interuniversitario CINECA, Innovation Technology Group SA and University of Stuttgart, High Performance Computer Centre as members of the plugIT consortium for the cooperation of this publication.

The authors especially acknowledge the contribution from Prof. Dr. Dimitris
Karagiannis (University of Vienna), Prof. Dr. Plexousakis (Foundation for Research
and Technology-Hellas) and Prof. Dr. Hinkelmann (Fachhochschule Nordwest-
schweiz) for their contribution to this publication.

---

[4] www.openmodels.at

References

1. ACS. Governance of Information and Communication Technology Committee (2009), `http://www.acs.org.au/governance/` (accessed May 29, 2009)
2. Andrea, J.: An Agile Request For Proposal (RFP) Process. In: ADC 2003: Proceedings of the Conference on Agile Development. IEEE Computer Society, Washington (2003)
3. Bloomberg, J.: SOA Governance – IT Governance in the context of service orientation (2004), `http://www.zapthink.com/report.html?id=ZAPFLASH-10272004` (accessed May 29, 2009)
4. BREIN. Business objective driven REliable and Intelligent grids for real busiNess (2009), `http://www.eu-brein.com/` (accessed May 29, 2009)
5. Calvanese, D., Giacomo, G., Lenzerini, M., Nardi, D., Rosati, R.: Description Logic Framework for Information Integration. In: International Conference on Knowledge Representation and Reasoning (KR), pp. 2–13 (1998)
6. Carr, N.G.: IT doesn't matter, HBR, BCG Analysis (May 2003)
7. Charlsworth, I., Davis, D.: Getting to grips with SOA governance. Ovum Report #040077, 2006-23 (2006)
8. CISR. Center for Information Systems Research (2009), `http://mitsloan.mit.edu/cisr/research.php` (accessed May 29, 2009)
9. COMPAS. Compliance-driven Models, Languages, and Architectures for Services (2009), `http://www.compas-ict.eu/` (accessed May 29, 2009
10. Dostal, W., Jeckle, M., Melzer, I., Zengler, B.: Service-orientierte Architekturen mit Web Services: Konzepte - Standards - Praxis, 2nd edn. Spekturm Akademischer Verlag, München (2007)
11. EITO. In cooperation with IDC, European Information Technology Observation (2006), `http://www.eito.com` (access: 04.04.2008)
12. Esswein, W., Weller, J., Stark, J., Juhrisch, M.: Identifikation von Sevices aus Geschäftsprozessmodellen durch automatisierte Modell analyse. In: Proceedings of WI 2009, pp. 513–522 (2009), `http://www.dke.univie.ac.at/wi2009/Tagungsband_8f9643f/Band2.pdf` (accessed May 15, 2009)
13. Forrester Research, European IT Services (2007), `http://www.forrester.com/Research/Document/Excerpt/0,7211,38932,00.html` (accessed: April 4, 2009)
14. Hedin, M.: SOA-Driven Organizational Change Management: A Market Trends and Vendor Landscape Analysis of Major Service Players to Address this Emerging Opportunity. IDC Competitive Analysis #204727 (2006)
15. Hochstein, A., Ebert, N., Uebernickel, F., Brenner, W.: IT-Industrialisierung: Was ist das? Computerwoche, 15 (2007)
16. ISACA. Information Systems Audit and Control Association (2009), `http://www.isaca.org/` (accessed May 29, 2009)
17. ITGI. IT Governance Institute (2009), `http://www.itgi.org` (accessed May 29, 2009)
18. ITIL. IT Infrastructure Library (2009), `http://www.itil-officialsite.com/home/home.asp` (accessed May 29, 2009)

19. Kappel, G., Kapsammer, E., Kargl, H., Kramler, G., Reiter, T., Retschitzegger, W., Schwinger, W., Wimmer, M.: On Models and Ontologies – A Layered Approach for Model-based Tool Integration. In: Mayr, H.C., Breu, R. (eds.) Modellierung 2006, pp. 11–27 (2006)
20. Karagiannis, D., Höfferer, P.: Metamodels in Action: An overview. In: Filipe, J., Shishkov, B., Helfert, M. (eds.) ICSOFT 2006 - First International Conference on Software and Data Technologies:IS27-36. Insticc Press, Setúbal (2006)
21. Karagiannis, D., Utz, W., Woitsch, R., Eichner, H.: BPM4SOA Business Process Models for Semantic Service-Oriented Infrastructures. In: eChallenges e-2008. IOS Press, Stockholm (2008)
22. Kätker, S., Patig, S.: Model-Driven Development of Service-Oriented Busienss Application Systems. In: Proceeding of Wirtschaftsinformatik 2009, pp. 171–180 (2009), http://www.dke.univie.ac.at/wi2009/Tagungsband_8f9643f/Band1.pdf (accessed May 29, 2009)
23. Kohnke, O., Scheffler, T., Hock, C.: SOA-Governance – Ein Ansatz zum Management serviceorientierter Architekturen. Wirtschaftsinfor 50(5), 408–412 (2008)
24. Kühn, H.: Methodenintegration im Business Engineering, PhD Thesis (2004)
25. Lamberti, H.-J.: Banken Technologie als Schlüssel für die Bank der Zukunft. Leistung aus Leidenschaft Deutsche Bank (2009), http://wi2009.at/fileadmin/templates/downloads/2009_0227_Lamberti_WI2009_Wien_Versand.pdf (accessed May 29, 2009)
26. Lembo, D., Lenzerini, M., Rosati, R.: Review on models and systems for information integration, Technical Report, Universita di Roma "La Sapienza" (2002)
27. Manakanatas, D., Plexousakis, D.: A Tool for Semi-Automated Semantic Schema Mapping: Design and Implementation. In: Proceedings of the Int. Workshop on Data Integration and the Semantic Web (DISWeb 2006), pp. 290–306 (2006)
28. Mhay, S.: Request for. Procurement Processes, RFT RFQ RFP RFI (2009), http://www.negotiations.com/articles/procurement-terms/ (accessed May 29, 2009)
29. Mitra, P., Noy, N., Jaiswal, A.R.: OMEN: A Probabilistic Ontology Mapping Tool. In: Gil, Y., Motta, E., Benjamins, V.R., Musen, M.A. (eds.) ISWC 2005. LNCS, vol. 3729, pp. 537–547. Springer, Heidelberg (2005)
30. Murzek, M.: The Model Morphing Approach - Horizontal Transformation of Business Process Models, PhD Thesis (2008)
31. OASIS. OASIS (2009), http://www.oasis-open.org (accessed May 29, 2009)
32. OCG. AK IT-Governance – Aufgaben und Ziele (2009), http://www.ocg.at/ak/governance/index.html (accessed May 29, 2009)
33. plugIT D 5.1: Use Case and Evaluation Criteria (2009), http://plug-it-project.org
34. Offmann, P.: SOAM – Eine Methode zur Konzeption betrieblicher Software mit einer Serviceorientierten Architektur. Wirtschaftsinformatik 50(6), 461–471 (2008)
35. plugIT D2.1: Use Case Analysis and Evaluation Criteria Specification (2009), http://plug-it-project.eu/CMS/ADOwebCMS/upload/plugIT_D2.1_Use_Case_Description_Evaluation.pdf (accessed May 29, 2009)
36. plugIT. EU-Project FP7-3ICT-231430, plugIT HomePage (2009), http://www.plug-it.org (accessed May 29, 2009)
37. Rahm, E., Bernstein, P.A.: A Survey of Approaches to Automatic Schema Matching. The VLDB Journal 10(4), 334–350 (2001)

38. Shawn, J.: Beyond the Template: Writing a RFP that Works (2009),
    `http://www.sourcingmag.com/content/c070228a.asp`
    (accessed May 29, 2009)
39. SOA4ALL. Service Oriented Architectures for All (2009), `http://www.soa4all.eu`
    (accessed May 29, 2009)
40. Strohm, O., Ulich, E.: Unternehmen arbeitspsychologisch bewerten: ein Mehr-Ebenen-
    Ansatz unter besonderer Berücksichtigung von Mensch, Technik und Organisation.
    Hochschulverlag AG an der ETH, Zürich (1997)
41. SUPER. Semantics Utilized for Process Management within and between Enterprises
    (2009), `http://www.ip-super.org/` (accessed May 29, 2009)
42. TEC. Technology Evaluation Centers (2009),
    `http://www.technologyevaluation.com` (accessed May 29, 2009)
43. Teubner, A., Feller, T.: Governance und Compliance. Wirtschaftsinformatik 50(5), 400–
    407 (2008)
44. The Open Group. TOGAF Version 9 (2009),
    `http://www.opengroup.org/togaf/` (accessed May 29, 2009)
45. Thomas, O., Leyking, K., Scheid, M.: Vorgehensmodelle zur Entwicklung Serviceorien-
    tierter Softwaresysteme. In: Proceedings of Wirtschaftsinformatik 2009, pp. 181–190
    (2009), `http://www.dke.univie.ac.at/wi2009/Tagungsband_8f9643f/`
    `Band1pdf` (accessed May 29, 2009)
46. Viering, G., Legner, C., Ahlemann, F.: The (Lacking) Business Perspective on SOA -
    Critical Themes in SOA Research. In: Proceedings of Wirtschaftsinformatik 2009, pp. 45–
    54 (2009),
    `http://www.dke.univie.ac.at/wi2009/Tagungsband_8f9643f/`
    `Band1.pdf` (accessed May 29, 2009)
47. Willcocks, L.P., Lacity, M.C.: Global Sourcing of Business & IT Services. Palgrave Mac-
    millan, New York (2006)
48. Windley, P.J.: Teaming up for SOA. InfoWorld (2007),
    `http://www.infoworld.com/t/architecture/teaming-soa-620`
    (accessed May 29, 2009)
49. Zimmermann, S.: Governance im IT-Portfoliomanagement – Ein Ansatz zur Berücksichti-
    gung von Strategic Alignment bei der Bewertung von IT. Wirtschaftsinformatik 5, 357–
    365 (2008)
50. Woitsch, R., Karagiannis, D., Plexousakis, D., Hinkelmann, K.: Business and IT-
    Alignment: the IT-Socket. Elektrotechnik & Informationstechnik, 7–8 (2009)

Author Index